POWERFUL LEARNING COMMUNITIES

POWERFUL LEARNING COMMUNITIES

A Guide to Developing Student, Faculty, and Professional Learning Communities to Improve Student Success and Organizational Effectiveness

Oscar T. Lenning, Denise M. Hill,
Kevin P. Saunders, Alisha Solan,
and Andria Stokes

Foreword by Vincent Tinto

Sty/us

STERLING, VIRGINIA

Sty/us

COPYRIGHT © 2013 BY
STYLUS PUBLISHING, LLC.

Published by Stylus Publishing, LLC
22883 Quicksilver Drive
Sterling, Virginia 20166-2102

Library of Congress Cataloging-in-Publication Data
Powerful learning communities : a guide to developing
student, faculty, and professional learning communities to
improve student success and organizational effectiveness /
Oscar T. Lenning . . . [et al.].
    p. cm.
Includes bibliographical references and index.
ISBN 978-1-57922-579-7 (cloth : alk. paper)
ISBN 978-1-57922-580-3 (pbk. : alk. paper)
ISBN 978-1-57922-581-0 (library networkable e-edition)
ISBN 978-1-57922-582-7 (consumer e-edition)
    1. Professional learning communities—United States.
    2. College teachers—In-service training—United States.
    3. Teacher-student relationships—United States.
    I. Lenning, Oscar T.
    LB1738.P69   2013
    378.0071—dc23   2012026180

13-digit ISBN: 978-1-57922-579-7 (cloth)
13-digit ISBN: 978-1-57922-580-3 (paper)
13-digit ISBN: 978-1-57922-581-0 (library networkable
e-edition)
13-digit ISBN: 978-1-57922-582-7 (consumer e-edition)

Printed in the United States of America

All first editions printed on acid-free paper
that meets the American National Standards Institute
Z39-48 Standard.

Bulk Purchases

Quantity discounts are available for use in workshops
and for staff development.
Call 1-800-232-0223

First Edition, 2013

10 9 8 7 6 5 4 3 2 1

THIS BOOK IS DEDICATED TO DR. RUSSELL EDGERTON

Most people involved in powerful learning communities have reaped the ongoing benefits of Dr. Edgerton's work without knowing about him. Over the past several decades he has done more than anyone else to motivate institutions of higher education to implement and examine the success of innovative and effective student learning communities. As special assistant to Secretaries Robert Finch and Elliot Richardson in the Department of Health, Education and Welfare, he initiated and became a principal contributor to the Newman Task Force on higher education reform that issued the landmark Newman Report.

Russell Edgerton was the primary architect of the Fund for the Improvement of Postsecondary Education (FIPSE) and served as its deputy director; over the past forty years, FIPSE has funded and served as a catalyst to innovation throughout postsecondary education, including the renowned Washington Center's focus on learning communities and numerous other projects on student learning communities. He then served as president of the American Association for Higher Education (AAHE) for two decades, and led that association's new focus on reforming methods of achieving and assessing college student learning. Dr. Edgerton continued to contribute to learning and learning communities in higher education as the Pew Charitable Trusts' director for undergraduate learning.

Dr. Russell Edgerton's contributions to funding and stimulating effective new approaches to student learning established a strong foundation for learning community theory and practice, which continues to have a powerful impact on higher education to this day.

CONTENTS

ADDITIONAL APPENDICES

These appendices are incorporated into the e-book edition
and may also be found at www.styluspub.com/resrcs/other/PLC.pdf.

APPENDIX G—A BRIEF HISTORY OF LCs

APPENDIX H—A CALL FOR AND EVIDENCE OF
   EDUCATIONAL CHANGE

APPENDIX I—WITHIN-CLASS LCs DEFINED

ACKNOWLEDGMENTS

S pecial thanks and "bouquets of flowers" for exemplary service to our project go to Lorene "Renie" Lenning, wife and helpmate to the senior author for 48 years. She is the author of *More Than Money* and taught K–8 in five states for 40 years and also served as an adjunct college professor. Renie conducted and recorded all interviews for the "100-Institution Survey" designed for this study and tabulated the results. In addition, she commented on and edited all the draft chapter manuscripts from the perspective of a master teacher who has always conducted her classroom as a bona fide and preeminently successful student learning community.

The authors also wish to thank the senior author's son, Rev. Chris Lenning, and his wife, Jennifer (LICSW), for reading the manuscript from their perspectives in the human services profession. In addition, we express sincere appreciation to Dr. Jade Solan, tenured, communication faculty member at Grossmont College, who assisted in reviewing and editing the manuscript.

Special thanks are also extended to three individuals who originally agreed to be coauthors of this book and were intimately involved in its original conceptual formulation but later had to withdraw from the project because of other important personal commitments: Dr. Larry Ebbers, then university professor of higher education and director of the Community College Leadership Program at Iowa State University, and coauthor of the forerunner of this book; Dr. Patricia Kelvin, then coordinator of teaching and learning in the Center for Learning and Advising at Thiel College; and Dr. Robert Reason, then professor in charge, College Student Affairs master's degree program at Penn State University.

We are grateful to the many students and professional mentors we worked with over the years who helped us learn to appreciate even more the importance of effective learning communities for student success. We thank as well our professional friends and colleagues who shaped our understanding of powerful learning communities, including Sandy Astin, Corly Brooke, Art Chickering, Pat Cross, Larry Ebbers, Jerry Gaff, Zee Gamson, Doug Gruenewald, Mary Huba, George Kuh, Steve Mickelson, Bob Pace, Ernie Pascarella, John Schuh, Joan Stark, Pat Terenzini, and Vince Tinto.

Finally, thanks to our respective families for their ongoing love and support. In particular, Oscar wishes to thank his grandchildren—Aspen, Bradyn, Hannah, Jackson, and Johnny—for their inspirational joy in learning. Andria would like to acknowledge Mike Stokes for his love and support during this project; Judy and Andy Hilvitz for their time reading through many versions of her writing; and her grandchildren, Taylin Lewis and Joshua Sherman, for keeping her focused on the importance of continued excellence within the field of education. Denise would like to acknowledge her best friend and husband, Jeremy Hill, for keeping her sane and the family running smoothly as she juggled writing the book, teaching full-time, and representing clients at her law firm. She is also grateful to her three children for their patience, unconditional love, and daily inspiration. She has been blessed with many personal and professional mentors including her parents, in-laws, Hon. K. D. Briner, Jeanine Freeman, Bill Hamm, Dr. Norma Hirsch, Jon and Connie Pagel, Sally Reavely, Carla Stebbins, and Kent and Anne Zimmerman.

Oscar T. Lenning
Denise M. Hill
Kevin P. Saunders
Alisha Solan
Andria Stokes

FOREWORD

Much has been written about learning communities and their potential to reshape student experience and enhance student success. Yet research tells us that their potential has yet to be fully realized. This is the case not because learning communities cannot achieve those goals, but because they are frequently not fully or correctly implemented. Many programs that institutions call learning communities are often no more than co-registration strategies that have students share two or more classes without any clear linkage. As Oscar Lenning and his colleagues take pains to describe, there is much more to learning communities than just co-registration. Among other things they require that the learning activities in the classes in which students are co-enrolled are coherently linked in both content and pedagogy so as to form a community of shared learning experiences that span what otherwise would be discrete, disconnected learning in the individual classes. Implementing such learning communities, however, is not a trivial process. For that reason the authors have made sure to delineate various strategies institutions have employed to successfully implement learning communities and the types of commitments and partnerships that institutions, faculty, and staff have to make to see them fully implemented. In these and many other ways, Lenning and his colleagues have put into one place information and insights that we would otherwise have to glean from a wide range of resources, some more difficult to locate than others. All who are interested in developing learning communities owe them a debt of gratitude.

Vincent Tinto
Syracuse University

INTRODUCTION

Why Write This Book?

> People in higher education often pay lip service to the concept
> of learning communities; therefore, the powerful potential of this
> concept may be unrealized. In order to realize the potential of
> learning communities, higher education needs to become com-
> mitted to identifying and implementing the learning community
> models that are best for their students and faculty and learn
> how to implement this process. The powerful potential of learn-
> ing communities is clear, however, good planning and as-
> sessment must play key roles in their development and
> implementation.
>
> —Rusnak and Stout (n.d., p. 4)

Readers may ask: Why is this book needed when there are already so
many quality sources of information about learning communities
(LCs)?[1] The answer is that there is no overall comprehensive guide
for those who seek a broad strategic view and wish to implement multiple
types of LCs that help one another maximize student learning and
compare/contrast delivery formats. This book is designed with that need
in mind.

Our book was also inspired by responses to Lenning and Ebbers's (1999)
The Powerful Potential of Learning Communities, of which this current volume is intended to be a follow-up. (The initial volume addressed the potential impact of LCs, while the current volume addresses how to make LCs
more powerful now that there is conclusive evidence of that potential.) The
opening quote here is from a *NOVAtions Journal* book review comparing
the Lenning and Ebbers's book to Palloff and Pratt's (1999) award-winning
Building Learning Communities in Cyberspace. The reviewers discovered a
remarkably complementary parallel between the two books, even though one
focused on LCs in the physical classroom and the other on LCs in the virtual
classroom—in essence, regardless of delivery format the same general principles and guidelines apply.

As the quote indicates, the potential power of LCs in higher education will be realized only when individuals at all levels of the organization commit to identify LC models that fit their institutional needs and learn how to implement the process meaningfully. That is true even though an effective LC within a single classroom will also help improve student learning.

Most institutions would benefit from practical guidance about best practices and appropriate action steps they can follow, particularly given the ever-changing style, format, and technology used in higher education. We have designed this book to assist individuals and institutions in purposefully designing LC format, membership, linkages, and programming in ways that meet their particular institutional goals while maximizing learning.

The Audience for This Book

This book was designed with an eye toward individuals in higher education who wish to champion, develop, or redesign student LCs (SLCs) or professional LCs (PLCs) and perhaps encourage development of their institution into a true "learning organization" (LO). When used as discussed in the "How to Use This Book" section, it is a practical tool. LC champions from all levels of an organization can use the book to engage and inform other institutional stakeholders (e.g., instructors, academic affairs staff members, student affairs staff members, students) in the move toward becoming more powerful LOs. Top-level administrators and academic/student affairs administrators and educational policy makers will also find guidance for setting appropriate policies, allocating resources, and making other decisions that support powerful LCs.

The book may also serve as a valuable primary or secondary textbook for graduate courses in institutional leadership and policy studies, curriculum and instruction, student affairs, or assessment/evaluation. (Although the main thrust of the book is higher education, helpful generalizations to secondary, middle, and elementary education can also prove relevant for those levels.) Finally, in this environment of tighter government economies and increased scrutiny from accreditation agencies, state education departments, and the US Department of Education, this book can orient and inform public policy decision makers and accreditors about how LCs can be a worthwhile investment for maximizing student learning.

How to Use This Book

Although its chapters are not formally organized into distinctive sections as such, because the functions are interactive and overlap, this book is organized around three themes: (a) setting the stage, (b) designing a powerful LC, and (c) building/enhancing a powerful LC. Each theme was created to aid in planning for, creating, or enhancing LCs.

Reading the book in its entirety will provide maximum benefit for readers involved in the administration, design, and implementation of powerful LCs. However, each chapter is also designed to stand alone in informing readers with a primary interest in a particular subject area. Regardless of the reader's intended focus, it is strongly recommended that individual chapters be read in conjunction with the introduction and chapters 1 and 2, which provide key information and context that support every chapter.

The first part of each chapter contains a scenario of hypothetical individuals in real-life situations called "What's the Story" (in chapter 6 a scenario is given in each major section). Each was constructed to provide a context in which to place the chapter content. The chapters also include sections that provide evidence from best practice research essential in creating an effective LC as well as sections that provide strategies to ease the process of choosing a best implementation tool. In addition, all of the chapters have a section called "The Rest of the Story" (chapter 6 includes this at the end of each major section) that offers a short recap of the scenario and possible actions that could be applied. Finally, after a descriptive conclusion, each chapter contains reflection questions, providing an opportunity for the reader to integrate the information. The section also points the reader to the relevant sections of Appendix C's Powerful LC Planning Form that apply the material from the chapter. The intent of this final section is to provide the metacognitive structure to support the reader's implementation of powerful LCs.

Creating powerful LCs can seem like a daunting task. Therefore, tools and resources are included in the book's appendices to assist readers in creating, implementing, and promoting powerful LCs. In particular, readers will find it helpful to refer to Appendix B: "Compendium of Key Factors Recommended in the Research to Build Powerful LCs" and Appendix C: "Powerful LC Planning Form." Appendix B provides, in tabular form, a quick glance at current themes in evidence-based research regarding building powerful LCs. Appendix C is a strategic planning tool to guide readers in designing (or restructuring) powerful SLCs, PLCs, and/or LOs. This customizable tool helps readers to apply the research, principles, and strategies discussed in this book to their own LCs in a concrete way. Until readers become familiar with the terminology and approach outlined on the form, it is most effective when used in conjunction with the corresponding chapters in this book.

New Data: The "100-Institution Survey"

In addition to being based on the authors' personal knowledge and experience, and updating of previous research, this book incorporates new qualitative data on best practices gleaned from a survey of 100 institutions with active SLCs. These colleges and universities, selected from the Washington Center's Learning Communities Directory (available at www.evergreen.edu/washcenter/project.asp?pid = 109), were chosen because they had the most years and breadth of experience working with SLCs. LC representatives from these institutions were contacted from March to May 2011 for a telephone interview.

The primary purposes of this survey were (a) to identify issues encountered and practices employed by institutions developing and using LCs, (b) to collect information regarding attributes that schools felt made their LCs unique and powerful, and (c) to gather experience-based recommendations for institutions that are considering LCs (see Appendix A for a list of the institutions contacted). Although the survey was directed to institutions specializing in SLCs, questions pertaining to PLCs and LOs were also included. The desire was to obtain a layperson's perspective about those types of LCs and to observe whether campus experts in SLCs would acknowledge PLCs and LOs as legitimate LCs.

The directory listed a contact person for each institution, and phone calls were placed to all those persons to conduct or arrange for a telephone interview. When a contact person could not be reached or was no longer at the institution, pertinent central offices were contacted to identify who on campus should be interviewed. After an appropriate introduction and overview of the study, those interviewed were asked the following 10 questions:[2]

1. Why and how did your institution create **student** LCs?
2. What do you consider to be unique or innovative about your **student** LCs?
3. What do you think are the most important aspects of your **student** LCs, that is, what makes them effective/powerful?

4. What are potential problems or pitfalls to consider in implementing **student** LCs?

5. What do you feel are the top legal and ethical issues faced in implementing **student** LCs?

6. Does your institution have a formal institution-wide **professional LC** that focuses on student learning? If so, please tell me about it.

7. A *learning organization* is where **everyone throughout the institution** is focusing **continually** on innovations to improve learning. Does this describe your institution?

8. Do you have any written material or policy statement about your institution's LCs?
   Would you be willing to e-mail it/them to us?

9. Would you have possible interest in being considered for inclusion in a "sharing best practice examples" section of the book?

10. Are there any other information/resources we should review or other people or institutions we should consult with?

The survey was not intended to be a quantitative statistical study but rather a qualitative and descriptive one that would suggest improvements/ assist practice. When the study ended, 81 of the 100 institutions surveyed had responded, yielding a response rate of 81%. The survey generated a great deal of stimulating and useful information regarding implementation and improvement strategies for more effective/powerful SLCs, PLCs, and LOs. Herein the survey is referred to as the 100-Institution Survey.

Definition of Concepts and Key Terminology

Throughout the literature on LCs and the responses to the 100-Institution Survey, and in the authors' experience, there is variance in terms used to describe concepts relevant to LCs. Similarly, different meanings may be intended when a relevant term is used. Given the lack of commonly accepted terminology and/or definitions, we have selected terms and definitions to be used throughout the book. Some of these are outlined in Table 1 to ensure that readers understand the intended meaning when they are used. The following subsections provide definitions and discussion of other primary terms used throughout the book.

What Is Community?

Webster's New World Dictionary of American English, Third College Edition, indicates that *common* and *fellowship* are root words for *community*. In other

TABLE 1
Terms and definitions used throughout the book.

Alternate Terms	Selected Term Used	Reason Term Was Selected
Type-of-interaction mode, delivery format	Delivery format	It seemed to be more commonly used.
Real time, synchronous	Synchronous	It seemed to be more commonly used.
Asynchronous, delayed communication, threaded discussion	Asynchronous	It seemed to be more commonly used.
Classroom, face-to-face, on-ground	Face-to-face	It is more concrete and descriptive.
Electronic, online, virtual, distance education	Virtual or online (both are used synonymously)	Such LCs may be other than online; however, online is more dominant in the literature.
Hybrid, blended	Hybrid	Until recently "hybrid" predominated.
LC coordinator, LC director, LC instructor	LC coordinator	This term is the most generic and applies to all the types of LCs; e.g., the LC coordinator often facilitates rather than directs, and may or may not be an instructor (plus non-coordinator instructors are often involved in LCs).

words, community members have something in common that "ties" them together for "friendly association" or "a mutual sharing" pertaining to common goals, experiences, activities, interests, and so on. McEwan (1993) states:

> The Hellenistic Greeks used the word "koinonia" to develop the idea of "fellowship" or "partnership." In its richest sense, the word denotes something shared in common with others: common language, common ownership, common relationship, or common ideas. Of the many forms of the word "common," the concept of community is easily the most dynamic. (p. 4)

What Are LCs?

The concept of LCs developed naturally over a period of many years, and knowledge of that history assists in understanding what LCs are all about. For the uninitiated, we recommend that you read the brief "General History of 'Community'" and "History of LC Development" in Appendix G, available in the e-edition of this book and at www.styluspub.com/resrcs/other/PLC.pdf, for such meaningful background context.

For purposes of this book, we define an LC as an intentionally developed community that exists to promote and maximize the individual and shared learning of its members. There is ongoing interaction, interplay, and collaboration among the community's members as they strive for specified common learning goals.

LCs can be in the form of teams or groups, but not all small-group interactions are LCs. It is the intentional design of the LC that is the power behind its effectiveness. It is the interaction and interplay among the members of an LC that bind them into a true community. An example would be teams of students in the health professions that are established following the recommendations in Michaelsen, Parmelee, McMahon, and Levine's (2007) highly regarded *Team-Based Learning for Health Professions Education*. Their book promotes development of SLCs because effective teams that have been developed and are led in a proper manner promote diversity and minimize barriers to cohesiveness.

What Are the Three Primary Types of LCs?

As indicated earlier, this book focuses on three primary types of LCs that can measurably contribute to student learning in higher education: SLCs, PLCs, and LOs. All three can contribute jointly to maximizing student learning.

SLCs are small groups of students intentionally organized (structurally and process-wise) for student-student, student-faculty, and student-curriculum interactions that will enhance student learning both for the group as a whole and for individual members of the group. Interaction and interplay among the members of the group over time bonds participants into a true community that maximizes their learning. This is achieved through intentional group organization, facilitation, tasks/techniques provided by the instructor or facilitator, and timely process orientation and training provided to the group. Grouping on many campuses involves, for example, various entering student groups, student housing groups, and curricular area groups that are intentionally organized in particular ways for small-group learning experiences and interaction that will lead to optimum group and individual learning.

PLCs are groups of faculty, staff, or both organized into small study, planning, and implementation groups for collaboration on developing and implementing strategies for contributing to optimum student learning. For faculty (whose learning might include changing their focus from how they teach to how students learn best), PLCs also develop strategies for building effective SLCs and other means of attaining improved learning outcomes for both students and teachers. As Falk and Drayton (2009) point out, PLCs can also extend across institutions or continents and be either face-to-face or online.

The Learning Enhancement Action/Resource Network (LEA/RN) at Iowa State University illustrates an effective PLC. It consists of faculty learning teams within various colleges and departments of the university that have been studying and promoting student learning and LCs for 15 years.

LOs are organizations in which the entire institution (or a primary structural entity therein) succeeds in organizing itself—including the organization-wide culture, leadership, and a preponderance of its members throughout—in ways that authentically transform the whole organization into an intentional LC organized to maximize all members' learning in relation to one or more dimensions of knowledge. This book focuses on only one such dimension, that pertaining to knowledge and understanding of how to maximize the quantity and quality of student learning.

The only examples of an LO in higher education that we could point to prior to writing this book were colleges with declining enrollments that attained a charismatic leader who was able to motivate everyone on campus to analyze together how to improve student learning and success; those environments lasted only a few years; for example, see Lenning and Ebbers's (1999) description of the 1990s transition at St. Gregory's University (pp. 92–93). However, developing and sustaining LOs became a "hot topic" at the elementary-secondary school level at the turn of the century and is now being discussed and written about more and more within higher education circles.

All three basic types of LCs should work together in concert to maximize student learning; in other words, they should become powerful and have in common the true community characteristics discussed later. The body of our book provides specific guidelines and suggestions for making each type of LC powerful and long-lasting. It also illustrates how they can best relate meaningfully and support one another.

What Are Powerful LCs?

In a powerful LC, there is optimally effective and ongoing interplay and collaboration among the community's members as they strive for specified common learning goals, and the result is deep learning that is maximally insightful and useful as it pertains to those goals. The members of the group express mutual trust and loyalty, share ideas, and support one another. They treat one another with respect and common courtesy, appreciate diversity and the expression of new ideas, enforce group and self-discipline, unite in a common purpose, and celebrate group traditions and accomplishments together. Success of the group depends on effective facilitation, special team-building activities, an emphasis on participants being actively involved in learning, and collaboration that promotes learning of the group *and* the individual group members.

John Gardner (1990) said good academic communities—in other words, "powerful LCs"—do the following:

1. Incorporate and value diversity.
2. Have shared learning.
3. Foster internal communication.
4. Promote caring, trust, and teamwork.
5. Have links with the outside world.
6. Foster the development of young people.
7. Have group maintenance processes and governance structures that encourage participation and sharing of leadership tasks.

Many of these criteria center on how the group functions more effectively as a community. Thus, "true community" is a key component in how powerful LCs promote more effective learning.

What Is "True Community"?

True community refers to the interaction and interplay among the members of a community that bind them into a true community, as suggested by the alternative views of true community presented in Table 2. There are, however, different views as to what other specific components LC scholars highlight as characteristic of true, healthy community despite many similarities. It may be that all these views apply, that they are merely "different faces" of a true community.

In a landmark report more than a decade ago, "Involvement in Learning," Ernest Boyer and the Study Group on the Conditions of Excellence in American Higher Education (Boyer Commission on Educating Undergraduates in the Research University, 1998) lamented the loss of community throughout higher education, concluding that colleges were administratively

TABLE 2
Alternative views of true community.

Peck (1987)	• Honest communication between members • Deeper relationships than mere member masks of composure • Openness to risk • Acceptance of human vulnerability • Ability to live through community • Inclusiveness • Commitment • Consensus • Differences acknowledged and processed • Contemplation • Vulnerability • "Graceful fighting" in which conflict is not avoided, minimized, or disregarded
J. W. Gardner (1990) and Kouzes & Posner (1987)	• Shared values • Caring for one another • Appreciation of cooperation as a generic characteristic of community
Bennis (1993)	• A place where individuals discover unity • A place where individuals learn • A place where individuals exhibit leadership
Sullivan (1995, p. 15)	• Individuals committed to celebrating together • Individuals committed to mourning together • Individuals committed to risking together
Barth (2001)	• Members acknowledge their own inadequacies. • Members share about their own problems. • Members are risk takers. • Members exhibit humor. • Members collaborate with the other learners. • Members show compassion. • Members serve as a model. • Members have a moral purpose for participation.
Boyer Commission on Educating Undergraduates in the Research University (1998, p. 327)	• Purposeful community—faculty and students share academic goals and work together to strengthen teaching and learning on campus. • Open community—freedom of expression is uncompromisingly defended and civility is powerfully affirmed. • Just community—the sacredness of each person is honored and diversity is aggressively pursued. • Disciplined community—individuals accept their obligations to the group and well-defined governance procedures guide behavior for common good. • Caring community—the well-being of each member is sensitively supported and service to others is encouraged.

	• Celebrative community—the heritage of the institution is remembered and rituals affirming both tradition and change are widely shared.
Wenger, McDermott, & Snyder (2002)	• Develop unique identity that is meaningful to and energizes all participants. • Conduct intensive joint and coordinated effort to develop optimum strategies for solving the problems at hand.
Doolittle, Sudeck, & Rattigan (2008)	• There is a sense of common purpose. • Members view peers in the group as colleagues. • Self/group actualization is sought. • There is a perception of outside groups as similar to their own. • All members have a clear understanding of the communication process. • A clear mission with goals and objectives is in place and understood by all. • A well-defined strategy for accomplishing the group's work is in place and understood by all. • Group membership and decision making criteria are clear-cut.

and socially so divided that common purposes were blurred or lost altogether. They related the penchant of Americans for social involvement/interaction to a centerpiece recommendation, a call for colleges to focus on the involvement of students within the institution:

> Many features of the teaching and learning environment in colleges and universities can be altered to yield greater student involvement in higher education. The fact that more learning occurs when students are actively engaged in the learning process has extensive implications for each faculty member and administrator in every institution . . . [including]
>
> 1. The amount of learning/personal development associated with any educational program is directly proportional to the quality and quantity of student involvement in that program.
> 2. The effectiveness of any educational policy or practice is directly related to the capacity of that policy or practice to increase student involvement in learning.
> 3. The amount of student learning and personal development associated with any educational program is directly proportional to the quality and quantity of student involvement in that program.
> 4. The effectiveness of any educational policy or practice is directly related to the capacity of that policy or practice to increase student involvement in learning. (p. 19)

Why Create LCs?

Many features of the teaching/learning environment in colleges and universities can be altered to yield greater student involvement. The fact that more learning occurs when students are actively engaged in the learning process through powerful LCs has extensive implications.

Appendix H, available in the e-edition of this book and at www.stylus pub.com/resrcs/other/PLC.pdf, highlights a "clear-cut call for educational change" directed at higher education institutions across the United States. It states: "Various voices are advocating for [a] fundamental transformation in the efforts to better meet individual and societal needs for education. Included in this transformation is a new vision of what constitutes 'good learning' and the types of learning experiences that support good learning."

Then the case is made that powerful LCs must play a central role in achieving such positive and dramatic educational change. The second section of Appendix H provides concrete evidence from major studies that effective LCs do in fact lead to the desired outcomes discussed earlier in the appendix. The evidence is clear-cut that powerful LCs do lead to deep learning and many other important outcomes, and that if they become prevalent they can in fact revolutionize higher education throughout the land.

Readers new to LCs or who are unfamiliar with the LC outcomes literature are encouraged to read Appendix H. Even those who have long been involved in planning and creating LCs may find its content stimulating and helpful in discussing LCs with others.

Notes

1. For example, see DuFour and Eaker, 1998; Falk and Drayton, 2009; Levine, Laufgraben, and Shapiro, 2004; Palloff and Pratt, 2007; Peckskamp and McLaughlin, 2010; and Soven, Lehr, Naynaha, and Olson, 2013.

2. If respondents requested to receive a copy of the questions electronically and respond electronically at their convenience, that was allowed.

I

THE SCOPE AND
TYPES OF LCs

What's the Story?

Dr. Bert Whelms is the learning communities (LCs) coordinator at Liberal Arts College. The college has been recognized as an outstanding learning organization, and it is hosting a conference on LCs for a team of LC coordinators from other local institutions. The coordinators are Greta Livas, Pablo Girard, Ann Sprinks, and Ray Freeman. Dr. Whelms is supposed to take the team on a tour of the campus, but he has been delayed, so the visiting coordinators head toward the campus coffeehouse. They chat together about their various jobs and institutions. Pablo asks Greta about the cluster courses she teaches, because he has been invited to teach a linked course. Based on her experience, Greta shares her insights about best practices.

When Greta, Pablo, Ann, and Ray reach the coffeehouse, they order coffee and sit down at a central table, where they can see and hear many other interactions around the coffeehouse. As they observe the activity around them, Ann is pleased to note that there is live music. A trio of music majors, who team up to perform there on a regular basis, are softly playing acoustic guitar. Ray overhears four students at the next table planning a group presentation for a face-to-face business course. The students' presentation focuses on their work on a campus food drive. Pablo observes another student who appears to be adding a comment to a lively discussion for an online course.

A group of faculty, staff, and students chat informally as they get coffee to take down the hall for their task force meeting. They are discussing how to improve the college's program for military veterans.

At last, Dr. Whelms arrives. He suggests that they begin their tour at one of the residence halls. He explains that the first-year students in that dorm are housed together based on their chosen majors.

How many different LCs are referenced in this scenario?

> A wide variety of outcome information without any structure is analogous to possessing a file cabinet in which the contents are arranged randomly. The ability to retrieve and communicate the contents of the file improves as the organization of the material within it becomes more explicit.
>
> —Lenning, Lee, Micek, and Service (1977, p. 1)

Although this quote refers to educational outcomes in higher education, the importance of structure is also true for learning communities (LCs). Which structure is appropriate for a given LC will be dependent on the purpose(s) and context(s) in which it was created. To follow the analogy, different types of LCs function like distinct filing systems, and although there may be common data filed in each, certain types of LCs will access some files more easily than others. Without clarity about the diversity of LCs—how different types relate to one another and what distinct purposes each type serves—the best LC system for a given context will also be unclear. This chapter introduces the wide variety and scope of LCs and proposes an LC typology that can be used to stimulate effective structural organization in planning for LCs.

The Scope of LCs

The scope of LCs is vast. Given that learning occurs within all disciplinary and multidisciplinary professional fields, the practices and potential of LCs also span across all such fields. For example, LCs or teams in business and management might deal with problems such as maximizing worker productivity, solving a product distribution bottleneck, or increasing the attractiveness of a particular product to the public. Diplomatic LCs might focus on resolving boundary disputes, proposing agreements to end a war, or negotiating trade agreements. Economic LCs might focus on developing more equitable insurance longevity tables, figuring out economic crises, or solving poverty issues. Scientific LCs might focus on discovering a cure for a fatal disease, discovering relationships between human characteristics and the tendency to experience social dilemmas, or developing new social networking methodology.

The focus of this book primarily limits itself to LCs intentionally designed to promote and maximize optimal student learning in higher education. However, as stated in the introduction, almost everything in the book can be generalized and applied directly to elementary and secondary education.

Similarly, we should acknowledge that LCs exist outside of educational settings and will inevitably aid members in workforce and other noneducation settings. Numerous "teams," "project teams," "committees," "task-forces," and other groups that focus on learning exist in workplaces, professional associations, volunteer groups, and government organizations. Although LCs in higher education are the intended focus of this book, the same general principles and guidelines discussed in this book will apply to LC groups in these other settings. When members of powerful LCs in collegiate disciplinary programs are exposed to principles and guidelines, gain experience through case simulations that emphasize role playing, and develop group problem-solving skills, they enhance their ability to effectively lead and contribute to LCs in those other settings.

Factors/Facets of LCs

Our review of the literature suggests that three primary factors/facets are used to distinguish among different types of LCs: (a) membership, (b) delivery format, and (c) duration.

Membership

The membership facet is based on who constitutes the primary membership of the LC. There are three primary membership facets:

1. *Student LCs (SLCs)* are primarily groups of students working toward learning goals together. They can range from a small group of students within a class, to the total group of students in a class, to students taking a number of classes together, to students living in the same residence who also take several courses together, to students taking the same major, to students with a common interest. Such types/subtypes of SLCs may operate simultaneously, and students may be members of more than one SLC at the same time.

2. *Professional LCs (PLCs)* are primarily groups of professionals whose focus is on learning pertaining to the profession or related entities; this book focuses on PLCs in higher education that have a primary goal to improve some aspect of student learning. These PLCs can include many combinations of professionals from various levels within the institution or larger community working together, such

as faculty groups, educational staff groups, faculty and staff joining together, and parents or community professionals joining with faculty and staff. A number of such PLCs may operate simultaneously, focusing on the same or similar student learning concerns from different perspectives and often cooperating with one another.

3. *Learning organizations (LOs)* have primary memberships that include the majority of members of an organization. They are organizations whose PLCs consist of a preponderance of college/university people continually planning and working together to maximize student learning to such an extent that the institutional culture of the organization as a whole functions as a distinctive LC.

Membership is the most complex of the three facets of LCs. LCs within the different membership types may be used and organized in a variety of ways. Further, many different subtypes of SLCs, PLCs, and LOs exist, serving to meet various learning concerns. These various uses and subtypes are discussed later in the chapter.

Delivery Format

LC members can interact in the following ways:

- *Face-to-face LCs:* LC members interact in person; they are physically in the same location at the same time.
- *Virtual LCs:* LC members interact electronically from different physical locations that may or may not be far apart; the interaction may or may not be in real time.
- *Hybrid LCs:* LC members interact face-to-face part of the time and online or electronically part of the time; online interaction may or may not be in real time.

Duration

The LC can involve the following types of relationships:

- *Long term:* The relationship exists for more than one semester or term.
- *Short term:* The relationship exists for only one semester or term.
- *Very brief:* The relationship exists only a week or two, a class period, or even less.

The duration of LCs can occur officially or unofficially. For example, freshman interest group SLCs are generally designed for the first term in college (short term) with an option to continue with their initial advisor through the remainder of the first year in college (long term). Typically academic program, curricular area, and residential SLCs at four-year institutions are officially designed to last several years. By contrast, SLCs such as ones designed around the concept of students in a cohort taking several specific courses together generally last only one term or year officially. However, when an LC has been successful, it may unofficially extend into a second or third year due to initiatives by its members.

SLCs within a course can vary in duration based on the philosophy of the instructor. To illustrate, compare the teams developed following Michaelsen, Parmelee, McMahon, and Levine's (2007) team-based learning approach, which promotes having permanent student teams for the term, with Beichner et al.'s (2007) SCALE-UP approach, which subscribes to using three-person teams with rotating members throughout the term.

PLCs and LOs are usually long term, unless specifically assigned to deal with a project or problem that is limited in scope. Those designed to accomplish a certain task or solve a particular problem may be more transient in nature, however, fitting more into the category of a short-term or very brief duration.

A Typology of LCs

We have used the three primary LC factors/facets—membership, delivery format, and duration—to develop a typology of LCs. These primary LC facet relationships are depicted in Figure 1.1. Within this typology, any given LC can be characterized by its particular blend of membership, delivery format, and duration. Any of the membership categories can use any of the delivery formats. Table 1.1 shows the relationship of membership and delivery facet categories in a two-dimensional matrix with specific example institutional LCs. In addition, any of these paired facets can apply different durations. For example, an SLC can be hybrid and long-standing or face-to-face and somewhat brief. Figure 1.2 portrays all three primary facets with the first-order categories listed within each. Any of the first-order categories can be joined with any combination of other first-order categories in the other two primary facets, so a total of 27 distinctive combinations at the first-order category level are possible.

FIGURE 1.1
The primary LC facets related to one another.

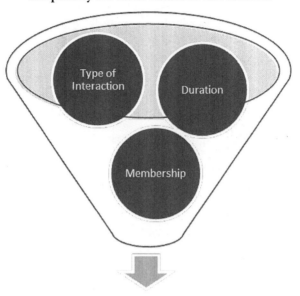

Distinct Types of Learning Communities

Although the typology characterizes distinct types of LCs, the categories within each primary facet are not mutually exclusive. These categories reflect the primary or majority nature of the LC, rather than a measure of what can occur within any given LC. For example, SLCs usually also include the involvement of one or more faculty members, and in this day and age, face-to-face LCs may quite often also communicate online. Despite the ambiguity of the categories, this typology is important for the following reasons:

- It emphasizes the breadth and variety of LCs that can help maximize student learning and calls attention to the fact that one may need different kinds of LCs for different purposes and contexts. In the past, many of these types of LCs were not recognized as "LCs." It was assumed that they were merely instructional strategies or pedagogical practices. Such an assumption implies (erroneously in our view) that LCs are *not* instructional strategies and pedagogical practices, which in turn limits some of the potential of those groups for impacting

TABLE 1.1

Interaction of the membership facets' (first column) and the delivery format facets' (first row) major categories.

	Face-to-Face LCs	Hybrid LCs	Virtual LCs
SLCs (Discussed in depth in chapter 5)	Examples: • Evergreen State College integrated courses • Kingsborough Community College thematic linked SLCs • Residential SLCs at University of Illinois • Roberts Wesleyan College organizational management academic program • The California State University, Los Angeles cooperative learning groups of Paulson and Faust (2008) • Wagner College first-year experience, intermediate, and senior SLCs	Examples: • The variety of hybrid SLCs at the College of DuPage as described by Snart (2010) • Master of Education in Educational Studies program at University of Alberta • University of Illinois Masters in Library Science hybrid SLC • University of Massachusetts blended learning programs	Examples: • Excelsior College online SLCs • Fielding Institute online SLCs • Lehigh Carbon Community College online linked courses • Santa Barbara City College online SLCs • Skagit Valley Community College online paired-course SLCs

(continues)

TABLE 1.1 (Continued)

	Face-to-Face LCs	Hybrid LCs	Virtual LCs
PLCs (Discussed in depth in chapter 5)	Examples: • Florida Atlantic University Faculty Showcase • Iowa State University LEA/RN • Miami University of Ohio FLCs • Portland State University Faculty Inquiry Council and Center for Academic Excellence • Skagit Valley Community College advisory committee • University of Iowa Student Success Team • Wagner College scholarship circles • Western Washington University Teaching Learning Academy	Examples: • Bronx Community College faculty development program for blended learning • Marist College Office of Academic Technology & eLearning • Pace University FLCs that involve both face-to-face and online interaction • The Sloan Consortium on blended learning, which interacts both face-to-face and online	Examples: • Dialogues in Methods of Education (D.I.M.E.) inquiry group • Inquiry Learning Forum (ILF) • The Math Forum • Multimedia Educational Resource for Learning and Online Teaching • National Science Foundation's Math and Science Partnership • Tapped In network
LOs (Discussed in depth in chapter 5)	Examples: • Lenning and Ebbers's (1999, pp. 92–93) description of St. Gregory's University in late 1990s • Iowa State University • Kingsborough Community College • Villanova University Lunchroom • Wagner College • West Valley College mission statement	Examples: • A number of colleges and universities are both campus- and online-based, and some may have a total institutional culture and practice that meets Peter Senge's defining standards for a true LO as a type of LC. None have yet been specifically identified, however.	Examples: • Some if not all of the sponsoring online organizations that organize and provide the online professional LCs listed above appear to have an institutional culture and practice that meets Peter Senge's defining standards for a true LO as a type of LC.

FIGURE 1.2
A typology of LCs designed to impact student learning.

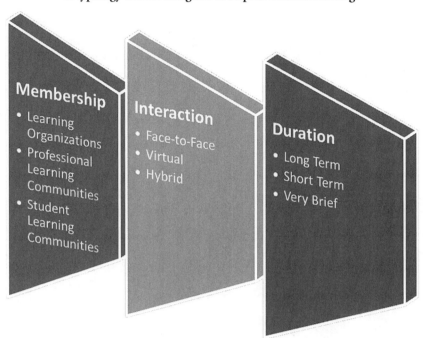

student learning. For example, traditionally it has not been recognized that collaborative/cooperative learning groups are in fact legitimate LCs, yet all entities and subentities within the typology can conform to the definition of LC presented earlier.

- It indicates that common principles and processes apply to all of these types and subtypes of LCs, and that understanding those principles and processes can help design all of them into what we have called powerful LCs.
- It highlights how each type/subtype of LC is distinctive in ways that must also be considered in designing powerful learning for its members.
- It makes clear that any of the types or subtypes of LCs can work individually as well as in concert to help maximize student learning.
- The various combinations within the typology encourage one to think creatively about new types of LCs that can prove powerful in

improving student learning. For example, prior to developing this typology we had not realized how many of the face-to-face LC strategies can be applied within the virtual environment.

Distinctive LC design factors predominate for the different primary membership categories. For the predominant design factors for each category, see Figure 1.3.

FIGURE 1.3
Breakout of the LC design factors important for each membership category shown in Figure 1.2.

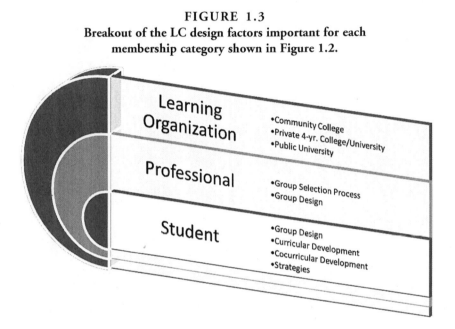

LC Subtypes for Membership Facet

The primary facet of membership has a large, complex array of LC subtypes, and unique design factors apply for each subtype. Table 1.2 assembles the general array of subtypes in one place for an easy overview. Within the SLC type, subtypes are further subdivided. The following sections define and address each subtype in the same order as presented in the tables.

Learning Organizations (LOs)

The guru of the "learning organizations" movement, Peter Senge, referred to LOs as "LCs" (Kofman & Senge, 1993, p. 5), as did early proponents of

TABLE 1.2
A typology of LCs as differentiated by membership.

Learning Organizations	*Professional LCs*	*Student LCs*

K–12 Schools as LOs
Colleges as LOs
Universities as LOs
Small LCs
LOs Outside of Education
	Learning Circle PLCs
	Communities of Practice
	  (CoP) PLCs
	Project Team PLCs
	Educational Faculty PLCs
	Educational Staff PLCs
	Educational Faculty-Staff
	  PLCs
	PLCs in Other Professions
	Parent PLCs
		Curricular Groups as SLCs
		Student-Type SLCs
		External SLCs
		Course/Class as SLCs

Note. K–12, college, and university LOs are addressed together in the text.

SLCs (Angelo, 1997; Ryan, 1994). Furthermore, the preeminent characteristics and operating principles discussed in the introduction of this book also apply to these entities. The five learning disciplines identified by Senge, Kleiner, Roberts, Ross, and Smith (1994) provide core thoughts for the establishment of an LO and ultimately the foundation of LCs as we know them. These five disciplines—personal mastery, mental models, shared vision, team learning, and systems thinking—are key ingredients for creating SLCs. Senge refers to them not as subjects for study but as a "body of techniques" (p. 7) that help enhance LC development.

Thoughtful integration of the five disciplines is key to enhancing an LO's success. Fundamental to the practice is to provide all members of the organization the incentive and the desire to take control of their own learning through *personal mastery.* No LC will ever be successful without empowering the learner through a variety of techniques. *Mental models* become crucial in that an individual's insight into and picture of the importance of the LC help assess the quality of both the individual's and group's learning. They will also shape individuals' actions and thoughts about the LC and the world around them.

Shared vision is the creation of a mutual understanding of the possibilities and intentions for the LC. That shared vision—and the resulting in-depth engagement among LC members—leads many of them to have a truly special, personal connection and appreciation for one another. In addition, it creates an environment and synergy within the LC that results in the application of creative new learning paradigms and a unique sense of worth for the individual and the group. For many LC members that sense of worth can affect their quality of learning on into the future.

Team learning is also important. Breaking down previously held beliefs about individualized learning and an emphasis on individual performance is a key to developing a truly powerful learning environment. To move to true team concepts outside postsecondary education, such concepts must be taught in our laboratories and classes.

Ultimately at the crux of all these disciplines is the *systems thinking* approach. To incorporate the value of LCs beyond the classroom, we must begin to think about how to make these LCs part of the institutional system. The challenge for all LCs is to provide some format, forum, or avenue for dealing with the larger picture.

Senge's concept of the LO is a powerful undergirding structure for our understanding of how to create true, powerful LCs. The integration of these concepts, along with the thoughts of the innovators on our campuses today, can harness the potential of how people will learn and work together to lead productive, successful, and challenging lives.

LOs can be divided into five subtypes: K–12 schools, colleges, universities, small LCs, and LOs outside of education. K–12, college, and university LOs have a common educational purpose although the learning outcomes/needs differ by each level, so they are discussed together.

K–12 Schools, Colleges, and Universities as LOs

At all levels of education—from K–12 schools to community college to four-year universities—schools that function as LOs embrace an institutional culture marked by a focus on learning. All members at all levels, individually and collectively, must aim to increase the capacity to produce desired educational results and the corresponding institutional transformation needed for that purpose.

Small LCs

Small LCs (e.g., see www2.ed.gov/programs/slcp), referred to by some as smaller LCs, have been prominent within secondary education since the turn of the century, but they are equally applicable to college and university education (e.g., Ashby Residential College at the University of North Carolina–Greensboro and the Residential Colleges at the University of Central Arkansas).

Essentially, the idea is to form a school within a school and subdivide large student populations into smaller, more-manageable and autonomous groups of students and teachers. The intention behind small LCs is to provide a more personalized environment that will better meet individual student needs. It is not uncommon for the same student/teacher community to move up together from grade level to grade level over a period of years. However, even with extraordinary funding by the Gates Foundation and the federal government, the concept has not impacted secondary students to the extent anticipated, probably because the focus has been more on smaller size of the community than on effective ways to maximize student learning.

LOs Outside of Education

PLCs and LOs are important outside of education for solving business or social problems, or issues within any professional field of study. Although they are not the focus of this book, the same general principles and guidelines apply to these LOs as to student learning in educational institutions.

Professional LCs (PLCs)

PLCs involve specialists with expertise in one or more fields of study working together in intentional community to learn and apply perceived solutions to problems. PLCs can be divided into several subcategories, which we discuss next.

Learning Circle PLCs

Learning circles are small groups of people who meet regularly, with no particular leader, to discuss particular problems, issues, or concerns. The meetings can take place either face-to-face or online. Riel (2009) defines them as follows:

> A highly interactive, participatory structure for organizing group work. The goal is to build, share, and express knowledge through a process of open dialogue and deep reflection around issues or problems with a focus on a shared outcome. . . . It is a task-based LC in contrast to a practice-based or knowledge-based LC. . . . The outcome of the circle is a written document. . . . No single person is the expert with the final say on what is, or is not, the truth. Rather the group is charged with finding the basis for their knowing. . . . Instead of everyone cooperating on one established project where the need for a single leader is pressing, the members of a learning circle are joined by a common interest or goal. Each member of the circle agrees to be leader of a task that they believe will help the group deepen their knowledge. They present this idea to the group during the planning phase and the group refines each of the projects. Once the group

has established the set of often overlapping or intersecting projects, the learning circle is an exercise in participatory management. Each participant is the leader of one project, and all members participate in the projects of others. . . . [There] are as many leaders as participants.

Examples include informal faculty discussion groups and brown-bag discussions.

Communities of Practice (CoPs) PLCs

Communities of practice are more formal groups of practitioners in which acknowledged and relevant members of a CoP continually discuss, share, and ask questions of one another. For example, departments and divisions can often function as CoPs when they discuss teaching practices, curriculum development, and/or new research within their field.

Project Team PLCs

A project team is a group of individuals with different, yet complementary skills that is assigned to solve a particular problem or achieve a particular learning goal. After an agreed-on length of time, or when the problem is solved or goal is achieved, the group disbands. The task may or may not be divided into components for which subteams are assigned. For example, a number of project teams or task forces might be created to prepare for institutional accreditation review.

Educational Faculty PLCs

An educational faculty PLC is composed entirely of educational institution faculty members. For example, faculty departments, divisions, and faculty senates (or any subgroups therein) can all function as an educational faculty PLC.

Educational Staff PLCs

An educational staff PLC is composed entirely of educational institution staff members who do not have faculty rank. For example, residential life staff, admissions staff, and maintenance staff can serve as educational staff PLCs when they work to learn about and problem-solve concerns within their functional areas.

Educational Faculty-Staff PLCs

An educational faculty-staff PLC is composed of both educational faculty and staff members working together on an equal basis. For example, members from faculty, student affairs staff, and residential life staff working together to plan and develop a residential SLC could function as an educational faculty-staff PLC.

PLCs in Other Professions

PLCs exist outside of educational settings, but the learning in those PLCs does not focus on student learning. Rather, the focus is on problems and issues within professional fields such as government, law, health care, business, and management. Although such LCs are not the focus of this book, except for curricular/training programs within those professions, the same general principles and guidelines apply to them. Furthermore, such problems frequently are dealt with by college students in disciplinary case simulations that emphasize student role playing, in preparation for enhancing students' ability to effectively lead and contribute to such LCs when they become full-time practitioners within that professional field after graduating from their undergraduate or graduate educational program.

Parent PLCs

A parent PLC is composed of parents whose purpose is to learn about and assist their children's learning. In addition to being professionals in their own career fields, the parents of college students are presumed to be professionals in relating to their children and can organize or be organized to study and work together in intentional community to learn and apply solutions to problems pertaining to their children's transition to college life. For example, the Berklee College of Music states that the Berklee Parents Learning Community offers "educational programming and resources to partner with you as you guide your student through opportunities and transitions during the college years" (www.berklee.edu/parents/learning-community.html).

Student LCs (SLCs)

As seen in Table 1.3, SLCs can be divided into four subtypes (which in turn each have subcategories): curricular groups, student type, external, and course/class. Because of the variety of SLCs, particularly within-course SLCs, the types listed in Table 1.2 and the discussion here are intended to be representative rather than exhaustive.

Curricular Groups as SLCs

A curricular group SLC pertains to students taking the same courses in the curriculum together as a group or in some other way interacting as a community with a focus on a course, multiple courses, and/or curricular content.

TABLE 1.3
Further subdivisions of SLCs.

Curricular Groups	Student Type	External	Course/Class
1. Cross-Curricular SLCs	Background	1. Cocurricular LCs	1. Total Class as an LC
a. Student Cohort/Integrative Seminar	Race/Ethnicity	2. Internship LCs	2. Within-Class LCs
Seminar	Ability	3. International Study LCs	a. Groups of Four
b. Linked Courses/Course Clusters	Gender	4. Living-Learning Communities (LLCs) or	b. Learning Pairs
Clusters	Military/Veteran	Residential LCs	(1) Think-Pair-Share
Federated LCs (FLCs)	Urban/Rural	5. Service-Learning LCs	(2) Three-Step Interview
Freshman Interest Groups (FIGs)	Other Types		(3) Pairs Check
Team-Taught Courses Across Fields			c. Roundtable
c. Coordinated Studies			d. Numbered Heads Together
2. Academic Program LCs			e. Send a Problem
3. Curricular Area LCs			f. Circles of Learning
			g. Student Teams and Achievement Division (STAD)
			h. Jigsaw I, II, and III
			i. Group Investigation
			j. Co-op Co-op
			k. Teams-Games-Tournaments (TGT)
			l. Team-Assisted Individualization
			m. Tribes LCs
			n. Peer Teaching
			(1) Supplemental Instruction
			(2) Mathematics Workshops
			(3) Writing Fellows
			o. Other Within-Class LCs

Note. All student types are discussed together in one section in the text.

Curricular group SLCs can be divided into three subcategories: cross-curricular, academic program, and curricular area.

1. *Cross-Curricular SLCs.*

In the cross-curricular SLC, students take courses as a group across the curriculum or integrate classwork jointly in some other way. This subcategory can be divided into subcategories originally suggested by the Washington Center for Improving the Quality of Undergraduate Education at Evergreen State College (www.evergreen.edu/washcenter): student cohort/integrative seminar, linked courses/course clusters, and coordinated studies.

These multidisciplinary/interprofessional LCs can also cross institutions. For example, when author Denise Hill was teaching the master of health administration (MHA) health law and ethics course at Des Moines University and the health law survey course at Drake University Law School, each course was divided into SLCs of four to five students. Professor Hill then designed case-based interventions that essentially combined the SLCs from each institution into larger teams with both MHA and law students for purposes of working on the project case.

a. *Student Cohort/Integrative Seminar.*

In a student cohort/integrative seminar, a relatively small cohort of students enrolls in large classes and the students attend them together. These classes are not coordinated by the faculty teaching them. During the same term, an additional integrative seminar is provided just for the students in the cohort. The seminar is designed to help the students make intellectual connections across the large courses they are taking together and build a sense of community for that group of students.

b. *Linked Courses/Course Clusters.*

Linked courses are sets of courses, as determined by the institution, for which specific groups of students co-register. The faculty members for the courses are independent of one another and may or may not be expected to collaborate on their syllabi, assignments, and activities. When only two courses are linked—usually a skills course in combination with a content course—they are called paired courses. The goals for the students are as follows:

- See the courses as an integrated and correlated set.
- Apply what is learned in one course to the content and assignments in the other courses.

- Feel encouraged to study the courses collaboratively in relationship to one another.
- Complete common assignments across the courses.
- Hear common problems, themes, and concepts presented from diverse perspectives by the different instructors; share concerns regarding learning; brainstorm common themes; and identify concepts that may have multiple perspectives based on the instructors' background.

What is considered enough linkage/integration from course to course in terms of realizing these objectives varies from instructor to instructor, and among groups of instructors. Linked courses may require lower-division courses from different disciplines, because they conceptually fit well into an interdisciplinary grouping, because they have common themes or issues, and so on. Courses most commonly linked are freshman (and sometimes sophomore) courses in English composition, speech, history, humanities, social sciences, and science.

For example, in the nationally recognized Interdisciplinary Writing Program at the University of Washington, in operation since the late 1970s, the expository writing instructors cooperate with the instructors of 27 general education lecture courses in a variety of disciplines. Generally about 20 students in a lecture course of 200 students are part of a linked writing course. Often incoming students are automatically assigned to an LC (from which they may opt out), but in the University of Washington program, students must volunteer for participation in linked courses.

There are different approaches to linked courses. To illustrate with paired courses, (a) both courses may share the same students and no other students are in either class; (b) the two courses may enroll significant percentages of students who are outside of the LC; (c) both courses may be taught by the same instructor; or (d) the two courses may be combined into a linked course that enrolls twice the number of students and is team taught by the two instructors.

Federated LCs (FLCs). Philosophy professor Patrick Hill created and implemented the FLC model in the mid-1970s at SUNY Stony Brook prior to his becoming provost at Evergreen State College. In the manner of "freshman interest groups," this model invites groups of up to 40 undergraduate students to volunteer to study together for a special set of three disciplinary courses ("federated courses") that relate directly to an overarching theme. In addition, the student group participates separately (with no other students) in a specially prepared "program seminar" related to all three federated courses. This seminar is taught by a "master learner," a faculty member from another discipline, who enrolls and participates in the three courses alongside the students.

Because of the cost involved in having a master learner, other colleges and universities have deleted that faculty position from the model, although proxies such as upper-division master learner students are sometimes used. That modified model retains the program seminar, however, and it is taught by the instructor of one of the federated courses.

Freshman Interest Groups (FIGs). The FIG model was originally conceived by the academic advising office at the University of Oregon as a way to provide effective advising assistance to entering first-year students and to build a sense of community among those students within each major. It involves interested incoming freshmen choosing from a list of special-interest group topics that may be career related (e.g., pre-law), social issues (e.g., world hunger), philosophical (e.g., what it means to be an educated person), and so on. Faculty members select specific courses that are deemed most pertinent to the topic. Then the students are grouped by their chosen topics into small groups of 20–40 students, and they (as a group) take the topic-related courses together to meet freshman course requirements. As conceived at the University of Oregon, faculty of the selected courses are not expected to coordinate syllabi or co-plan classes during the semester, although they are invited to attend an initial group meeting of the FIG to introduce themselves and say a few words of introduction about their respective courses.

Depending on the institution, the FIG may or may not have a common faculty advisor/mentor or an upper-class student peer advisor/mentor. For example, Gabelnick, MacGregor, Matthews, and Smith (1990) said the following about the FIG program at the University of Oregon:

> The LC connection for each FIG is provided by a peer advisor. This older student organizes the first meeting of the FIG during Student Orientation Week and then convenes the group weekly during the semester to explore issues and resources related to student life on campus, form study groups, or just spend some informal time together. The peer advisor receives some upper-division academic credit in leadership for leading his or her FIG. (p. 24)

Team-Taught Courses Across Fields. SLCs may involve interdisciplinary courses that faculty members team teach. The course work is embedded in an integrated program of study and involves a synthesis of two or more disciplines to establish a new level of discourse and integration of knowledge.

c. Coordinated Studies.

Coordinated studies, a yearlong LC endeavor for first-year college students, modeled after the groundbreaking approaches of Meiklejohn in 1932 and Tussman in 1969 (Tussman, 1997), was built into the curricular design of Evergreen State College for its opening in 1970. "Coordinated studies" means that the students and faculty assigned to the LC are involved together in a complete program of study. This program of study requires participating faculty to focus on collaborative learning. The size of these LCs is proportionately larger than that of course clusters; they generally involve groupings of 60–100 students, and 3 to 5 faculty members who teach only in the coordinated studies program. The number of faculty and the size of the total group depend on the number of courses involved. The faculty-to-student ratio in such a program is generally 1:20, and the faculty involved in such an LC as well as the program offerings change each academic calendar term.

In this model, faculty and students are working together full-time in active, interdisciplinary, thematic learning. However, the modes of delivery and subject-matter emphases can be quite varied from program to program. Some coordinated studies programs are extremely specific in terms of content and skills and are highly sequenced; others are not sequenced nor focused thus.

2. Academic Program LCs.

The students within any academic program can be organized into an effective LC based on a particular shared certificate or degree program. A very successful example occurred at Roberts Wesleyan College in Rochester, New York, when the senior author helped initiate an upper-division accelerated bachelor's degree program called "Management of Human Resources," later renamed "Organizational Management" (for more information see the description in Appendix D).

3. Curricular Area LCs.

Throughout the history of higher education, faculty, students, and alumni have viewed themselves as members of a specialized profession that represents a distinctive community of scholars. By the time students are juniors and seniors majoring in a disciplinary area, they tend to begin seeing themselves as members of that disciplinary community. Furthermore, they have a number of common courses with their disciplinary student peers. As a result, upper-division students tend to interact more with their disciplinary peers and faculty within their major than with other students and faculty.

Generally, the faculty and/or students within the college or university department organize their own disciplinary clubs that provide targeted learning and fellowship experiences for their specialized LC. Through application of the principles and guidelines emphasized in this book, LC activities within a curricular area may be organized on an even more formal basis and lead to enhanced student learning outcomes.

Student-Type SLCs

For a variety of reasons—personal, historic, and systemic—students from similar backgrounds or students who perceive themselves as sharing some common student-type characteristics have tended to congregate together socially. Therefore, they are also more likely to study together. Examples of these types of students include international students from the same country, region, or culture; students of the same race; students of the same gender; students with disabilities; rural students; urban students; and student athletes. Whether such groupings facilitate student learning depends on the orientation and goals of the group, and on whether the students are practicing effective LC methods. Often, the group's common interest in a particular social activity may distract the students from effectively studying together.

It should be emphasized that college students of particular types are sometimes organized into formal SLCs by the institution, faculty, or staff in order to take advantage of common background, ability, and interests. Targeted honors programs often are designed to form such SLCs. Support for international students can also be provided by organizing them into formal SLC academic clubs. As we were writing this book, many institutions had started to organize academically oriented SLCs designed to support returning veterans and military members. Others have College Assistance Migrant Programs for children of migrant workers and/or LCs for students who are the first generation in their family to go to college.

The range of student-type categories is wide and emergent. LC developers should consider the unique populations and interest groups that already exist within their institutions as they determine what student-type LCs might be of benefit.

External SLCs

External SLCs focus on student learning occurring in the extracurricular realm of the institution or experientially at off-campus settings. They can revolve around informal activities that occur within the institution but are *not* a formal part of the curriculum, or they can involve activities that occur outside of the institution's boundaries completely, through loose or tight affiliation. The latter may be located in the surrounding community, across the nation, or in international settings around the globe.

1. *Cocurricular LCs.*
Cocurricular or extracurricular LCs have students interacting in important learning activities complementary to but not formally part of the curriculum. Examples of cocurricular LCs include honor societies, performance groups, interest clubs, disciplinary organizations, altruistic or social networks, athletics, and out-of-class civic or service activities.

2. *Internship LCs.*
Internships involve formal, applied involvement in workplace communities under the auspices of an employer. Students serve as trainees and can often earn college credit for their internship activity if faculty members oversee the internship. Interns across a wide variety of settings often meet together in community to share experiences.

3. *International Study LCs.*
International study programs, also called study abroad or overseas study programs, allow students to study in LCs outside US borders. These LCs may be formally structured, such as when a cohort of students goes abroad together on a guided learning experience such as a tour of historical sites and museums or foreign fieldwork such as an archeological dig. Other times, learners studying abroad may get together and form informal LCs; this is especially common when students seek out others from their own culture or who speak the same language.

4. *Living-Learning Communities (LLCs) or Residential LCs.*
Residence halls and student housing are commonly associated with student community. Over the years, many colleges and universities have developed residential life programming to direct a community impulse toward supporting academic success for students in the same residence hall (or on the same floor). Research has determined that residential hall community living and LC programming is often a primary factor explaining the superior academic performance of those students.

For example, Schein (2005) reported dramatic student learning and retention impact for students in the LLC whose development he led at the University of Illinois, Urbana–Champaign. As reported in chapter 5, similar success for LLCs has been found at Ball State University, Bowling Green State University, Earlham College, University of Iowa, University of Maryland, University of Michigan, Michigan State University, Missouri University, Stanford University, Syracuse University, Truman State University, Wagner College, and Yale University.

5. *Service-Learning LCs.*
Service-learning programs allow students to join together in serving the external community in ways that meaningfully assist that community while also encouraging students to reflect on application of concepts, methodologies, and principles learned within the curriculum.

Service-learning projects are frequently managed in collaboration with nonprofit organizations in the community, and they can be either tied directly to course curriculum or part of extracurricular clubs and activities on campus. Service-learning can involve short- or long-term projects and can range across a wide spectrum of activities, including but not limited to peer mediation, tutoring, campaigning for public health and safety issues, collecting survey data, running energy audits, collecting local or oral histories, and organizing food and clothing drives.

Course/Class as SLCs

A professor and her or his student class can function as a separate, effective LC like those discussed previously. In addition, through the professor's leadership, student subgroups within the class can be helped to form other LCs that can positively improve academic success.

1. *Total Class as an LC.*
Particularly in the self-contained elementary classroom where students and the teacher interact and work together on a continual daily basis, the entire classroom of students has been viewed as an LC. Generally, in classes where the teachers work to effectively develop a sense of family or community across the classroom, all of the students in the class view themselves as members of a distinctive LC. Although the time spent together in a college-level class is much less, professors can still cultivate a community approach to learning in their classes.

2. *Within-Class LCs.*

Within-class LCs are what is generally called cooperative learning in elementary-secondary education and collaborative learning in higher education, although the use of "cooperative learning" is becoming more common in higher education as a result of the efforts of Johnson, Johnson, and Smith (1991); Paulson and Faust (2008); and Millis (2010). Without differentiating between effective and ineffective applications, Pascarella and Terenzini (2005) calculate that cooperative education at colleges and universities contributed 19% to the improvement of student content learning over traditional methods of instruction (lecture and question/answer).

Cooperative learning is often referred to as a technique or method, but note how it also functions as a "micro" LC that helps support and sustain larger LCs; they are LCs within other LCs. Within-class LCs are generally very brief but can be short term if groupings are maintained for the duration of the semester/term or can even be long term if a class spans more than one semester/term. There are numerous variations for within-class LCs. Table 1.3 lists some significant, specific within-class LCs. (These are defined and discussed in Appendix I, which is available in the e-edition of this book and at www.styluspub.com/resrcs/other/PLC.pdf.)

The Rest of the Story

Look back at the scenario at the beginning of the chapter. Eleven potential LCs are directly referred to in the scenario—1 LO: Liberal Arts College; 2 PLCs: the team of directors (CoP) and the task force (project team); and 8 SLCs: the course clusters, the linked courses, the music majors (curricular area), the presentation group (within class), the service-learning, the online discussion (total class), the veterans program (student type), and the residential LC. Remember that powerful LCs can exist in a variety of settings.

Conclusion

LCs cover a broad landscape. All LC types in the typology can be powerful if they are designed and implemented in ways that contribute to maximizing student learning. Awareness of this breadth is important because different institutions, purposes, and contexts require different types of LCs to best serve their needs. Although there are many types, some common principles and guidelines for maximizing student learning apply to all of them. However, each particular type and subtype of LC may require distinctive guidelines for maximum effectiveness. In planning and implementing LCs, it is important to consider what array of powerful LCs will best work together to maximize learning for your targeted students.

For Reflection

As you create your own meaning from ideas in this chapter, begin to think about a specific LC at your institution (or at an institution you know about if you are in a governmental or other noninstitutional role) and how it can inform your work or interests. Use that LC to answer the following questions and help you reflect on practical implications of the material in this chapter:

- What are the membership, focus, context, purpose, specific objectives, and scope of this LC?
- From the broad array of LC types presented in this chapter, which come closest to serving the needs for this particular group?
- What creative combinations of LC types and subtypes can help maximize learning for this particular group? Will specific LC subsets be needed at specific points in time to help maximize learning for the total group?

Now that you have read and reflected on this chapter, you should be able to complete the following item on the Powerful LC Planning Form in Appendix C:

- Section II: #1. "What will the LC look like?"

2

PREPARING FOR
POWERFUL LCs

What's the Story?

Roxie Evans is a faculty member at Nearby Community College (NCC). She is concerned and frustrated that she is serving on a Diversity and Equity Committee that does not seem to be meeting its goals. On the committee are four other faculty members: Babette Fields, John Wilson, Trish Woo, and Pat Snipe.

Recent institutional data indicate that retention and graduation rates among students of color at NCC are significantly lower than at other similar institutions in the state. In addition, the most recent accreditation report for the institution raised a concern about the college's lack of attention to diversity in general. In response, the provost assigned Roxie to chair a Diversity and Equity Committee. The committee is specifically charged with developing an LC to address the matter of retention and graduation rates among students of color. However, the provost has not allocated any money to the project.

At the first meeting, Roxie shares the institutional data with the committee members. She finishes by saying, "It is a serious concern that our school is not serving a significant proportion of its students."

"I agree," John says. "But I have been on various diversity committees on this campus for the past 15 years. Whatever we say and do here is just going to be filed in a report and put on a shelf in some administrator's office to satisfy accreditation."

"I think people are just tired of hearing about diversity," Pat says with a sigh.

"And what about other types of diversity? People who are overweight or have disabilities experience a lot of discrimination, too," Babette adds.

At the next meeting, Trish brings flyers for the upcoming World Arts Festival on campus. Pat and Babette get excited about the festival and suggest that the committee consider having a booth at the festival.

"Yes, and something for Black History Month," Pat adds.

Much of the rest of the meeting is spent discussing the festival. Pat and Babette discuss designing flyers for the booth. Roxie looks at John and he shrugs.

How could Roxie create a more powerful PLC in order to develop a successful SLC?

A Networked Learning Community is constructed as its members collaborate to achieve common goals, learning together as they develop solutions for problems they are addressing in common. As the learning community grows, the members of the community develop new knowledge and skills through their participation and contributions. Everyone becomes a learner. . . . The distinctions between students and teachers fade away.

—My eCoach at http://my-ecoach.com/project.php?id = 12003

This quote states well the underlying intended purpose of any powerful learning community (LC). In addition to expanding on and broadening that purpose, this chapter introduces principles for designing such LCs and discusses the importance of building institutional partnerships for creating and sustaining powerful LCs.

The introduction discussed in some depth the concept of "true community," which is a key characteristic of powerful LCs. Whether working toward creating learning organizations, professional learning communities (PLCs), or student learning communities (SLCs) the notion of using a well-defined community to support learning and application of desired goals is essential. As authors we know that this book would probably not be read by those who do not already believe that building community is essential for learning. However, there are key factors that support building and sustaining a community for learning. Thus, we recommend that you go back and read the introduction if you have not already done so.

The following sections discuss considerations of purpose, environment, designing, and building of a powerful LC.

Creating Purposeful LCs That Are Powerful

There are usually trigger events that cause institutions and individuals to decide to create an LC; often it is perceived to be the answer to a charge or concern from within or without the institution. For example, a particular faculty member or administrator may become interested in enhancing learning for a particular group or an accreditation review may charge the institution to improve student learning and retention. Identification of this event begins to bring the purpose into focus. Yet, many LCs are "working in circles" based on lack of purpose. For example, the following comment by a faculty member reveals what can happen when LCs lose sight of their purpose:

> I have worked with many faculty and administrators over the years and when we discuss LCs, there seems to be a loss of purpose after creation occurs. Simply stated, we get together to collaborate and make changes, but do not identify the academic, retention, social, or emotional reasons for existence of the LC. We several times establish goals and norms, and then somehow become involved in minute details that cause confusion. My question is a simple one. How do we as an LC stay on track and make sure the decisions we make relate back to student learning and the growth of our program?

Both purpose and design considerations should be addressed when creating LCs. Using the trigger event helps to define the existence of the LC. It addresses and/or responds to important questions such as: Will we be creating a new program? Is revision of the curriculum needed? How can we provide more effective support for students academically and socially? What about the first-year experience—can structures be put into place to support the myriad experiences that happen on campus? Because there are many purposes for creating LCs within educational structures, identification and definitions should be established within the LC and/or for the LC.

Shapiro and Levine (1999) identify the following purposes for creation of LCs, in their book *Creating Learning Communities: A Practical Guide to Winning Support, Organizing Change, and Implementing Programs*:

> At their best, learning communities generate their own synergy, creating a campus culture where the whole is greater than the sum of its parts. Learning communities create opportunities for greater faculty-student interaction, build on the strengths of interdisciplinary curricula, foster collaboration between academic affairs and student affairs, and generally provide creative space for thoughtful members of the college community to work together. (p. 43)

With these purposes, Shapiro and Levine provide clarity for future programming decisions by discussing the use of purpose as a way to create direction, precision, transparency, and buy-in when implementing any program into an institutional structure. Each of the purposes revolves around creating successful collegiate learning that will enhance functioning within the greater society.

The selection or creation of a stated purpose can guide the group toward what type of LC should be created to support intended outcomes. In addition, selection of a specific purpose using a tool such as Table 2.1, developed by the authors, can also enhance group construction and strategies that might need to be put into place to assist in goal attainment.

Conducting an Environmental Scan

Every LC is operating within an external/institutional complex of social, cultural, and physical conditions—the environment surrounding it—that can affect the success of the LC in a positive or negative manner. When setting the stage for powerful LCs, it is important to take stock of the environment that will support or detract from the active change necessary for effective LC efforts.

Lewin (1943) defines *active change* through a model called the force field model of change. This model considers two forces that compete against each other to maintain the status quo. There are those forces that drive change

TABLE 2.1
Identification of specific intended learning purposes for creation of an LC.

Purpose	*Overarching Goals*
Build community	• Share knowledge • Build a solid foundation • Promote shared experiences • Maintain process of governance structures
Create meaning	• Promote a variety of perspectives of content • Create quality ideas • Provide an opportunity to learn through depth and breadth
Establish identity	• Introduce or support diverse cultural lenses • Promote shared experiences • Build communities of support
Provide opportunities for practice	• Solve problems • Learn the culture • Provide emotional support

and those that restrain or obstruct the act of change. Only when the driving forces are more powerful does the desired change in behavior occur. Thus, identification and consideration of environmental pushes and pulls are extremely important when creating or building an LC. Identifying environmental qualities, stakeholders, resources, and sources and noting potential barriers and solutions will help guide the process and support creation of an LC that is strong, effective, and sustainable.

Cox (2004) discussed 10 environmental qualities that contribute to the true sense of effective community needed for powerful faculty learning communities (FLCs): (a) safety and trust, (b) openness, (c) respect, (d) responsiveness, (e) collaboration, (f) relevance, (g) challenge, (h) enjoyment, (i) esprit de corps, and (j) empowerment. These qualities must also be present in *all* types of LCs. Each quality is discussed at www.units.muohio.edu/flc/qualities.php.

Potential stakeholders are also part of the environment, and they can become either barriers to LC success or solutions that can help guide the process and support the creation of an LC that is strong, effective, and sustainable. Early on, LC designers must identify all stakeholders within the organization as well as within the surrounding community, evaluate each of the stakeholders as to their potential to be barriers or contributors to LC success, and determine what incentives can help them to become the latter.

It is crucial to obtain broad-based institutional buy-in to the LCs, including faculty from various departments, administration, and all staff members in every department. According to Peckskamp and McLaughlin (2010), LC designers should reach out to the following campus stakeholders: "academic department, the registrar, housing, residence life, and admissions offices" (p. 1). These stakeholders provide guidance, resources, and information exchange options that will sustain an LC. Developing such partnerships is so important that we discuss this topic in more depth later in the chapter.

LC resources and access to potential sources of them is an important aspect of the environment. Lack of necessary resources often serves as a barrier to LC success. Alternatively, timely access to needed resources can contribute to LC success.

First, identify what the LC requires to function effectively in terms of resources, such as space, staff/people, money, time, training, tools, and technology. Then seek out sources for acquiring these necessary resources. Some resources may be readily available and can easily provide for the LC's needs. For example, an all-purpose room on campus can serve as a space for the LC to meet, or time and money already dedicated to faculty/staff development may be earmarked for conferences and/or training related to LC efforts. However, sometimes the sources must be more aggressively pursued, such as requests for budget reallocation or grant acquisition. Often these sources require much time and energy in and of themselves, and LC designers must provide a clear rationale for the need. Shapiro and Levine (1999) well state the rationale for such resource needs:

> Throughout this book we return to the centrality of faculty for the success of a LC. How an institution estimates the budgetary implications of faculty involvement is a complex issue. . . . To change the nature of undergraduate education on a campus, there must be an investment in faculty develop-ment. At the same time, the reward structure must be rethought. . . . LCs are among the most cost-effective ways to involve faculty in sustained professional development activities around teaching and pedagogy. Faculty in LCs are constantly reporting that the experience has changed the way they teach in all their classes. . . . Costs associated with faculty release time to work collaboratively with others in different departments, summer stipends, incentive grants, and travel support are investments in improving undergraduate education. (pp. 49–66)

Alternatively, LC designers may need to consider other ways to think about or meet their needs. As an illustration, if an LC has a project designed to expose members to other cultures, it may be too costly to send members to another country. However, American immigrants from that culture could be invited to participate in the activity on campus or LC members could meet at an ethnic restaurant. LCs should also explore more creative ways of acquiring resources, such as seeking out nontraditional partnerships in the private sector with mutual interests.

Principles for Design of Powerful LCs

When considering the idea of principles, most agree that these are the stated beliefs that one holds about a particular topic, such as life, profession, or conduct. The use of principles within LCs relates to those beliefs that will guide the creation and sustenance of the community. When we discuss prin-ciples pertaining to a powerful LC we are taking into account actions and beliefs that will become the architecture that guides the operation/functions of the individuals in the LC.

Bielaczyc and Collins (1999) identified four characteristics that should be evident within the culture of the organization: (a) a population of mem-bers who are diverse in knowledge and skills, (b) a desire to create and build a collective knowledge, (c) a shared belief that the process of learning is the key component to academic success, and (d) the creation of a device to share what is learned. Before implementing a plan, faculty and staff should reach a consensus that these four characteristics exist.

Bielaczyc and Collins (1999) propose 14 principles for LC design, as presented in Table 2.2. They are not introduced in a specific order but combined to help emphasize intent and identify purposes that aid the LC process as based on prior attempts to create and maintain successful LCs. The development of effective LCs often requires a paradigm shift for most individuals who work in institutionalized forms of education. These principles are shared with the intent of helping individuals move beyond such prior perspectives when beginning or refining LCs.

First and foremost, the guiding principle for any type of LC should be community growth: the power of many versus the power of one. Intentional growth occurs through assembling professionals with differing strengths and knowledge bases. Combining individual knowledge leads to expansion of skills, general knowledge, and growth in perspective. The intent of this principle is to create a cycle that expands the LC's knowledge exponentially through collaboration and communication. Without a desire to expand the LC's knowledge and skills, the LC will quickly lose sight of purpose and be open to a variety of pitfalls.

At this stage, institutions may start to ask the following: Do we need to consider new ways of doing things? What processes and procedures hinder collaboration? How can we jump-start an initiative, or what are ideas for beginning? Iowa State University started a path of collaboration as various planners from multiple parts of the institution brought various goals: improving undergraduate education, increasing retention, focusing on student learning, and building connections across department and college silos (Brooke & Gruenewald, 2003). The principle of growth invites the community to develop common purpose and to explore future possibilities.

The next several principles work in concert to begin forming the framework needed to support the LC. These principles are emergent growth, articulation of goals, structural dependence, respect for others, and sharing. They focus on *co*-construction of goals to increase collective buy-in while identifying participant strengths and weaknesses. Whether working with students, colleagues, the outlying community, or all three, each participant must be able to participate fully. Simply constructing goals does not guarantee that perceptions will be equal.

TABLE 2.2
Fourteen principles for design of powerful LCs.

Principle	Description	Example
1. Community growth	Confirm that the ongoing intent is to enrich and grow the entire LC.	New diverse and talented students join the program, department, and/or institution as a result of the LC.
2. Emergent growth	Construct LC goals through conversations with its members.	Faculty and students hold brainstorming sessions on LC goals and objectives.
3. Articulation of goals	Be sure goals, objectives, and measures are clearly identified, effectively communicated, and understood and agreed upon by all LC members	Faculty committees draft and approve a goal to increase the number of campus students actively involved in powerful face-to-face SLCs by 10% during the academic year of 2012–13.
4. Metacognition	Ensure that there is continual monitoring of thought, identification of strengths and weaknesses, and reflection on prior actions within the LC	Staff agree to record attempts to attract new students and to realize it is important to involve students in recruitment because they may have more access to prospective students even though they may not know the details of the program. They have never tried using students to help recruit bur decide to try it out.
5. Beyond the bounds	Try new things that seem to be "out of the box."	The department chair decides to try having students from the department SLC create a video about the department and post it on social media.
6. Respect for others	Encourage and allow all voices in the LC to be heard and respected.	The administration invites feedback by providing diverse options: publicly in groups, and privately in e-mails or on note cards.
7. Fail-safe	Take risks with ideas.	Supervisors remind staff that they accept and appreciate that learning comes from failure.

8. Structural dependence	Focus on collaboration that is created with purpose in mind.	One department invites another to assist in completing a task.
9. Depth over breadth	Give time for group investigation into the purpose of and connection between matters under consideration, allowing participants to realize who has expertise in the area.	Each recruit completes a personality test that identifies likes and strengths. Pairs or groups are then matched to build in-depth connections.
10. Diverse expertise	Utilize individual strengths by connecting abilities to tasks.	Those who are excellent writers create the script for recruiters, those who speak well go out to schools to gather data, and those who are strong statisticians track data.
11. Multiple ways to participate	Ensure that the community is designed with a variety of ways to participate and be heard.	Administrators invite all LC members to be cheerleaders, elaborators, facilitators, initiators, questioners, responders, summarizers, and other roles.
12. Sharing	Encourage knowledge sharing as essential throughout the LC.	LC coordinators encourage LC members to engage in both face-to-face and online discussion, including the use of tweeting, blogging, and other social applications of the latest technology.
13. Negotiating	Encourage energetic questioning and exchanges of ideas, and provide practice in honing effective negotiating skills.	LC coordinators make use of the Socratic Seminar to hone the individual's and the group's negotiating skills.
14. Quality of products	Establish standards of practice that support the inside and outside community and stick with them.	Students are not badgered to participate or give information; well-thought-out, creative, pertinent, stimulating, and workable ideas and solutions result.

Note. For more information see Bielaczyc and Collins (1999).

As institutions consider these principles, individuals will often begin to consider a series of questions that move beyond the initial visioning steps and turn attention to the purpose, structure, function, and ethos of the program. Questions at this stage might include: Who owns the program? What organizational structures support partnerships and collaboration? What ongoing structures and practices will support ongoing partnerships? An important consideration in this phase is how the structure of the program supports the established goals. For instance, several institutions developed intentional partnerships between student affairs and academic affairs in the development of SLCs (see B. L. Smith & Williams, 2007).

It is important to remember that the intent of LCs is to help expand the community's knowledge and effectiveness; all members need to be in agreement regarding goals and their achievement. Without careful articulation and agreed-upon assessment, goals could be interpreted as being met by some members whereas others might disagree. Use of identified activities that require dependence within and among groups can help to unify the work at hand.

Use of the correct grouping will provide growth of expertise as well as identify new information. Homogeneous grouping will help strengthen like knowledge bases and heterogeneous grouping will provide different perspectives. Without interdependency, rogue groups or individuals could derail the LC's work.

Finally, consideration of and respect for individual personalities, backgrounds, and experiences plays a large role in achieving LC goals. Specific rules for respect should be created by the group so that all members feel empowered and heard as the LC moves forward toward completion of goals. Establishment of sharing mechanisms is essential, including the use of collaborative, real-time devices such as Google Docs or asynchronous methods such as e-mail, to ensure that each voice in the community is heard, respected, considered, and challenged.

The next group of interconnected principles consists of depth over breadth, use of diverse expertise, and metacognition. Research conducted by A. L. Brown, Bransford, Ferrara, and Campione (1983) supports these principles. When considering operation of the LC, individuals and groups need sufficient time to investigate deeply and foster a sense of expertise to support the meaning derived through collaboration. As interests expand, there may be a need to departmentalize and create small groups within a larger one that presents a passion and drive that brings new expertise to the LC.

Planning for meaningful discourse, exchanging ideas, and wrestling with the presentation of new topics or ideas can help create deep learning and understanding of content. Reflection, intentional use of personal monitoring, and awareness of collective knowledge provide the tools needed to guide and refine the LC's work. As all individuals work in unison, new or modified versions of goals may come to light. With the metacognitive principle in place, all members are reminded to ask themselves what is needed to continue moving toward the goals.

Finally, the creation of quality ideas and learning requires the fail-safe and out-of-bounds principles, provision of multiple ways to participate, and skills in making one's case and challenging the ideas of others (effective negotiation) so that the best ideas survive and result in exceptional quality for the groups' results, outcomes, and products. The fail-safe principle is the ideal way to create and maintain risk taking that includes trying "out-of-bounds" ideas. If members of an LC know that they can fail and that the group will collectively learn from that failure, individuals and interest groups will attempt to move beyond ideas considered within the status quo and find new, exciting ways to extend learning. One way to support this principle is to establish numerous ways for individuals within the LC to participate.

For instance, there are many aspects to running a successful community and not all have to do with writing, public speaking, or researching. Sometimes, individuals will need to participate by watching and listening instead of doing. Bielaczyc and Collins (1999) noted that learning by doing may mean learning by watching someone else do it first. Observations can be just as powerful as experiences. This principle encourages co-collaborators to create a community that respects all roles and participation levels and understands that learning is a process and takes time.

The last principle, quality of products, must be valued by the community and those outside the community. When creating products, the LC should take stock of the audience, the level of background knowledge, and the expectations for standards of completion. Although the LC, as a whole, may agree on one set of standards, consideration of the outside community will determine the worth of the community's collective output. Each LC should keep in mind who its audience is and what standards of performance are expected.

The Powerful LC Planning Form presented in Appendix C includes items pertaining to the principles, such as for structural dependence, respect for others, diverse expertise, and knowledge sharing. Identification as a group or an organizer of how the structure of the community will have inter- and intradependence, respect for all members, intentional grouping or member selection to maintain diverse expertise, and identification of specific venues for knowledge sharing help make an LC strong and effective. These elements are often discussed at the creation stage, but they sometimes get lost along the way. The use of these components can take an existing or fledgling community and guide it toward one of power.

Designing Powerful LCs

In designing powerful LCs, building effective partnerships with relevant institutional stakeholders that can help support the LCs is important. So is devoting attention to effective member criteria and selection procedures.

Building Partnerships to Support Powerful LC Development

As discussed previously, the stakeholders can provide important guidance, resources, and information exchange options that will help sustain an LC. However, more is needed than identification of one's stakeholders that can help guide the process and support the creation of an LC that is strong, effective, and sustainable. Effective partnerships not only must be developed but also cultivated in an ongoing manner so that they last.

Within any college or university, effective partnerships between different relevant organizational units to support the development of long-lasting powerful LCs are crucial. Several issues should be considered when creating a plan for implementation, including the role of administration and other partnerships that need to be developed. As B. L. Smith, MacGregor, Matthews, and Gabelnick (2004) indicate, "LCs require leadership at many different levels" (p. 303). They explain that establishing a collaborative leadership team is the single most important step in initiating and sustaining LCs, which was also a key finding from the National Learning Community Project (1996–2003). One strategy is to develop an advisory board for the LC consisting of multiple stakeholders. This board can provide diverse opinions, support cross-campus communication, develop policies and procedures, and establish an egalitarian structure (Brooke & Gruenewald, 2003).

B. L. Smith et al. (2004) further suggest that having many individuals with different institutional roles and perspectives is truly valuable in institutionalizing an LC program. Thus, attention can be brought to the functional support needs of the LC to ensure that critical support people are involved (e.g., recruitment, development, cocurricular connections, marketing, advising, registration, space and scheduling, library, administrative support, and evaluation).

There are a number of crucial, key partnerships. It should be realized, however, that there are both primary and secondary stakeholders, and that developing pertinent and effective partnerships with secondary stakeholders can also be crucial to the development and sustenance of LCs. Secondary stakeholders include institutional offices such as admissions, registrar, bursar, and affirmative action. Also included are noninstitutional organizations such as nonprofit agencies, employers, and alumni involved in service-learning and internships for students.

Developing an Effective Partnership Between Academic and Student Affairs

This section echoes the pertinent comments from various contributors to B. L. Smith and Williams's (2007) monograph *Learning Communities and Student Affairs: Partnering for Powerful Learning* and summarizes the successful strategies that seem most pertinent to LCs. It is useful to note that while recent literature points to the powerful potential in collaboration between academic affairs and student affairs (Kinzie & Kuh, 2004), the two groups often bring different approaches to decision making, debating, and establishing priorities (Blake, 1996).

B. L. Smith and Williams (2007) note that institutions with successful LCs overcome divisional boundaries and rely on the unique contributions of each partner; for example, it is impossible to imagine a successful residential LC that does not rely on the expertise of both residence life staff and faculty. Ways to support powerful student affairs/academic affairs partnerships include the following:

- Ensure that administrative/organizational structures include an academic/student affairs partnership. One way to accomplish this is joint leadership with the responsibility to coordinate design/implementation of the LC (Gruenewald & Brooke, 2007).
- Recruit individuals who bring a spirit of cooperation and collaboration to the table. Use this talent to develop a community based on shared vision and positive intentions (Gruenewald & Brooke, 2007). Senior academic and student affairs administrators need to demonstrate support to the collaboration by devoting resources (human and

fiscal) to collaborative initiatives (Levine Laufgraben, O'Connor, & Williams, 2007).

- Cultivate community and build relationships that are vital to success (Watson-Derbingy, 2007).
- Develop an approach that places community and empowerment-oriented education first. Think about fitting the institution to the needs of the LC participant, even if that reconfigures traditional roles and boundaries (Hardiman, Smith, Washington, & Brewster, 2007; Watson-Derbingy, 2007).

Developing an Effective Partnership With Institutional Research/Student Assessment

Institutional researchers, acknowledged as the institutional planning and assessment experts at most colleges and universities, must play a leading role in order for the comprehensive approach to optimal LCs to become a reality. Swing (2009) argues that institutional researchers will engage in the process of managing and leading institutional change by blending data skills, strategic planning, outcomes assessment, and advocacy for improvement.

Swing also argues that the change process begins with building awareness and developing focus. In the planning stages, institutional researchers can communicate database information that identifies and disaggregates components of complex issues. Institutional researchers can support these steps through careful collection, analysis, and reporting of information before the initiation of LCs. Peterson (1999) noted a shift in the focus of institutional research from organizational improvement to institutional redesign and transformation. Institutional researchers contribute to organizational learning by participating in mixed work groups, serving on campus committees, and facilitating forums that support discussions of relevant data (Delaney, 2009; Leimer & Terkla, 2009). In this sense, they can help foster collaborative conversations that allow the institution to explore the bigger questions that relate to LCs.

Other ways that institutional researchers can assist in making LCs effective are as follows:

- They can set an example of how to conduct evaluation by providing relevant research and information from peer institutions (Swing, 2009).
- They can support program faculty in the development of measures that inform improvement efforts (Delaney, 2009).

- They can provide data about LCs on campus for institutional press releases or promotional publications, or reports to accrediting or state coordination agencies.

In short, the institutional research office can provide critical information and support as LCs look to demonstrate impact, determine areas that need improvement, and identify learning success.

Selecting Members

As the creation of an LC moves forward, consideration of member selection is the next key component. Although the intrinsic nature of an LC is to bring together those who have a single or agreed-upon purpose, access and diversity are essential considerations that come into play. Both depth of perspective and legal considerations are at stake. If the group is limited in membership, then selection, perspectives, ideas, and expertise could become extremely narrow and cause the LC to stall. In addition, there could be legal implications for exclusion of desired participants (chapter 6 covers legal implications within LCs in depth).

As indicated in Table 2 in the introduction, Barth (2001) stresses that true community is fostered by appropriately encouraging and facilitating community members to acknowledge their own inadequacies, share their own problems, be risk takers, exhibit humor, collaborate with the other learners, show compassion, serve as a model, and have a moral purpose for participation. Wenger, McDermott, and Snyder (2002) add to this list that a powerful LC develops a unique identity that is meaningful to and energizes all participants and conducts intensive joint and coordinated effort to develop optimum strategies for solving the problems at hand.

Doolittle, Sudeck, and Rattigan's (2008) view of ideal participants in an effective LC adds to Barth's view:

> Learning community members exhibit seven propensities: a sense of common purpose; viewing peers in the group as colleagues; seeking self/group actualization; perceiving outside groups as similar to one's own group; individual and communal reflection; giving and seeking help; and celebrating accomplishments. . . . [Individuals also] must infuse four critical components of group process to be successful: a clear understanding of the communication process; a clear mission, with goals and objectives; a strategy for accomplishing the group's work; and group membership and group decision-making. Additionally, two features of the group communication

process are essential: having opportunities for meaningful feedback, and having a strategy to deal with group tension and defensiveness. Underpinning this is clarity of mission with a written set of goals and objectives. (pp. 305–6)

Data collected by Ajjawi and Higgs (2008) indicate that it is important for pertinent role models and mentors to be included as active members of PLCs. If one is talking about FLCs, for example, every faculty has members who are especially listened to and influential, and that group should be represented among the LC membership. DuFour (2004) indicated that homogeneous cohorts can create deeper learning by removing barriers to success, while grouping students with quite diverse strengths can "strengthen all voices within the group to create intellectual and psychological development due to the mismatch of skills" and the resulting interdependence "creates a bridge between the learners" (p. 6).

The Rest of the Story

Look back at the scenario at the beginning of the chapter. Roxie, the director of the NCC committee, is concerned and frustrated for good reason. It is clear that the provost is only giving lip service to the value of the committee: The provost is unwilling to commit money to the project, and as John observes, reports by various diversity committees over the years have merely been filed away. There seems to be a general lack of buy-in by major stakeholders.

The committee has been specifically charged with developing an LC to address the problem of low retention and graduation rates among students of color. However, Babette shifts the focus of purpose too broadly by talking about diversity and discrimination in general. Later, other members of the committee lose sight of the big picture when they get sidetracked into tangential concerns and direct their attention to details of participation in a festival.

Roxie needs to refocus her group on the purpose of the LC; get stronger buy-in; do an environmental scan to identify stakeholders and develop partnerships; and identify alternative sources and resources, because the provost provided none. She can also apply the principles of LC design to the committee as well as the SLC they are to develop.

Conclusion

This chapter proposed guiding principles for constructing and sustaining powerful LCs of various kinds and discussed practical steps for creating or improving powerful LCs. It emphasized the importance of having a clear purpose for the LC and performing an environmental scan. In addition, it offered practical tools for operationalizing and applying design principles, such as building significant partnerships among stakeholders.

For Reflection

As you create your own meaning from ideas in this chapter, begin to think about a specific LC at your institution (or at an institution you know about if you are in a governmental or other noninstitutional role) and how it can inform your work or interests. Use that LC to answer the following questions and help you reflect on practical implications of the material in this chapter:

- Why is this an LC? What traits does it have? How interdisciplinary is the focus?
- What special significance does the research evidence referred to in Appendix H, available in the e-edition of this book and at www .styluspub.com/resrcs/other/PLC.pdf, indicate about your LC?
- Is there a specified purpose for the LC? Is there agreement about the LC's purposes?
- How can you best sustain LC support efforts over time?
- Is it a powerful LC? If not, what would it take to make it powerful?
- How can you best get administration/faculty buy-in to this LC? Who owns the program?
- Which partnerships are important, and which are especially important, for this LC?
- What organizational structures support partnerships and collaboration? How can you best establish needed partnerships to support the LC in maximizing student learning?
- How does the LC connect to the broader community?
- What intentional strategies are being used, and what should be used, to enhance this LC?
- Is your institution a true learning organization in the sense described here? Does it have effective institution-wide PLCs? What can you do about the situation?

Now that you have read and reflected on this chapter, you should be able to complete the following items on the Powerful LC Planning Form in Appendix C:

- Section I: #1. "How did this idea for an LC come about? What was the trigger event?"

- Section I: #2. "Why are you doing this?"
- Section I: #3. "What are your overarching goals?"
- Section I: #4. "Purpose Statement" and "Conduct an environmental scan."
- Section I: #5. "Who are the stakeholders?"
- Section I: #6. "What resources (or sources of resources) are available to support the LC?"
- Section I: #7. "What are potential barriers to your powerful LC?"
- Section II: #1. "What will the LC look like?"
- Section II: #2. "How will you select members for your LC?"
- Section II: #3. "What are the overarching goals of the LC?"
- Section III: #1. "How will you build community?"
- Section III: #2. "How will you develop a culture for learning?"
- Section III: #3. "What norms do you want members to follow and how will you ensure accountability?"
- Section III: #4. "What resources are needed for your LC to be successful?"

3

CREATING AND IMPLEMENTING OPTIMAL FACE-TO-FACE, VIRTUAL, AND HYBRID LCs

What's the Story?

Private College has received a generous donation from a couple of alumni in support of the school's mission of "accessible education." The administration has earmarked the money for improving learning communities (LCs). A committee has been formed to determine how best to use these resources. The committee is made up of three faculty members, two student representatives, and two staff members. The committee members are crammed into a small conference room, because the only larger meeting space is already in use and there are no other places for groups to meet on campus during that time period.

"Liz Geets can't make it today," says Professor Joni Davis. "It's tough being the only full-time IT staff member on a campus of this size. Liz thinks we should dedicate a significant portion of the funds to beefing up the online and hybrid courses."

Professor Ron Rather says, "No way! We don't need extra money for online or hybrid classes."

"Are you kidding?!" exclaims student member Leah Spitz. "Have you seen this school's online learning site? It's so boring and so slow."

"At least you can get on it," mumbles Larry Fish in a dejected voice as he slumps in his chair. He is having difficulty navigating the site because he does not have a personal computer at home and there is little help in the Tech Mall. He thinks he will have to drop the course. The others ignore him.

"It's not just the site," Professor Davis adds. "They need to give course reductions for online teachers. They want me to teach two new hybrid sections and an online one without any reduction in the rest of my workload."

"Who needs a course reduction?" Professor Rather counters. "I start teaching online next semester. I'm just uploading my lecture notes and sitting back to watch the learning."

Just then K. C. Glib bursts into the room with a huge stack of papers. "Sorry I'm late. The parking just gets worse and worse around here. All the students have been complaining about it. It affects the morale of the whole campus." K. C. adds, "By the way I printed out some articles I got off the Web that we can go through today."

The rest of the group members moan and roll their eyes.

In what ways are LCs generally failing at Private College?
In what ways could LCs be improved in each of the delivery formats?

We have concluded through our work that the construction of a learning community, with the instructor participating as an equal member, is the key to a successful outcome and is the vehicle through which online education is best delivered. . . . What is most effective about our approach is its simplicity. And the fact that it does not depend on any one form of technology. It is about using our best practices as educators and applying them in a completely different environment. Tried and true techniques used face-to-face in the classroom often do not work when the classroom is virtual. . . . When learners cannot see or even talk to one another, the use of collaborative assignments becomes more challenging but far from impossible. . . . Learning in the distance education environment cannot be passive. . . . Successful online teaching is a process of taking our very best practices in the classroom and bringing them into a new, and for some faculty, untried, arena. In this new arena, however, the practices may not look exactly the same. . . . Development of a strong learning community and not just a social community . . . is the distinguishing feature of online distance learning.

—Palloff and Pratt (2007, pp. xvi, 5–6, and 43)

As noted in this quote, the benefits of LCs apply across delivery formats. Yet in comparing face-to-face and virtual student learning communities (SLCs) adaptations may be necessary to fully realize such benefits. Furthermore, the hybrid delivery format (a combination of face-to-face and virtual) is gaining popularity in many local settings and also deserves unique attention. This chapter provides an in-depth and in-breadth comparison and contrast of powerful LCs in all three delivery formats.

Astin (1993) was a forerunner in proposing peer networks to support student learning, and Dawson (2010) has discussed the use of "social" inter-action to educate, based on the positive correlation between learning and peer-peer interactions. In 2001, Light noted that "a student's propensity to participate within study groups was an accurate predictor of academic suc-cess" (p. 737). Yet how do instructors reach the "digital natives" of the "yuk/wow" generations (McWilliam, 2008) while still providing learning environ-ments for Generation X? Understanding how face-to-face, virtual, and hybrid delivery formats are alike and different helps answer that question.

Comparison of Outcomes in Face-to-Face, Virtual, and Hybrid LCs

At the time this book was being written, the latest available data collected by the National Center for Education Statistics (NCES, 2008) showed that during 2006–7 two-thirds of all US postsecondary degree-granting institu-tions offered online and/or hybrid courses, 97% for public two-year institu-tions and 89% for public four-year institutions. A total of 61% of all the institutions offered online courses, and 35% offered hybrid courses. The overall combined percentage for all the institutions (66%) increased from 52% in 2000–2001.

In July 2009, the US Department of Education released the findings of a carefully performed meta-analysis evaluating the outcomes of learning in online education (Means, Toyama, Murphy, Bakia, & Jones, 2009) that may accelerate the prevalence of virtual and hybrid LCs. The findings showed that online students performed better academically than equal-ability students in the same courses learning face-to-face across a wide range of subject disciplines. Although the study's primary focus was on pre-college students, the stated conclusions were generalized to include undergraduate (and graduate) students at all types of colleges and universities. Picciano, Seaman, and Allen (2010) drew on six years of extensive data collected through national studies of online learning at the elementary through college levels of American education. They documented that online education is having a growing transformative impact on American education in terms of its increasing compatibility with institutional missions and increases in stu-dent access, faculty acceptance, instructional quality, student satisfaction, and student learning.

Note, however, that this study and the Department of Education study make no mention of the impact of online learning on student retention. The many studies that have compared retention rates for face-to-face and online courses have all found lower student retention for college online learning courses and programs. It should be mentioned that this finding may result from factors other than the method of instruction. One example is Pratt's (1996) finding that extroverts probably should not be taking online courses because it is more difficult for them to establish their presence in an online environment than a face-to-face environment; the converse was found to be true for introverts. Another example is Gednalske's (2010) finding that adding a greater sense of human presence to online courses at Santa Barbara City College increased the student retention rate by 10%. As students discover that online courses are not for them—whether it is because they are extroverts, because online seems too impersonal to them, or for some other reason—they will tend to drop the course rather than try to finish it. There may be additional factors that also account for this finding.

The Department of Education study referred to previously (Means et al., 2009) found several key factors to explain the superiority of online education for student learning. These factors seem to be important for effective LCs. They include students' "control of their interactions" (p. xvi), greater active learner reflection and self-monitoring, more opportunities for collaboration, and greater time on task. We suggest that such factors, generally more prominent in online education, are the critical factors—not the medium used. As the Department of Education study states, "When groups of students are learning together online, support mechanisms such as guiding questions generally influence the way students interact, but not the amount they learn" (p. xvi). Thus, the study concludes that online learning is not a superior medium, but, rather, that it leads to better results because it emphasizes such types of interaction much more than face-to-face instruction.

In addition, the study found that hybrid (blended) courses, courses that involve a combination of online and face-to-face learning, offer even greater student learning than online courses. Here again, the student interaction and time factors noted are the key. It is now abundantly clear that in the future face-to-face and virtual LCs must work in concert and support one another, because even though they each have important qualities of uniqueness they have commonality as well.

Appendix D demonstrates from two personal experiences of the senior author that exactly the same principles and techniques are operating in powerful online LCs as are operating in powerful face-to-face LCs. And as will become apparent later in this chapter, research and theory within the literature also supports this conclusion.

Although our discussion has focused on SLCs, it is important to realize that all three delivery modes can also be applied to powerful professional LCs (PLCs) and learning organizations (LOs).

Essential Processes Common to All Three Delivery Modes

As technology continues to advance and hybrid LCs become ever more popular, the similarities between online and face-to-face LCs will probably become even more pronounced. Palloff and Pratt (2007) comment: "Many of our colleagues have postulated that the technology enhancement of face-to-face courses has effectively begun to blur the distinctions between online and face-to-face classes. The use of synchronous media and virtual classrooms has grown and is affecting how we view community" (p. xv).

One process all three delivery methods have in common is the use of online learning management systems/learning content management systems (LMSs) designed to develop, manage, and deliver digital learning content for courses, administration, and university committees. Most aspects of a course and/or an LC can be delivered through an LMS including posting of key documents (e.g., course syllabi, meeting agenda), announcements, assignments and due dates, and lectures; links to relevant online videos, modules, and websites; discussion/feedback forums; grading and assessments; and wiki, RSS feeds, online chat, and social media. Although several common traits are found in most LMS products, there is wide variation in the placement, labels, use, operations, and overall features offered by each. Accordingly, effective LMS training for all faculty, students, and LC members is crucial to success, regardless of the delivery format. Similarly, LMSs that separate out announcements, discussion boards, folders, wiki, and other communication areas by team or group can aid in managing multiple SLCs whether face-to-face, virtual, or online.

LMSs are particularly important for courses offered in the virtual delivery format because the system essentially becomes the online cyberclassroom, connecting the instructor and course participants. The same would likely be true for a virtual and/or hybrid LC.[1] However, many institutions are making LMSs available and/or mandatory for all courses, even those offered in a face-to-face format. As face-to-face instructors use LMSs and become more comfortable with their use for posting course materials and grades, they increasingly incorporate the more interactive LMS features into their courses. This would also appear to be the case with face-to-face LCs. In that regard, LMSs have played a key role in eliminating some of the historical distinctions between face-to-face and virtual online courses and LCs.

Even absent this trend, powerful face-to-face, hybrid, and virtual LCs—whether SLCs or PLCs—have many critical characteristics and processes in common. In addressing these commonalities, the following discussion identifies 25 essential processes based on characteristics that the three delivery modes share in common. These essential processes are grouped according to whether they deal primarily with planning and preparation, implementation and operation, or sustenance and improvement of powerful LCs; however, it should be realized that most of them have important relationships to all three types.

Quotes throughout the following subsections sometimes refer specifically to face-to-face LCs or virtual LCs. In every case, however, what is said applies equally to the other types of LCs. Despite slight differences in application (e.g., each mode necessitates adjusting the interaction activities and techniques in different ways to achieve maximum positive effect), essentially the same processes and activities can be utilized to achieve success.

Planning and Preparation of Powerful LCs

1. *In planning, promoting, and initiating the group, define the purpose and outcome goals and objectives for the group in unequivocal, clear-cut, succinct, and focused terms.* This is essential for all three primary membership types of LCs (SLCs, PLCs, and LOs). If intended aims are not unambiguous to all LC members, how can one expect that they will cooperate in achieving the intended learning goals? All experts in LCs agree that clear goals are essential to group learning success, whether the learning focus is on, for example, understanding and mastering content, stimulating higher order thinking, or finding solutions to practical problems. Most experts would add that in order to sustain the LC, it is important to remind the community members periodically of the purpose and goals of the LC, using appropriate and stimulating terms. LC members should internalize and express the LC purpose and goals.

Goodsell Love (2004) states emphatically:

> LC programs can be tremendously flexible in addressing the needs of specific student populations or specific curricular issues. Too much flexibility, however, can lead to a lack of focus. Clearly defining the purpose of LCs

during implementation, and continuously revisiting purpose(s), is essential to sustainability. Although this sounds obvious, it is often glossed over. . . . LC leadership with a broad mandate for sweeping change must be able to articulate the program's purposes and expected outcomes in detailed, observable, and measurable ways. (p. 20)

2. *Be certain that the LC contributes to and is integral to the institution's core mission and vision and has the full and committed support of the institution's leadership.* For an LC to be "powerful," the institution sponsoring the LC, whether it be a college or university or some other organization (often true of PLCs), must reflect its core mission in the mission of the LC. This will contribute greater commitment and support on the part of leadership throughout the institution—the administration, the various service department heads, and in the case of colleges and universities the academic department heads and the faculty (who are traditionally responsible for the curriculum/courses offered).

While support of the formation and activities of LCs by the central administration is crucial to the success and power of LCs, stringent top-down mandating and control by the central administration is counterproductive and undesirable. Such oversupport and interference will generally lessen or destroy LCs' power to impact member and group learning.

Goodsell Love (2004) adds additional reasons why the institutional mission is important to the success and sustainability of LCs:

Congruence between a LC initiative and the institution's mission is essential, since the mission relates to and influences systems such as faculty rewards, recruitment of students, and allocation of financial resources. . . . [It is] instrumental to the program's longevity. Typically, they have an administrative champion, someone who advocates for and protects program resources. This person's deep commitment to the program can provide a buffer from leadership changes higher up in the organization. . . . Developing a stable core of faculty is equally important for the sustainability of LCs. . . . Related to the need for a stable core of administrators and faculty is the need to expand the LC leadership network. . . . Increasing the number of people committed to and responsible for a LC program helps sustain the program even if key leaders leave or early adopters "burn out." (pp. 23–25)

3. *In addition to faculty, be certain to obtain buy-in and commitment to the LCs from important stakeholder groups across the institution.* It is crucial

to expand institutional buy-in to the LCs beyond faculty, including the administration and all staff members in every department. Peckskamp and McLaughlin (2010) identify specific stakeholder groups on a campus that should be reached out to: "Successful LCs require the participation and support of many different campus stakeholders, including academic department, the registrar, housing, residence life, and admissions offices, and others" (p. 1).

The positive impacts of LCs should be shared with the stakeholders. For example, it is important for them to know that SLCs create strategic and reflective learners who are intellectually and socially adept within society and that faculty and staff find involvement in LCs pleasurable and intellectually rewarding. Regarding the latter, Hurd (2010) states:

> Faculty and staff who work with LCs report that they both enjoy the experience and learn a great deal from collaboration that crosses the sometimes seemingly impermeable boundaries between academic affairs and student affairs, as well as boundaries between the disciplines. They also enjoy the kind of boundary crossing that happens as they connect multiple kinds of learning experiences to develop a more holistic learning environment for students. (p. 4)

4. Decide ahead of time what methods will best promote rich exchanges of knowledge and experiences among members for the expected composition and culture of that LC. This recommendation came from Falk and Drayton (2009). They talk about the importance in PLCs of applying craft knowledge (professional knowledge regarding how best to accomplish the specific task), contextual knowledge (knowledge of how the particular context may change the approach or application that is needed), and emerging experiences (the pertinent new knowledge gained from discussing and actually trying out an application).

Stimulating back-and-forth dialogue and questioning/querying continually occurs in powerful LCs, and it is important that there be a variety of effective ways for LC members to share insights and other relevant learning. For example, introverts may prefer to have time to organize their thoughts before sharing, whereas extroverts may want to talk through their thoughts in the moment.

In an LO, which by its nature includes a wide range of levels of education, skills, and experiences—from administrators to faculty to professional staff to students to maintenance and security personnel—not all members may feel equally comfortable or skilled with all forms of communication. Support staff in maintenance or groundskeeping may be hesitant to share in activities involving formal writing. Face-to-face faculty may feel quite comfortable with public speaking, but less comfortable with computer chats. Other staff may feel nervous if asked to speak publically. Finally, be aware that different stakeholders may be hesitant to contribute honestly if they fear their opinions are undervalued or not welcome; for example, adjunct or part-time faculty/staff and full-time faculty up for tenure may fear reprisals for contributions oppositional to the overall cultural attitudes within the institution. In such cases, options for anonymous input may be useful.

Planning for and providing multiple avenues for contributing insights can allow for greater diversity of voices, shared knowledge, insights, and experiences. In addition, the LC can make use of the diversity of individuals' skills during interactions and colearning.

5. *Plan for construction of an LC environment that will maximize learning outcomes.* In their principles of good practice, Chickering and Gamson (1987) call for encouraging active learning environments to promote transfer of student learning (see chapter 5). The environment within and surrounding the LC impacts member learning positively or negatively in many ways. It is crucial to create an environment that promotes the deep learning found in powerful LCs.

6. *Identify, plan for, and gather all necessary resources in a timely manner.* Although the introduction of LCs can often make use of program funds budgeted for programs that they are replacing, significant long-term additional costs in personnel, material, equipment, and other financial needs should be expected. This is especially true for complex LC programs and where start-up funding was provided by foundation or government grant funds that are now being phased out. Goodsell Love (2004) identifies a number of specific operational costs that need to be budgeted: "Depending on the features of the program, funds may be required for out-of-class activities, field trips, research projects, events or fairs highlighting and celebrating the work of students and faculty, or for external speakers or performers" (p. 28). For personnel, not only do salaries and benefits apply, but there is need for faculty and staff development.

It is crucial to conduct effective assessment into priorities, creative ways to economize without adversely impacting the LC's quality and outcomes (e.g., through cooperating with other institutional departments or centers), and how to maximize "bang for the buck" through improving organizational and operational efficiency and effectiveness. However, it should be remembered that such assessment studies also require financial resources.

Making your case to the institutional policy makers and decision makers for such budget items requires a rationale that is well thought out and communicated effectively. Shapiro and Levine (1999) state well the rationale for such resource needs:

> Throughout this book we return to the centrality of faculty for the success of a LC. How an institution estimates the budgetary implications of faculty involvement is a complex issue. . . . To change the nature of undergraduate education on a campus, there must be an investment in faculty development. At the same time, the reward structure must be rethought to include recognizing and valuing teaching. LCs are among the most cost-effective ways to involve faculty in sustained professional development activities around teaching and pedagogy. Faculty in LCs are constantly reporting that the experience has changed the way they teach in all their classes. . . . Costs associated with faculty release time to work collaboratively with others in different departments, summer stipends, incentive grants, and travel support are investments in improving undergraduate education. (pp. 49–66)

In addition, Strine Patterson (2010) states, "Creating learning communities requires resources, time to plan and collaborate, and commitment from staff, faculty and students . . . not a 'quick fix' to the ills of higher education. . . . The benefits of LCs, however, usually outweigh the costs" (p. 24).

Implementing and Operating Powerful LCs

7. *Take concerted steps to maximize "social presence" and thus over time to have the community of inquiry be emotionally bonded.* This promotes ongoing group cohesion, coalescence, esprit de corps, camaraderie, and sense of identity, which leads to the members working together effectively toward a common goal or cause. Boston, Ice, and Gibson (2010) contend it is crucial that models of student retention for virtual LCs be developed (like the ones that have been developed for face-to-face LCs). In their analysis of 28,000 student records and survey data, they identified "social presence" as the most critical variable to consider in such a model.

Palloff and Pratt (2007) define "social presence" in online contexts as "the person we become when we are online and how we express the person in virtual space" (p. 28). They emphasize that to achieve social presence the instructor must model it, empower the participants to help build community, and establish shared goals/purposes and mutually agreed-upon guidelines pertaining to participant behavior and communication guidelines. For them, presence correlates with both coalescence and the formation of a sense of community. According to Garrison and Vaughan (2008),

> Students in a community of inquiry must feel free to express themselves openly in a risk-free manner . . . and gain a sense of belonging to the community. The formal categories of social presence are open communication, cohesive response and affective/personal connections. . . . Social presence must provide the cohesive tension to sustain participation and focus. Although participants must be respected as individuals, they must also feel a sense of responsibility and commitment to the community of inquiry. Open communication establishes a community of inquiry, but social cohesion sustains it. As an environment of comfort and trust evolves, over a period of time the emotional bonding and camaraderie typical of a powerful LC will become established. (pp. 19–20)

Most experts on virtual LCs would probably say that social presence pertains only to virtual LCs, because it is so crucial in that realm. However, Garrison and Vaughan (2008) point out that because all of the characteristics that they mentioned are crucial factors in powerful face-to-face SLCs, the term should apply equally in face-to-face settings. The term *social presence* is not used in the literature that we reviewed pertaining to the PLCs and LOs. Nevertheless, it seems clear that social presence is equally critical to PLCs and LOs.

8. *Provide and emphasize group and individual norms for conduct at the start, and follow up with periodic reminders as needed.* Because a powerful LC has such open, free interaction and member bonding is so strong, behavioral expectations need to be stressed up front, and members may need to be reminded appropriately if there are hints that interactions could get out of hand. Conduct stimulating orientation information sharing and activities to help members get to know one another as well as the purpose and goals/objectives of the community. It is essential to offer explicit explanations of the learning activities being utilized and why they are important so that members come to understand and respect the customs, roles, autonomy, powers, and responsibilities and expectations that will assist all members in being optimally effective as they relate to and communicate with one another and the total group. The behavioral expectations should also be related to what the LC is designed to accomplish.

9. *Develop a shared vision of what the LC is all about, and promote a sense of excitement, vitality, group identity, and loyalty from the very beginning.* With regard to this charge, Palloff and Pratt (2007) state:

Most instructors begin their classes with student introductions as a way for the class to begin to know one another as people. Simply jumping into the course material without this creates an atmosphere that is dry and sterile, devoid of any sense that there are real people engaged here. Many instructors . . . use . . . designed group activities, simulations, and group projects as another means of facilitating a sense of being part of the group. (p. 113)

Recent developments at Northern Illinois University, which was not selected for our 100-Institution Survey, are illustrative of the importance of developing such a shared vision throughout the entire institution. In early 2010, President John G. Peters launched a Vision 2020 Initiative that involved intense campuswide discussion at all levels about the university's goals. In a September 2010 promotional document titled *Vision 2020* (Northern Illinois University, 2010), President Peters announced to the world the preeminent vision coming out of that process: "We will become the most student-centered public university in the Midwest" (p. 3). In his *President's Report 2012* (Northern Illinois University, 2012), Peters highlighted two new student programs, both pertinent to this book, developed and designed to help the university achieve its new vision: (a) "Research Rookies," which "pairs talented underclassmen with faculty mentors and allows them to participate in research and the creation of new knowledge early in their college careers"; and (b) "Themed Learning Communities," which "[provide] students with opportunities to learn in deeper, more significant ways by allowing them to examine a common theme across disciplines such as the humanities, natural sciences and social sciences" (p. 7).

10. *Create a distinctive meeting place or places for the group to meet regularly and encourage and facilitate member interactions between meetings.* A designated space or spaces is needed for exchange of ideas and perspectives. In every powerful LC there is a designated location or locations (virtual and time-delayed/elastic in the case of online LCs, physical and real time in the case of face-to-face LCs, and both for hybrid LCs) for everyone to meet and dialogue, conduct group activities, reflect as a group, and so forth. The leader should clearly identify the location(s) from the start. Furthermore, in the case of online LCs, it is important to use language that clearly marks the "location" as a virtual site, so that members do not confuse it with a physical space.

For the LC to be powerful, it should meet regularly with not too much time elapsed between meetings in order for group bonding to be maintained and keep increasing. Chickering and Gamson's (1987) principles of good practice call for activities that promote frequent contact of various kinds among community members. Moreover, the place to meet—whether it is a physical location with synchronous interaction or a virtual location with asynchronous interaction—should be interesting and engaging, not boring. This is particularly important for sustaining the power of an LC and is the responsibility of the LC leader/facilitator.

11. *Make use of cohorts working together and having common experiences over significant lengths of time.* DuFour (2004) indicated that homogeneous cohorts can create deeper learning by removing barriers to success. Grouping students with quite diverse strengths can result in group learning that is much greater and deeper than would result from an equally effective group consisting of participants with homogeneous strengths. Furthermore, the participants rely on one another more, which strengthens group bonding.

12. *Make ongoing and effective intellectual connections to ensure LC success.* In a powerful LC, the focus continually needs to be on building connections: grounding concepts and generalizations as they relate to facts, linking content and theory to the practical and applied, mutually reinforcing themes related to individual and group activities and assignments, and making intellectual connections that promote both understanding and creativity. Proficiency in connecting and making meaning from what appears on the surface to be isolated experiences, facts, and topics is a hallmark of powerful LCs.

LC participants should be oriented and trained to always look for meaningful intellectual connections across the various individual and group activities. Making such connections in an efficient, effective manner facilitates information transfer across different spheres of thought. For example, it leads to comparing and contrasting—and integrating commonalities and differences—across academic disciplines and fields.

13. *Allow for and encourage a range of member roles, including leadership roles, and then promote effectiveness in those roles by providing orientation and other support.* A powerful LC involves creating a culture in which diversity of expertise is present, respected, and appreciated and in which all members are on equal footing. All members are empowered to share their thoughts, inquiries, and ideas and to assume leadership roles in the community that appeal to them and are needed. Such a culture cannot develop without effective encouragement, support, orientation, and training from the LC leader.

Chickering and Gamson's (1987) principles of good practice call for respecting diversity and talents within the group regardless of the ways in which particular individuals learn. In addition, all members—and especially the leader—must genuinely get to know all other members as well as their previous experiences. They should also continually encourage, affirm, and recognize member questions, ideas, suggestions, and other input.

14. *Develop a culture of trust, reward, and humility over ego, while encouraging LC members to resolve their own conflicts and disputes with one another.* Gregory and Kuzmich (2009) state the following about PLCs, which also applies to SLCs:

> It is a human basic need to feel that we belong and are accepted and included. The feelings of comfort, trust, respect, and affection increase the brain's feel-good neurotransmitter brain levels (Panksepp, 1998). As a member of a team that influences our natural tendencies and responses, we create more fertile conditions for our own learning and risk taking. Michael Fullan (2002) suggests that information only becomes knowledge through dialogue and meaning making. . . . It would provide the same for adults. Also, modeling and engaging in cooperative group learning will help teachers design successful group work in the classroom. (p. xiv)

To be a powerful LC, the LC's environment must become one of collaboration, trust, mutual respect, understanding, and cohesion. These characteristics are necessary to facilitate conflict resolution so that the LC facilitator should not have to be drawn into any member conflict that develops. Moreover, in the LC formation and orientation stage, the facilitator should discuss conflict resolution strategies with the members, thus giving them the tools to harmoniously resolve developing conflicts on their own. According to Gregory and Kuzmich (2009),

> People need strategies for conflict resolution and methods of making decisions and solving problems. This is also the conscious process of discussing openly what the team needs to succeed and sometimes redefining the tasks. Strategies to use are building climate, problem solving, and determining priorities. (p. xix)

15. *Remember that an effective mentoring relationship is critical for the development of powerful LCs.* According to Strine Patterson (2010), developing an effective mentoring relationship is crucial, especially for young or new PLC professionals. Regarding powerful SLCs, Thomas and Adsitt (2010) state concretely that "the formal and informal mentoring relationships that participating undergraduates develop with influential faculty members and administrators are at the heart of the program's success" (p. 93). Include

well-trained peer mentors who have experienced a successful LC of a particular type. In addition, having the peer mentor meet regularly and work very closely with the leader or facilitator also contributes power to the LC.

Astin's (1993) data indicate that the peer group is "the single most important environmental influence on student development" (p. xiv). According to Strine Patterson (2010):

> There are very positive benefits attained by observation of the action of another person who has gone through similar changes and experiences. Peer mentors can participate in LCs by advising, tutoring, instructing, modeling roles or facilitating conversations, formally and informally. (p. 23)

16. *Not only allow but encourage and assist subgroups of the LC members to form and meet.* A variety of cooperative/collaborative learning subgroups, which can become true and powerful LCs, are identified and described in the typology. Without the formation, effective operation, and internalization of such subgroups, the LC lacks power in positively impacting member and group learning. They may be onetime or ongoing subgroups, depending on the need for division of labor or other important learning purposes.

17. *Include a focus on inquiry- and problem-based learning, active learning, reflection, and other approaches that will meet the desired goals and diverse learning styles.* Levine Laufgraben and Shapiro (2004) state that "within the universe of LCs, there is a sense 'no one size fits all.' . . . LCs vary to adapt to distinct campus cultures" (pp. 2, 13). Every learner has his or her learning style and it is important to respect diverse talents and ways of learning through multidimensional approaches.

This does not mean that we should tailor our instructional methods to particular learning styles; rather, it means that helping all of our students learn through multiple channels making use of diverse instructional methods (not just lecture) that are appropriate for the content being presented is important. The latter rather than the former is what both our personal teaching experience and research results in the literature on learning support.

It should be mentioned that Pashler, McDaniel, Rohrer, and Bjork (2008) found that "at present, there is no adequate evidence base to justify incorporating learning styles assessments into general educational practice" (p. 106) and subsequent articles in *The Chronicle of Higher Education* and *Change Magazine* highlighted this finding. We do not view Pashler et al.'s findings to conflict with our position. In the *Chronicle* article, for example, Glenn (2009) states:

The grandfather of this territory is David A. Kolb . . . who began to study learning styles in the late 1960s. In an interview, Mr. Kolb agrees with Mr. Sternberg that Mr. Pashler's review of the literature seems thin. . . . But Mr. Kolb also says that the paper's bottom line is probably correct: There is no strong evidence that teachers should tailor their instruction to their students' particular learning styles. (Mr. Kolb has argued for many years that college students are better off if they choose a major that fits their learning style. But his advice to teachers is that they should lead their classes through a full "learning cycle," without regard to their students' particular styles.)

18. *Be certain all LC members understand that each is responsible for and in control of contributing to the group's learning as well as her or his own learning.* In powerful LCs, all members know they have responsibility to themselves and the group. They must carry out their own learning responsibilities in an effective manner and also encourage one another to meet these responsibilities.

19. *Provide ongoing constructive feedback to each member and to the group.* Both individuals and groups need to know regularly how things stand. Clearly express the progress made in terms of both problems and accomplishments. Chickering and Gamson (1987), in particular, call for prompt constructive feedback to help refinement and reflection.

20. *Focus on learning principles and methods that build community.* Building LCs involves active learning methods and activities that promote meaningful intellectual engagement and deep learning. The key is active doing/ applying and teaching one another.

The LC leader must effectively encourage and demonstrate openness to risk and vulnerability, and acceptance of one another. Among other things, this involves moving from relatively safe and nonconfrontational to more challenging and uncomfortable activities, ideas, and categorizations.

According to Levine Laufgraben and Tompkins (2004) such pedagogy emphasizes that LC members and leaders share responsibility for both individual and group learning; LC members learn from one another; the LC facilitator's assignments are important in terms of both their content and the context in which they are given; and learning and community strengthen each other and each is both a process and an outcome, a means and an end. With good pedagogy, the LC can develop and gradually internalize a common identity that leads to natural loyalty, sharing, and the engaged and deeper learning desired.

21. *Focus on how people learn best.* Levine Laufgraben and Tompkins (2004) share insight into the special role of LCs in how many people learn best:

> The key development over the past two decades has been to take the "LC" with a new sort of inquisitive seriousness by asking how students learn best. Uri Treisman (1992) noticed that successful students studied in different ways, forming study groups to review material and reinforcing each other's learning. What is remarkable about this finding was that student learning had nothing to do with improved lecturing, better or more animated presentation by the teacher, or visual aids; it was a function of the social organization of students. (pp. 54–55)

Sustaining and Improving Powerful LCs

22. *Make effective, long-term professional development for leaders and program support a key to sustaining and improving powerful LCs.* The most effective professional development involves individual incentives/activities and effective PLCs. Goodsell Love (2004) devotes an entire chapter to training and professional development for faculty who will lead SLCs. Such training can be diverse, from costly and formalized conferences to frugal and informal faculty chatting about assignments. The best methods will consider the stage of program development and the level of experience of the faculty members involved. Goodsell Love uses the following analogy:

> Faculty development is the fuel needed to keep the luxury cruiser in motion—it energizes and invigorates the program. The content and process of faculty development should be planned so that it supports and guides the needs of the LC program. The content and process of faculty development should be planned so that it supports and guides the needs of the LC program. In this way it becomes an essential factor in sustaining LCs. (p. 18)

23. *To sustain the power of the LC long term, include strategies that are novel, unexpected, and stimulating.* Originally this item was assigned to the "Implementing and Operating Powerful LCs" subsection, but Gregory and Kuzmich (2009) make a strong case that it is the key to sustaining an effective PLC (the same is no doubt true of face-to-face and online SLCs). They state emphatically:

> Facilitating learning by providing information in a novel way that stimulates all senses . . . is what good teachers do. No less is necessary for

adults. . . . Allowing adults to read, view, process, and dialogue about new knowledge and skills creates multiple conditions for diverse learners to continue learning. (p. xv)

Gregory and Kuzmich's (2009) strategies have proven themselves over many years of application by experienced and innovative teachers. Their book *Teacher Teams That Get Results: 61 Strategies for Sustaining and Renewing Professional Learning Communities* can be a valuable resource in the creation of powerful SLCs. They devote much of their book to presenting 61 "strategies" that can help appreciably to keep things novel and stimulating for PLCs over the long term (see Table 3.1). They also say that these strategies are effective for SLCs, and though their book is targeted to elementary-secondary education, the authors do an outstanding job of presenting practical details for applying each of the 61 strategies. In addition, they provide the specific purpose(s) for each strategy, a variety of excellent factual information in tabular form, process directions, guidelines for when to use each strategy, application examples, relevant sources in the literature, and drawings that serve as interesting and useful templates. Furthermore, although intended for use in face-to-face LCs, virtual LC versions can be created for all of them.

24. *Understand, plan, and apply the proven practices for accomplishing major change.* It is important for LC planners, leaders, and facilitators to be knowledgeable about good practices in group and change processes, and to have the ability to apply them with skill and wisdom. According to Goodsell Love (2004):

> Indeed the process of implementing long-lasting learning communities is no less daunting than the process of institutional reform; on some campuses it may be more like institutional revolution. . . . Understanding the nature of change is crucial to the success of learning communities . . . especially for campuses trying to improve and sustain their programs. . . . Understanding organizational dynamics and organizational change, and their applicability to curricular reform, can help learning community practitioners meet the challenges of sustaining learning communities. (p. 15)

Such strategies for change must be intentional, well planned, and executed with precision even though unexpected barriers and situations (both positive and negative) are likely to occur. Goodsell Love also emphasizes the importance of a stable campus leadership, the expansion of the LC leadership

TABLE 3.1

Gregory and Kuzmich's (2009) 61 strategies for sustaining and renewing PLCs.

Creating a Growth-Oriented Climate	Sharing Knowledge and Skills	Building Resilience and Creating Solutions	Determining Priorities Creating Excellence
1. ABC Conversations	1. Four-Corner Cards	1. Dip Party	1. Building on Success
2. Birthday Months	2. Inside-Outside Circles	2. Checking the Oil	2. Cause-and-Effect Planning
3. Community Circle	3. Jigsaw	3. Communication Matters	3. Celebrations and Next Steps
4. Concept Formation	4. Know, What to Know, Learned (KWL)	4. Doubling Up	4. Current Snapshot
5. Appreciating Diversity	5. Perspective Lens	5. Environmental Scanning	5. Four Squares for Creativity
6. Find Someone Who	6. Pluses and Wishes or Plus, Minus, Delta	6. FLOW	6. Lesson and Unit Studies
7. Four-Corners	7. Plus, Minus, Interesting or Upside, On Side, Downside	7. Force Field	7. Prioritizing the Impact of Solutions
8. Give and Go	8. Promissory Note	8. Gallery Walk	8. Prioritizing Work and Learning
9. Map Our Journey	9. Right Angle	9. Graffiti Board	9. Probable and Preferred Future
10. 3-2-1	10. Round Robin, Round Table	10. Hot Buttons	10. Pros and Cons
11. Nominal Group Process	11. Round the Room	11. Journey Mapping (History-Mapping)	11. SWOT
12. Personal, Interpersonal, Task Model (P.I.T.)	12. Star Gazing	12. Musical Chairs (Consulting Line)	12. The Interview
13. Processing Pause	13. Think, Pair, Share	13. Parking Lot	13. The People Ladder
14. Random Partners and Find a Partner	14. Wallpaper Poster	14. Roadblock Removal	14. Think Abouts
15. Synectics		15. The Question Matters	15. Data Chats
16. T Chart and Y Chart		16. Two Sides of the Story	

network across the institution, and extensive curricular integration in accomplishing major change pertaining to LCs.

25. *Conduct ongoing LC assessment and evaluation, and use the results for improvement.* It seems that every book on LCs includes a chapter or primary section that deals with the assessment of such entities and outcomes for the members therein. Such activities must occur on a regular basis, be well designed, and be implemented effectively. They must involve qualitative and quantitative as well as direct and indirect measures, and inferential interpretation. Once the assessment and evaluation results become available, it is imperative that they be discussed extensively by all pertinent parties. Then agreed-upon improvements must be incorporated into LC improvement.

Again, the 25 essential processes that we have discussed are equally applicable to all three delivery modes. Regardless of whether the LC will be face-to-face, online, or hybrid, the concerns noted should be considered when planning, implementing, or improving LCs.

However, it is also necessary to consider the unique characteristics and necessary processes that arise with differences in delivery mode in order to make appropriate adaptations for that mode. The following sections identify and discuss essential processes required to adapt to the unique characteristics of each of the three delivery modes. (Because hybrids are a blend of face-to-face and online modes, be aware that they may alternately reflect the characteristics and process concerns of these other two delivery modes, depending on the specific mode that the hybrid LC is functioning in at any given time.)

Essential Processes Unique to Face-to-Face LCs

Traditionally, most educational institutions have relied primarily on face-to-face delivery. Essential processes that uniquely pertain to face-to-face LCs include the following:

1. *Make the most of the potential that powerful face-to-face LCs have in order to create synergy for the entire campus.* Because face-to-face LCs meet in real time and space, they necessarily bring members of a particular LC "on location" to the college or university campus (or its recognized satellite). As such, members of face-to-face LCs have greater opportunity to interact formally and informally with one another as well as others on campus. They

are more likely, then, to contribute in complex ways to an overall campus culture. As Shapiro and Levine (1999) state:

> At their best, LCs generate their own synergy, creating a campus culture where the whole is greater than the sum of its parts. LCs . . . generally provide creative space for thoughtful members of the college community to work together. They do this by bringing together different units of the campus that have separate and distinct missions. (p. 43)

2. *Be sure that many people across the campus are intimately involved in face-to-face LCs.* This point extends on the first characteristic. While coming together on campus allows synergy to build from LC members to the campus as a whole, the reverse is also true. The experience of members of face-to-face LCs is more directly affected by the experience of campus life as a whole. This is especially true for residential SLCs. What is needed is well stated by B. Smith and R. Smith (2000):

> The engaged classroom is rarely, if ever, produced naturally. All involved— professors, teaching assistants (TAs), academic and residential college administrators, and especially students—must consciously conceive of, plan, and implement these types of experiences. And when developing residential LC models, they must do so both in and beyond the classroom. (p. 70)

LCs must work to include all of these groups actively and fairly. For example, institutions that rely heavily on part-time or adjunct instructors need to welcome and value the contributions of these professionals. They must also be aware that most of these instructors—the majority of whom are excellent and dedicated professionals—frequently have other demands on them, such as a full-time job or commitments to multiple institutions. Thus, there may be a need to compensate these and other professionals for the additional time and energy that LC work may require of them.

3. *Decide on and implement ways that the physical space can be improved in order to support community interaction for face-to-face learning to be maximized.* The design of physical spaces on a campus can either detract from or contribute to the effectiveness of face-to-face LCs. Are they welcoming, comfortable, and conducive to informal back-and-forth small-group discussion? Are they flexible, so that they can easily and effectively be adapted to changing LC situations? Do they provide easy access to places to congregate

for informal community interaction? Being sensitive to such needs is essential. For example, in the classroom, having chairs on wheels, so that they can easily be moved to stationary lab tables, can dramatically affect the ease with which in-class group work can take place.

4. *Encourage multilevel dialogue and engagement in face-to-face LCs so that interactions can be richer both verbally and nonverbally.* According to Shapiro and Levine (1999), "stimulating verbal exchanges and interaction are the norm" in face-to-face LCs (p. 150). A number of other prominent authors on LCs have made similar statements. By its nature, in-person communication is "richer" than mediated communication. This richness comes from the greater availability of nonverbal messages carried by the voice and body, which in turn allows for more nuance, complexity, and subtlety in meanings. Such nonverbal messages are significantly limited or completely absent in mediated forms of communication, including online interaction. For example, Strempel (2010) notes of her experience leading a face-to face LC, "An additional advantage is that students tend to look out for one another more, wondering out loud why someone is not in class and calling (or text messaging) the missing student in order to keep the group together" (p. 44). Such absences are less immediately noticeable in online contexts. Furthermore, in-person communication has a dimension of simultaneity—communicators can, and do, send and receive messages at once.

Thus, interaction in face-to-face LCs is not limited by the linear nature of online interactions, in which communication is often asynchronous and communicators must alternate between sending and receiving messages. This, nonlinear quality of face-to-face interaction allows for more stimulating, holistic flow and nonlinear exchange in interactions in face-to-face and hybrid LCs. Leaders/facilitators of face-to-face LCs therefore must take full advantage of the richness of interaction available to them, and hybrid leaders/facilitators should also consider the relative richness of communication in planning which activities might be more appropriate for times dedicated to face-to-face interactions.

5. *Observe and pay special attention to whether body language, facial expression, and voice tone and inflection correlate to the words being expressed.* Nonverbal communication is frequently a more accurate indicator of a person's real feelings, perceptions, and views than what verbal communication may indicate. Therefore, when nonverbal communication conveys a different message from the person's verbal communication regarding the matter, it is usually best to trust the former.

6. *Encourage involvement in service-learning to help make face-to-face SLCs powerful.* Although there are online service-learning courses (e.g., see Guthrie & McCracken, 2010), service-learning itself is inherently a face-to-face activity. Involvement in service-learning can be a unique opportunity for SLCs, because as stated by Leavitt and Oates (2003), "LCs provide an intellectual environment that fosters student voice and active engagement with complex, capacious problems and ideas. Service-learning applies this knowledge in service to broader community needs" (p. 5). An effective way to deepen the LC participants' sense of community is to have the participants work together to accomplish a "greater good."

Essential Processes Unique to Online LCs

Online learning provides convenient anytime, anywhere learning opportunities and credentialing for individuals. Unlike the face-to-face LC literature, the virtual LC literature does not (with some exceptions, e.g., Carlen & Jobring, 2005) focus much on different categories of virtual LCs. Part of the reason may be that researching online methods of use, such as "cyberethnography," is a relatively new realm of scholarly activity (see Browne, 2003).

An examination of institutional websites reveals that when institutions mention that they have online LCs they do so without distinguishing what forms those LCs take (e.g., Excelsior College, the Fielding Institute, and Santa Barbara City College). However, two respondents to our 100-Institution Survey did report specific online categories. Lehigh Carbon Community College has "online linked courses," and Skagit Valley College has "online paired-course" SLCs. This suggests that online education could benefit from intentionally incorporating many of the different SLC categories used in face-to-face SLCs as identified in the LC typology in chapter 1.

Drayton and Falk (2009) discuss the application of virtual PLCs for needed professional learning in the areas of mathematics and science, and list many factors that are important in order to achieve effective virtual PLCs (such factors are also important for virtual SLCs):

> For the past two decades a growing number of professional developers, educators, Web designers, and programmers have collectively developed electronic communities to facilitate professional learning in the areas of mathematics and science. This book presents the work of a group of trailblazers who have been engaged in the creation of such communities over

a long time. In sharing their insights and decisions, they cast light on the building and scaffolding of many aspects of online communities: content selection, creation and management, site architecture, administrative structures, tools and interactive features to be deployed, facilitation of discourse, and the development of online leadership. (p. 1)

The critical characteristics and processes unique to online LCs are as follows:

1. *Designated spaces for exchange of ideas and perspectives in powerful virtual LCs must be welcoming and lively even though they are virtual spaces.* Although online LCs do not function in a physical space, the members of online LCs do come together in a virtual space, and the design of that "space" can dramatically impact how members relate. Wahlstedt, Pekkola, and Niemelä (2008) note that the designers of online sites are capable of "enabling social community building in e-learning environments, and most importantly, supporting the development of a user-friendly and motivating e-learning place" (p. 1020).

Palloff and Pratt (2007) provide the following list of important elements that they include in designing online course sites:

- A welcome area, which includes a place for important announcements or additional guidelines that emerge as the course progresses
- A social area or forum on the discussion board where group members can interact on a personal level, apart from the course material
- Course content areas, organized according to the way the syllabus was constructed (meaning either by week, topic, or readings)
- An area or forum on the discussion board devoted to reflections on learning and the course evaluation
- An area or forum for student questions
- A separate area for assignments and exams or for posting assignments as discussion items, depending on the course structure (p. 46)

These elements can serve as helpful criteria for designing online spaces for LCs in general.

2. *Participants in powerful virtual communities must meet the following criteria:* be comfortable with and skilled in written communication; have effective self-motivation and self-discipline, a desire to contribute and share knowledge and experiences, and an effective working knowledge of computer and Internet technology; and be committed to and confident in online

learning. These requirements are identified by the Illinois Online Network (n.d.). In a powerful online LC, stimulating written exchanges are the norm, and the good writing skills essential for LC member and group success have become apparent. If such writing skills are not present in particular community members, steps must be taken to remediate, compensate with other skills, or adjust the interactions.

If such skills are present, the LC members have the potential to move far beyond writing an essay (one of the hallmarks of traditional face-to-face courses that is also considered important for online courses). According to Snart (2010),

> The web communicates best, or it educates and engages most effectively, not when it is used to present a single thesis and to support that thesis in a linear fashion, as might the traditional college essay. The web works best when it is used to reflect associative, nonlinear thinking. (p. 2)

Yet, as the Illinois Online Network criteria suggest, such benefits are available only to LC members whose basic reading and writing skills are developed enough to engage at this level.

Individuals in an online LC who fail to meet the criteria—such as having underdeveloped writing or computer skills—can suffer from a lack of inclusion in the LC. Further, the potential for unsuccessful participation by such members also negatively affects the group as a whole through misunderstandings and/or losing the voice and contribution of such members.

3. *Re-creating a face-to-face LC as an online LC should not be attempted.* Miller (2009) documented how attempts to directly transfer a face-to-face LC into an online one are problematic. Such attempts generally lead to high participant dropout in the online version of the LC. This higher dropout rate is due to the differences in face-to-face and online interaction.

In contrast to courses designed for a physical classroom, which generally do not have any mechanism to force discussion, online courses are more dependent on full participation for any sense of community. As Miller (2009) points out, "In the online environment, all students can have a voice and can be required to contribute to a discussion. Students often feel that it is easier in an environment where you are 'faceless' and yet participation still can be a challenge" (p. 2). Thus, it is the norm in online environments to require everyone to participate. In addition, the online culture/environment is always uniquely different from the face-to-face culture/environment even with a strong sense of occupancy online.

4. *Leaders/facilitators of powerful virtual LCs must continually explore the applicability of pertinent new online technological innovations and developments.* No area of society is advancing more rapidly than the field of online and wireless technology. New technological tools of many kinds are continually being introduced, and some of them undoubtedly have the potential to contribute to online community. An example is provided by a research study at Syracuse University (see Gednalske, 2010) that explored how sense of true online community and social presence, and in turn student success, was affected by incorporating Skype, Elluminate, Wimba Voice Board, and a microblog into online courses offered by Santa Barbara City College. Study data gathered and analyzed at the college indicated that the higher level of human contact in these types of online courses increased the student success rate significantly. Class completion rates were up 10%, and student course satisfaction ratings and mean GPA averages showed similar increases.

After contending that low-tech online LCs can be very effective, Snart (2010) discusses a number of the newest current technologies that can "ultimately help to create within a class a sense of communal experience and to foster in individuals the sense that they are contributing to a public sphere of dialogue, debate, knowledge and ideas" (p. 141). Some of the technologies that Snart suggests can help make virtual LCs more powerful are blogs, wikis, sharing of content and community through Social Bookmarking (see http://synnd.com/bookmarking~software/social-bookmarking for information on social bookmarking concepts and software), ExitReality (for information on this technology, see http://3d.exitreality.com or www.crunch base.com), and Second Life (an online 3D world imagined and created by its "residents").

Essential Processes Unique to Hybrid LCs

Hybrid LCs include an integrated focus on both face-to-face learning and online learning. According to the Sloan Consortium, if a class meets face-to-face less than 30% of the time, it cannot be classified as a blended/hybrid course (Snart, 2010). Deng and Yuen (2010) describe hybrid LCs as follows: "The blended nature of a community is reflected through the interplay of the online and offline dimensions of a community and the mix of various media in support of community-wide interaction" (p. 228).

According to S. Kaplan (n.d.),

There are two core assumptions that underlie approaches to building blended [hybrid] LCs: (1) that the deeper the personal relationships between learners, the richer the collaborative learning experience; and (2) that relationships between learners may be strengthened through structuring group interactions (using technology) before and/or after a face-to-face training event.

He identifies three types of hybrid LCs: Ice Breaker, Follow-on, and End-to-End. Each type is defined in Figure 3.1.

Garrison and Vaughan (2008) stress that the hybrid approach "is fundamentally different . . . not simply an add-on" (p. x), that it is "a design approach whereby both face-to-face and online learning are made better by the presence of the other" (p. 5), and that the mix of delivery modes in hybrids is "distinguishable" as "learning that is multiplicative, not additive" (p. 7). They see creating a powerful LC at the heart of hybrid learning success: "At the core of this process is a community of inquiry that supports connection and collaboration among learners and creates a learning environment that integrates social, cognitive, and teaching elements in a way that will precipitate and sustain critical reflection and discourse" (p. 8). Rovai and Jordan (2004) found a stronger sense of community in hybrid courses than either face-to-face or online courses.

The critical characteristics and processes unique to hybrid LCs are as follows:

1. *In order to design, implement, and sustain powerful hybrid LCs, educators must have an in-depth understanding of the operation of both face-to-face and virtual LCs.* Powerful hybrid LCs require practitioners to understand and work effectively in both face-to-face and online modes. In addition to applying all 25 essential processes that the three delivery modes have in common, powerful hybrid LCs must also effectively apply all the essential processes that are unique to both face-to-face and online LCs.

2. *Designated spaces for hybrid LCs are both virtual and physical; the two must work together naturally and seamlessly in concert.* Garrison and Vaughan (2008) characterize the best blend, a hybrid LC, as "the thoughtful fusion of face-to-face and online learning experiences" in such a way that "it recognizes the strengths of integrating verbal and text-based communication and creates a unique fusion of synchronous and asynchronous, direct and mediated modes of communication in that the proportion of face-to-face and online learning activities may vary considerably" (pp. 5–6). In addition, they

FIGURE 3.1
Three types of hybrid (blended) LCs.

Icebreaker Hybrid LCs

Icebreaker communities involve LC members engaging in pre-event or warm-up activities to "break the ice" prior to the group's face-to-face training or other kind of sessions. (Presumably such activities could also be conducted prior to a primary online meeting.) Such activities introduce norms, ground rules, and a continuing esprit de corps among the group members. Icebreakers accelerate the group's ability to "form, storm and norm" so that they will be able to accomplish the learning and other tasks at hand more quickly and effectively. By engaging participants in structured introductions and pre-work prior to a face-to-face training—through web conferencing, online discussions, and conference calls—it becomes possible to accelerate openness, sharing, and collaborative learning when participants gather face-to-face.

Follow-on Hybrid LCs

Follow-on LCs continue relationship and learning development following a face-to-face training, problem-solving, or other learning event. (Presumably such activities could also be conducted prior to a primary online meeting.) To keep people engaged, connected, and productive for a designated period of time following the event, follow-on LCs can serve as vehicles for sharing such things as results of group projects, discussing field research findings, and receiving mentoring from peers and instructors. For example, a follow-on LC to a one- or two-day training event can allow participants to receive answers to questions that may arise when they return to their jobs and apply what they learned to the practical setting, plus peer and instructor feedback, instructor coaching, and sharing with one another.

End-to-End Hybrid LCs

End-to-end LCs include both icebreaker and follow-on learning activities. Because the face-to-face meeting is typically "sandwiched" between group interactions supported by e-learning and collaboration tools and technologies, some have compared such an LC to a "digital sandwich." For example, a leadership development program could include an icebreaker LC to provide pre-work and introduce participants, a face-to-face experiential workshop LC to help clarify and define individuals' leadership development objectives, and a follow-on LC for coaching and mentoring that will help participants overcome challenges as they strive to achieve their development objectives.

Note. Adapted from S. Kaplan (n.d.).

suggest that leaders/facilitators "take special consideration of social and cognitive issues at the front end" and build and sustain a community "framed by the three essential elements of a community of inquiry—social, cognitive, and teaching presence" (pp. 32–33).

Garrison and Vaughan (2008) devote a major section of their highly recommended book *Blended Learning in Higher Education: Framework, Principles, and Guidelines* to discussing the following seven principles for implementing hybrid learning: (a) plan to establish a climate that will encourage open communication and trust (pp. 33–35); (b) plan for critical reflection, discourse, and tasks that will support systematic inquiry (pp. 35–39); (c) sustain community by shifting to purposeful, collaborative communication (pp. 39–40); (d) encourage and support the progression of inquiry (pp. 40–42); (e) manage collaborative relationships to support students in assuming increasing responsibility for their learning (pp. 42–43); (f) ensure that inquiry moves to resolution and that metacognitive awareness is developed (pp. 43–46); and (g) ensure that assessment is congruent with intended learning outcomes (pp. 46–49). Christensen, Johnson, and Horn's (2008) book on blended learning, *Disrupting Class: How Disruptive Innovation Will Change the Way the World Learns,* can also be stimulating and helpful to those interested in blended learning even though it is targeted at elementary/secondary education.

3. *LC leaders/facilitators must determine when a particular approach will work best.* While both face-to-face and online learning can accomplish all of the following, they also each have their particular strengths. The best of face-to-face learning is usually considered to be clear presentation of content/meaning, confirmation of understanding, and content that is made meaningful through discourse/discussion. The best of online learning is usually considered to be purposeful interaction and high quantity and quality of reflection.

Snart (2010) compares the strengths thus: "The online component is ideal for allowing students to work through information and to craft written responses at their own pace, in a concentrated and reflective way. . . . Face-to-face . . . is best suited for the embodied experience of discussion and presentation" (p. 83). In hybrid LCs, where both modes are available, different activities can be matched to the relative strengths of each mode.

Snart (2010) recommends using face-to-face time "for energetic discussion, student presentations, and the introduction of complex concepts/topics" and online time "for regularly recurring time for reflection, substantial writing, [and] repeatable self-assessment" (p. 148). However, he points out, "Equally successful blended courses may look entirely different from one another, so there is no recipe to guarantee success" (p. 148).

Although experts in hybrid LCs would contend that creating powerful LCs is always much more than merely choosing and combining the best of face-to-face and online learning, this is a significant way that hybrid LCs differ from face-to-face and online LCs. As Snart (2010) states, "It is not so much the learning mode itself as the activities that are taking place in that learning mode that will affect the student experience" (p. 30).

The Rest of the Story

Look back at the scenario at the beginning of the chapter. The statements by the various members of the committee to improve LCs illustrate problems that institutions face in trying to accomplish the various steps focused on in this chapter. There are "turf" battles and no one on the committee seems to appreciate what an effective LC in any of the three formats is like. Problems exist in all types of LCs:

Face-to Face: As a PLC, members of this committee ignore important body language and tone of voice cues. LC synergy on campus is negatively affected by the lack of parking and the fact that there are not enough spaces for groups to meet.

Online: Technology support for online education gets shortchanged; there is only one IT staff member on campus. Workload accommodations are not available for instructors of online (or hybrid) classes. The site for the online courses is "boring" and not welcoming. The technology is slow and probably out-of-date. Professor Rather plans to make no changes in his face-to-face course when he is required to teach it online. There is no filter process to direct students to the best type of LC for them. Student member Larry does not have computer skills or easy access, so he is not a good candidate for success in an online LC.

Hybrid: The issues just described also affect hybrid LCs. In addition, K. C. fails to consider the best delivery mode by printing out online articles that could more easily have been sent to the committee members online well ahead of the meeting.

Conclusion

Palloff and Pratt (2007) contend that developing a powerful online SLC is more crucial for the success of online learning than for face-to-face learning; specialists in face-to-face SLCs would disagree. Though each delivery format is distinctive in terms of how LC members interact and relate to one another, powerful face-to-face, online, and hybrid LCs have much in common, whether they are SLCs or PLCs. A total of 25 common processes are essential for LC success across all three of these delivery modes, although the specific activities involved may need to be creatively adapted for the particular mode being used. In addition, each mode has particular characteristics and essential processes that are unique to it. Incorporating these essential processes in a flexible and effective manner should lead to powerful and effective LCs in each delivery mode, and in turn lead to increased member and group learning and sustenance of the LC.

For Reflection

As you create your own meaning from ideas in this chapter, begin to think about a specific LC at your institution (or at an institution you know about if you are in a governmental or other noninstitutional role) and how it can inform your work or interests. Use that LC to answer the following questions and help you reflect on practical implications of the material in this chapter:

- Based on what you have read, what delivery mode would be most beneficial for this LC?
- How would you organize or reorganize the delivery mode of that LC to make it more powerful in contributing to member and group learning?
- How could each of the essential processes that all three modes have in common be adapted for application to this LC?
- Based on the answer to the first question, how could each of the essential processes unique to the selected delivery mode be adapted for application to this LC?
- Which of Gregory and Kuzmich's (2009) 61 strategies for sustaining and renewing PLCs and SLCs (see Table 3.1) could be incorporated into this LC, and how should those strategies be adapted for the particular situation(s) pertaining to it?

Now that you have read and reflected on this chapter, you should be able to complete the following items on the Powerful LC Planning Form in Appendix C:

- Section II: #1. "What will the LC look like?"
- Section III: #1. "How will you build community?"
- Section III: #2. "How will you develop a culture for learning?"
- Section III: #3. "What norms do you want members to follow and how will you ensure accountability?"
- Section III: #4. "What resources are needed for your LC to be successful?"

Note

1. In regard to hybrid delivery format see Ellis, R. A., & Calvo, R. A. (2007). Minimum indicators to assure quality of LMS-supported blended learning. *Educational Technology & Society, 10*(2), 60–70.

4

CONCEPTUAL FRAMEWORKS
FOR CREATING POWERFUL LCs

What's the Story?

Robert Helms is chair of the Humanities Department at Public University. Faculty in the department frequently share how difficult it is to engage their students in learning activities during classes, especially when there is a large enrollment in the course. The institution recently reviewed responses to a national survey instrument and found that its students tended to provide lower ratings regarding levels of engagement in the learning environment. In response, increased attention is being devoted to students' engagement in learning activities.

Wanda Leeds, the associate provost for faculty development, wants to develop a plan for initiating a faculty learning community (FLC) that will engage in an ongoing discussion of the issues related to levels of student engagement in the learning environment, provide a supportive network for faculty colleagues, and share best practices. Although Wanda recognizes that the LC format can offer benefits over the typical workshop or lunch-and-learn format, it is not clear what structure the LC should take, what principles will guide interactions, and how best to facilitate the discussion in a meaningful way. Because Wanda knows that Robert has struggled with the challenge of engaging students in learning activities and that he was one of the people who highlighted the need for faculty development in this area, she invites him to lunch. The week before the lunch, she asks Robert to come up with some suggestions and he decides to formulate some ideas about how to best support the FLC.

How can Robert and Wanda best prepare for their meeting?

Teaching well . . . is like creating jazz. Jazz blends musical sounds from one tradition with theories from another. . . . It incorporates polyrhythm. . . . Like jazz, great teaching calls for

> blending different cultural styles with educational techniques
> and theories.
>
> —Tomlinson and Germundson (2007, p. 27)

The jazz metaphor may make learning sound mysterious and elusive. Instead, we use this metaphor to capture the dynamic nature of learning and teaching. As you will recall from chapter 1, learning communities (LCs) alone will not have a significant impact on learning if they do not incorporate other learning approaches. For example, Pascarella and Terenzini (2005) argued that LCs need to incorporate a broad array of learning experiences rooted in learning theory.

The purpose of this chapter is to provide readers with an overall framework of learning theory that can be used to assist the design, implementation, and maintenance of LCs. Our view is that LCs offer a rich environment that can support the implementation of multiple and various learning experiences. However, without explicit attention to how learning theory can shape and inform the practices within LCs, the impact on learning may well be limited to the 10% for LCs found by Pascarella and Terenzini (2005) (see Appendix H, available in the e-edition of this book and at www.styluspub .com/resrcs/other/PLC.pdf).

It is beyond the scope of this chapter to present an exhaustive overview of learning theories. Instead, we offer a historical overview of pertinent learning theories and then suggest an overall framework that can support a powerful and purposeful blending of learning experiences. The goal of this chapter is to promote understanding of ways to develop significant learning experiences within LCs. Building on the jazz metaphor, we seek to find a powerful blend of traditions, theories, and practices that produce significant learning. There are two important benefits that result from this blend. First, this type of learning produces engaged and motivated learners who enter the learning process with a high energy level. Second, this process produces learning that offers significant and lasting change that becomes a clear value in the learners' individual lives (Fink, 2003). Finding ways to identify and create truly significant learning experiences will yield significant progress in improving the quality of education.

As made clear in the introduction and Appendix H, there is a need for education to be responsive to changing societal needs and to demonstrate positive impact on student learning. Although institutional and national studies of LCs have found positive impact on learning, significant challenges remain. Fink (2003) notes that traditional universities are inflexible, focus on processes and outputs rather than significant long-term learning, and operate in a way that leads to high cost. He calls for new paradigms and new forms of teaching to change the design of instruction. Similarly, B. L. Smith, MacGregor, Matthews, and Gabelnick (2004) state, "We know more about what promotes learning than ever before, but we face considerable challenges putting what we know into practice" (p. 3). Furthermore, they caution against the tendency to develop innovative practices without a clear and coherent understanding of how these practices contribute to student learning.

Focusing on Learning in LCs

This section focuses on examples of distinctive learning that powerful LCs—both student LCs (SLCs) and professional LCs (PLCs)—are designed to produce and makes the case that this work must be shaped by an understanding of multiple learning theories. It also provides a learning framework to aid in the intentional design of effective LCs and offers specific principles and strategies for designing powerful LCs.

For LCs to fully support powerful learning, they should become "communities of practice" that have four components: *meaning*—learning that consists of one's experience; *practice*—learning by doing; *community*—learning that results from a sense of belonging; and *identity*—learning that is a constant state of becoming (Wenger, 1998). We use Wenger's four components as elements to frame the power of learning in community.

Meaning

Powerful LCs embrace an understanding that learners' experiences and how they make meaning from those experiences are both important components of the learning process. Theories of adult learning widely recognize that personal experience and individual understanding serve as a lens that shapes how we make meaning of new information. The concept of constructed knowledge is particularly salient for all members of LCs. Constructed knowledge positions knowledge as contextual, places learners as creators of knowledge, and values multiple strategies for knowing.

One strategy for enhancing student learning is to allow students to experience "connected teaching" (Belenky, Clinchy, Goldberger, & Tarule, 1986). In this model of teaching, teachers trust students' thinking and encourage them to expand on their thinking. The design of LC processes and experiences should consider ways to connect learning to LC members' great breadth of life experiences, knowledge, and previous education and help them relate theories and concepts to that knowledge.

Powerful experiences can lead to critical reflection and transformative learning (Mezirow, 1978; Perry, 1970). Perry (1970) concluded that when information cannot be easily assimilated or internalized, the "knowledge structure" for the individual must be changed in order for that knowledge to make sense in that person's mind. He contended that these knowledge structures, which he called "schemas," can be endlessly linked and woven as new learning is created/occurs either individually or collaboratively within groups. This process of changing the knowledge structure is transformative learning.

As a process, transformative learning involves the three phases of critical reflection, reflective discourse, and action. The group and its members first call into question their tacit assumptions, frames of reference, expectations, and mind-sets that may have long been taken for granted. Then the goal is to be more discriminating, open, and reflective in order to arrive at new, more defensible conclusions that point to and guide action. Suddenly, assumptions and understandings may seem new and point to additional possibilities for exploration and action.

Well-designed LCs challenge learners to question, adapt, and create their knowledge structures. Educators can support students in thinking more reflectively and making more reasoned judgments by designing difficult tasks, providing probing assignments and activities, and offering developmental support (see King & Kitchener, 1994b). Similarly, PLCs and learning organizations (LOs) can support individuals' efforts to make meaning by talking about professional practice, using tools to investigate and reflect on practice, and promoting changes in practice based on systemic inquiry (Levine, 2010). The group engages in a cycle of inquiry in which professionals formulate problems, collect and analyze data, share understanding, and plan for action. To promote more thoughtful reflection on past experiences and future efforts, this process relies on the group to scaffold learning through intentional experiences and to encourage the meaning-making process.

Practice

To apply the second component of communities of practice, an LC must provide learning experiences that allow members to practice new ways of thinking. Rather than approach the learning experience as a transmission of knowledge from teacher to student (which emphasizes lower levels of thinking such as memorization and recall), SLCs provide their student members with extensive opportunities to engage with other members in active learning strategies in which they continually develop new ways of thinking (including higher order thinking skills such as analysis, synthesis, and evaluation). Active learning techniques such as dialogue, debate, writing, problem solving, small-group exercises, simulations, case studies, and critical reflection encourage learners to practice applying and developing thinking skills (Bonwell & Eison, 1991; Meyers & Jones, 1993). It is important to note here that although active learning strategies are not limited to LCs, the structure and dynamics of an LC can be expected to foster a unique environment that supports integration of active learning techniques.

In powerful LCs, learning by doing occurs in a deliberate, effective manner through having community members and groups draw on their experiences and knowledge to explore objects, problems, ideas, questions, and controversies and to perform experiments. Such inquiry-based activity encourages active engagement, motivation, autonomy, responsibility, interdependence, creativity, enhanced problem-solving skills, and longer-term memory (Bruner, 1966). Wenger (1998) describes communities of practice in which groups of people learn and develop shared practices while engaging in a common enterprise. Powerful PLCs provide access to conversations that represent inquiry-based dialogue about effective practices; such dialogue is also important in SLCs even though most of the students may be hypothetically projecting ahead to future practice rather than being involved in such practice now.

Community

The third component of communities of practice discussed by Wenger (1998)—community—has a clear connection to the focus of this book. Powerful LCs make use of cooperative learning, which involves members working together in sub-LCs to attain a broad array of goals not possible when working alone or competitively. Cooperative/collaborative learning actively involves team members in the learning process, which requires knowledge to be discovered by members and transformed into concepts to which they all can relate. The knowledge is then reconstructed and expanded through new learning experiences.

The learning takes place through dialogue among team members. Because members perceive their success or failure to be dependent on their ability to work together as a group, they motivate and encourage one another to help each other with the needed tasks so that the whole group succeeds. Furthermore, because members must explain, discuss, and debate various perspectives, a greater understanding of the material is obtained and elaborative thinking is promoted. In an LC that effectively involves community in the learning process, emphasis is placed on acquiring knowledge collaboratively, developing social and interpersonal skills, and learning how to cooperate in order to find the best possible solution to a problem. Each individual team member is responsible for creating a community atmosphere of achievement (Johnson, Johnson, & Smith, 1991; Kegan, 1994).

The literature on PLCs also considers the importance of community for individual learning. DuFour and Eaker (1998) discuss the benefits of communities collectively and collaboratively undertaking in-depth dialogue, inquiry, problem solving, and reflection in an effort to develop shared learning and a commitment to implementation. In addition, they explain that effective communities encourage the development of each individual's skills, seek to improve the community's function, and share responsibility. These dialogues, interactions, and activities among community members become an essential component of how individuals learn and make meaning (Vygotsky, 1978).

Effective PLCs or LOs engage in systematic intentional inquiry as a community and promote learning by actively working to create or revise theoretical constructs that guide their work (Levine, 2010). Furthermore, such inquiry communities help individuals identify unexamined elements of practice that may represent tacit assumptions. Community inquiry supports movement from tacit to explicit knowledge. This supports systematic inquiry from multiple perspectives, which, in turn, questions existing knowledge and standard practices. Here the community develops a body of common knowledge, practices, and approaches (Jacobs & Yendol-Hoppey, 2010).

Identity

In addition to emphasizing a positive attitude, identity recognizes that learning is an ongoing process. If one subscribes to the goal of lifelong learning, then learning is a constant "becoming." One aspect of identity is the recognition that individuals learn in multiple ways (see H. Gardner, 1999). Powerful LCs should include a wide variety of effective processes and stimuli (e.g., open-ended problem solving, integration across disciplines, various types of learning activities that emphasize different skills); otherwise, it is possible that members with certain learning styles and preferences may not hear or see as much that has meaning. They may contribute less to the interaction/ group learning and exhibit no learning themselves.

This notion of identity, while reminding us to remain attentive to individual preferences and skills that learners bring, also presents the individual learner with an important responsibility in a community of learners. A central learning skill is the ability to see connections across diverse ideas, concepts, and bodies of knowledge. For example, in *College Learning for the New Global Century,* the American Association of Colleges and Universities (2007) identifies integrative learning (synthesis/advanced accomplishment across general and specialized studies) as one of four essential learning outcomes.

As individuals (and groups) seek to identify meaningful connections, it is important to gather knowledge from multiple sources, explore ideas from various bodies of knowledge, and solicit a diversity of opinions. Thus, individuals have responsibility to share their understanding and perspectives within the community, enhance the group's task of developing meaningful connections, and create actionable knowledge. Effective LCs represent high-impact practices in which members can learn how to become integrative thinkers and enhance the opportunities for others in the community to develop their integrative thinking through a collaborative effort.

PLCs and LOs also should attend to this concept of identity. For example, community members might have an activity that explores how learning can be fostered by active participation in discourses and practices that are unfamiliar or not part of their own traditions (Levine, 2010). In addition, pre-service teachers' engagement with students from different backgrounds (e.g., socioeconomic, ethnic, religious) asks them to engage with and make sense of perspectives and activities of students that may be different from their own. Powerful LCs should consider how the primary or majority identities of their members shape the dominant discourses and perspectives that may stifle competing voices or understanding.

Attention to intended learning and use of theory as a foundation is a critical starting point in the design and implementation of LCs. The following sections explore multiple learning frameworks that provide a variety of meaningful lenses for viewing LCs and LC designs. In addition, an integrated framework that can be used to aid in the design of powerful LCs is provided.

Instructional Design Frameworks

A number of theories provide insight into ways that the learning environment and experiences should be designed within LCs. First, the learning environment should take an eclectic view of learning; people learn in different ways. Second, complex learning requires an integrated set of learning goals. Third, instructional systems need to be fully aligned with human cognition by recognizing the learning process and individuals' learning capacities (van Merriënboer & Paas, 2003).

Design of instruction is underpinned by a theory of learning and a way of knowing or understanding the world. Moseley et al. (2005) offer an overview of 12 instructional design frameworks. Table 4.1 offers a time sequence of instructional design theories that make up these frameworks. For a more detailed summary of each framework, see Appendix K, available in the e-edition of this book and at www.styluspub.com/resrcs/other/PLC.pdf. A robust multidisciplinary literature affirms the importance of supporting learning through structures and opportunities that stimulate connection making and nurture deep learning (Bransford, Brown, & Cocking, 1999a).

A common element across the various instructional design theories is the importance of intentional learning environments. For example, several theories raise a concern that too many classrooms only elicit recall, and thus the theories advocate for increased attention to higher order reasoning skills (e.g., L. W. Anderson & Krathwohl, 2001; Bloom, 1956; Merrill, Jones, & Zhongmin, 1992). In powerful learning environments, teachers provide ways for students to practice higher order thinking, develop deep learning skills, and become more comfortable with complex problems.

LCs offer a strong environment for structured "bridging" experiences that allow learners to progressively increase the complexity and level of thinking. Consider, for example, Fink's (2003) sequence of activities in team-based learning. In the preparation phase, students have out-of-class reading followed by in-class pretesting, review, and corrective instruction. The application phase consists of ongoing out-of-class homework along with a sequence of group work, moving from simple assignments to more complex ones. The teacher provides feedback as students practice more complex tasks. The final assessment phase includes out-of-class review and a summative exam that is done either individually or in groups.

Note how this sequence offers a structured learning experience that scaffolds students' learning in a way that encourages higher level thinking, integration of individual understanding (homework), group knowledge

TABLE 4.1
Instructional design frameworks in chronological order.

Design Framework	Significant Design Elements
Bloom's (1956) taxonomy of educational objectives	Improves performance through the use of learning objectives that target increasingly complex goals (application, analysis, synthesis, evaluation)
Gagne's (1965) eight types of learning and five types of learned capacity	Similar to Bloom, offers a hierarchy of learning goals with problem solving at top; also highlights the need to establish conditions for learning according to individual needs
Ausubel and Robinson's (1969) six hierarchically ordered categories	Stresses importance of relating prior knowledge to new knowledge, scaffolding understanding, and teacher-structured learning
Williams's (1970) model for developing thinking and feeling processes	Develops individual talents through cross-curricular connections
Hannah and Michaelis's (1977) comprehensive framework for instructional objectives	Guides skill development and supports learner inquiry, critical thinking, and creativity
Stahl and Murphy's (1981) domain of cognition taxonomic system	Designs learning experiences to promote various cognitive processes
Biggs and Collis's (1982) SOLO taxonomy	Improves cognitive performance through assessment and feedback
Quellmalz's (1987) framework of thinking skills	Models metacognition and infuses critical thinking across the curriculum
Presseisen's (1991) models of essential, complex, and metacognitive thinking skills	Uses complex and challenging tasks to develop thinking skills
Merrill, Jones, and Zhongmin's (1992) instructional transaction theory	Designs interactive strategies to support learner's construction of mental models
L. W. Anderson and Krathwol's (2001) revision of Bloom's taxonomy	Improves cognitive performance from alignment of learning objectives, assessment, and instruction
Gouge and Yates's (2002) Art Project taxonomies of arts and reasoning in thinking skills	Promotes learning through peer coaching and collaboration

development, and deeper learning that moves from mastery of content to learning how to use/apply content in a meaningful way. Following this model, powerful LCs should offer students opportunities to engage in progressively more challenging learning tasks with supportive feedback along the way.

Similarly, PLCs and LOs can support deeper learning through guided discussions as a means of inquiring into practice. They might use conversation tools, called protocols, to push beyond individual private practices to inquire jointly about the shared learning experiences within the organization. For example, a "critical friend" protocol asks an individual to share a learning dilemma and its context in detail. Other members of the community then have several minutes to ask clarifying questions, and then they spend a set amount of time talking about the presenter's dilemma while the presenter listens. Specific techniques and strategies for instructional design are provided in subsequent chapters. What follows are alternative guiding frameworks that can help in the design and implementation of effective LCs.

Holistic Frameworks

Moseley et al. (2005) provide another set of thinking frameworks that they categorize as "all-embracing." They describe these frameworks as ambitious in that they address a wide scope of how people think and learn in a variety of contexts. These frameworks support an applied educational purpose, rather than simply trying to explain cognitive development. Table 4.2 provides an overview of the six thinking frameworks.

Common features exist among these holistic frameworks, such as the inclusion of metacognition and self-regulated learning, the addressing of learning outside the cognitive domain, and the deliberate use of skills in the application of knowledge (e.g., problem solving, decision making). This team-based learning as applied to successful LCs begins with gathering of information and formation of ideas, moves to a phase involving some kind of "doing" experience (e.g., case study, simulation, problem-based learning), and concludes with reflective dialogue (Fink, 2003).

One way to clarify this focus throughout various learning experiences is to create an integrating question for the LC. For example, LC teams of students could be given the key guiding question, "What is entrepreneurship?" During the information-gathering phase, LC members could write their own personal answers and ideas, research examples of entrepreneurs, and identify common characteristics of entrepreneurs. Teams could then revise this list of characteristics to see if they need to add, delete, or modify the group list. They could then

TABLE 4.2
Knowledge-building frameworks in chronological order.

Knowledge-Building Framework	Knowledge-Building Elements
Romiszowski's (1981) analysis of knowledge and skills	Guided discovery through learning or skill cycle
Wallace and Adams's (1993) thinking actively in a social context model	Collaborative problem solving in a practical context to develop transferable skills; movement from modeling, to guided activity, to autonomy
Hauenstein's (1998) conceptual framework for educational objectives	Cross-curricular links and experiential learning emphasized
Vermunt and Verloop's (1999) categorization of learning activities	Teacher-facilitated self-regulation and knowledge construction in learner, including cognitive (relating/structuring, analyzing, applying, memorizing, critical processing, and selecting), affective (motivation and management of feeling), and regulative (plan, do, and review) categories
Marzano's (2001) new taxonomy of educational objectives	Clearly developed objectives at multiple levels (individual knowledge acquisition, cognitive processing, and metacognition), with skills applied in meaningful ways
Sternberg's (2001) model of abilities as developing expertise	Challenges provided in analytic, creative, and practical learning

explore case studies of successful and unsuccessful entrepreneurial ventures and determine what aspects facilitated or interfered with success in light of their list of common characteristics. The last phase could include whole-team discussion, then individual reflection on the key question.

PLCs help with meaning making by inviting people to learn and develop best practices. Here individuals with various levels of experience and multiple perspectives share information about useful practices, invent new practices, or discuss challenges with current practices.

Development Frameworks

An additional set of frameworks focuses on cognitive growth as well as affective and behavioral changes (Evans, Forney, & Guido-DiBritto, 1998). While the learning process is complex and involves multiple levels of "development," these theories encourage professionals to think in purposeful ways about applying theoretical approaches in order to design learning experiences that recognize the holistic nature of development. A common feature in development frameworks is the recognition that individuals are at various development levels (cognitively, affectively, and behaviorally) and that individuals have different needs to facilitate growth. Table 4.3 provides an overview of the eight thinking frameworks.

Central to these developmental learning approaches is the notion that knowledge is socially constructed. Learning experiences challenge individuals to encounter discrepancies between the ways they view the world and their

TABLE 4.3
Development frameworks in chronological order.

Development Framework	Development Elements
Piaget's (1950) social interaction and constructivist learning theories	Well-designed external "inputs" encourage individuals to manipulate existing schemas in ways that allow new relationships to emerge and learning to increase.
Sanford's (1966) readiness, challenge, and support	Experiences with optimal dissonance maximize the level of challenge through a supportive environment.
Freire's (2000) dialogic model of educational practice	Dialogue within a community is designed to be a means of transforming social relations into new understandings of content and society.
Perry's (1970) theory of intellectual and ethical development	Individuals make meaning of their experiences in different ways (e.g., duality, multiplicity, relativism), which shapes how they learn.
Astin's (1984) involvement theory	Amount of learning and development is proportional to the quality and quantity of involvement.
Kolb's (1984) learning styles	Learning is a four-stage cycle in which learners need to master the four components: concrete experience, reflective observation, abstract conceptualization, and active experimentation. Learning style information helps design experiences that support the different components.
King and Kitchener's (1994a, 1994b) reflective judgment model	Individuals learn to address vexing or ill-structured problems through reflective thinking and reflective judgment.
Baxter Magolda's (1999) theory of self-authored learning	Learning is promoted by validating individuals as knowers, situating learning in individuals' experiences, and inviting groups to construct meaning mutually.

experiences, and then strike a balance by developing new understandings. Powerful LCs prompt individuals to work with others to reflect on knowledge and to remake meaning based on experiences. Learners' experiences in the LC become a foundation for this remaking of meaning. LC leaders need to guide this process, acknowledge learners' experiences, and attend to the holistic development of individuals in the community.

Overall Guiding Framework in the Creation of Powerful LC Strategies

Knowledge of the dynamics operating within LCs and the frameworks introduced in the last three sections can inform and support the development of powerful LCs. Here we present an integrated framework that incorporates aspects of the learning frameworks discussed earlier. What follows is an overall guiding framework that facilitates the design and implementation of effective LCs. It focuses on a shared vocabulary and understanding of learning as it pertains specifically to LCs and generally to learning in any setting.

Moseley et al. (2005) build on the Bloom-based taxonomy to identify four cognitive components. The Bloom model includes information gathering, building understanding, and productive thinking as the learner moves to more advanced learning activities. Moseley and his associates add a self-regulatory or metacognitive component called strategic and reflective thinking (see Figure 4.1). They note that cognitive skills are procedures that can become automatic, but strategic and reflective thinking requires highly conscious and sustained effort.

FIGURE 4.1
Integrated thinking and learning model (Moseley et al., 2005).

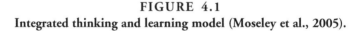

Strategic and Reflective Thinking		
Engagement and management of thinking supported by critical reflection		

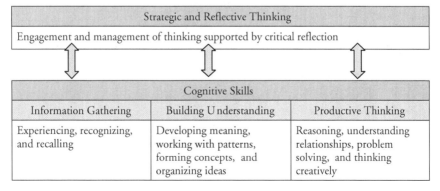

Cognitive Skills		
Information Gathering	Building Understanding	Productive Thinking
Experiencing, recognizing, and recalling	Developing meaning, working with patterns, forming concepts, and organizing ideas	Reasoning, understanding relationships, problem solving, and thinking creatively

In short, the model claims that when there is conscious and careful reflective thinking, meaningful learning is more likely. This model offers a practical tool for mapping different models, frameworks, and taxonomies in a way that supports intentional design of powerful LCs.

The remainder of this section explores the four cognitive components identified by Moseley et al. (2005) with specific attention to how they inform LC design and implementation strategies.

Information Gathering

The focus of the information-gathering component is the development of foundational knowledge through gaining understanding. Facilitators support understanding of the underlying conceptual structure in addition to teaching such knowledge. A powerful grasp of foundational knowledge requires an in-depth understanding of relationships among concepts and facts.

Teachers, facilitators, or other LC designers who wish to enhance foundational knowledge in LCs might consider the following suggestions (Fink, 2003). First, because teachers and facilitators often face a challenge in finding time to focus on students' ability to use knowledge as a result of a large portion of class time being devoted to communicating content, consider making better use of out-of-class time by moving the initial exposure to the content to out-of-class time. For example, a session on ethics would provide students with foundational readings ahead of time, and class time would be devoted to working on a series of case studies that provide a variety of ethical issues and questions. This strategy requires that students know that completion of out-of-class work is absolutely necessary in order to do the structured in-class activities.

Second, provide content in different forms. Many teachers use traditional means of providing content such as readings and lectures. LCs offer a rich environment for creative forms of learning. Field experiences, documentary film discussions, and out-of-class group projects offer an opportunity for students to engage in "doing situations" in which they gather information and engage in learning about the subject matter.

Third, link content information to other activities. For example, students in a business SLC might use basic concepts from core classes to operate a real business. In a chemistry SLC, students might take turns facilitating discussions by using an article provided by the teacher as a foundation, but supplementing the discussion with their own research on the topic. In a teacher education SLC, students might prepare for a field experience by reflecting on their own assumptions about teaching and learning, engaging in class discussions about key questions of teaching, and viewing videotapes of classroom instruction. After this preparation, students could then participate as "participant observers" in classrooms.

Leaders of PLCs should also consider ways of linking concepts or ideas with different points of view. Mezirow (2003) suggests that transformation does not occur in isolation, but through dialogue that involves finding agreement, welcoming difference, trying different points of view, searching for synthesis, and reframing understanding. In other words, powerful PLCs that consider a wide variety of possible solutions to problems of concern will be designed to include members with diverse perspectives and experiences. Consider the scenario at the start of this chapter. A successful FLC that explores ways to enhance active learning experiences would likely draw on the multiple experiences, successes, and failures of faculty to engage students in a variety of disciplines and through various pedagogical strategies.

Building Understanding

The second component of learning (and teaching) outlined by Moseley et al. (2005) is building understanding. Here learners develop meaning through elaborating, sharing, and representing ideas. Learners see patterns and concepts and organize ideas across content information. Teachers, facilitators, and other LC designers interested in enhancing students' efforts to build understanding might consider some of the following strategies.

SLCs should provide students with opportunities to learn about the various connected subjects and then reflect and think about the connection. This second part requires intentional opportunities for students to focus attention on making connections through specific activities such as thinking, writing, reflecting, or discussing. In a biology SLC, for example, students could work through a series of scientific case studies and explore the nature of science and how knowledge is transferred. Students could then explore how misconceptions about early communicable diseases inform how we construct and share knowledge. Or, students could consider how writing strategies influence successful communication and then write a response to a blog entry about the dangers of vaccinations, basing their response on current scientific knowledge. In a construction engineering SLC, students could learn about construction standards while exploring professional ethics practices. Students could research various ethics case studies to explore various issues related to legal responsibilities, ethical decision making, and improper construction practices.

Teachers and facilitators need to provide diverse modes of learning to help students understand that there are many ways to approach problems, multiple possible interpretations of information, and several possible alternative answers to important questions. A tangible way to encourage diverse modes of learning in an LC is to help students engage in constructive dialogue around a controversial issue. As students explore ways that various disciplines and methodologies might approach an issue, they can develop a tolerance for conflict and ambiguity as they seek deeper understanding.

Learning that lasts is active and interactive, independent and collaborative (Mentkowski & Associates, 2000). Note here that LCs offer an important tool in building understanding simply through the inclusion of multiple learners who can collaborate in problem-solving efforts, shape reflection through multiple perspectives, and enhance interactive learning opportunities. Effective LCs can provide a team structure that offers community members repeated opportunities to work on significant projects.

Through SLCs, teachers can facilitate learning from such experiences by encouraging collaborative reflection (dialogue) and providing opportunities for individuals to make new learning connections. LCs support this effort in two distinct ways. First, they allow students to practice what they are learning in multiple situations that encourage learners to make connections between individual experiences and the collaborative group efforts. Second, they invite students to identify how diverse fields and individual perspectives integrate to inform their approach to novel problems. LCs offer a rich environment that allows significant group projects, collaborative interaction, reflection on connections between learning experiences, and opportunities to practice integrating learning across disciplines.

Productive Thinking

LCs are primed to provide students with learning experiences that are grounded in a practical context, but that can also be applied to new and ambiguous situations (i.e., transfer). Consider the following strategies to promote situated and transferable learning in LCs. First, offer realistic simulations and practice situations. Second, offer opportunities for students to practice skills in varied contexts and tasks. Third, construct learning activities that require students to transfer or apply previous knowledge to new contexts or situations. And finally, provide structured opportunities for students to explore different perspectives and consider the merits of each.

Active learning strategies such as these invite students to develop connections between context-specific knowledge that is grounded in a presented task and possible applications or different contexts in which that knowledge could be applied in the future. Invitations to explore the relevance of concepts to everyday life, and to their future professional careers, offers students the opportunity to further develop these connections. LCs should provide students with repeated opportunities to practice skills and specific feedback on their efforts during practice activities.

Here are some examples of ways to offer students opportunities to practice various ways of thinking within an SLC. Students in an engineering LC could practice critical thinking by critically assessing published articles on current standards and practices that relate to sustainable development (e.g., LEED [Leadership in Energy and Environmental Design] standards, water conservation). Business LC students could practice creative thinking by designing a fictional business that incorporates new ideas and/or improvements on old ideas. Students in a horticulture LC could practice practical thinking by exploring landscape design case studies in a structured format in which they examine the presented information, decide what additional information is needed, diagnose potential environmental factors that either impacted previous plants or could impact future plants, and propose a strategy or solution for the client.

LCs can also provide students with opportunities to practice skills (e.g., communication, teamwork). Students in an LC could practice effective behavioral interviewing techniques by using the S.T.A.R. technique (situation, task, action, and result) to share how they served as an effective leader for a team project. In this example, the students develop the ability both to communicate about their personal skills and to reflect on their performance on a team. Students in a journalism LC could take a field trip to visit an office or business where they could practice interview techniques and learn more about the career paths of professionals.

Another area of practice that supports students' learning is the opportunity to manage large, open-ended, complex projects. Students in a business LC studying entrepreneurship could develop their own company in which they identify what to sell, how to organize the company, how to secure venture capital, how to manage production, and how to ensure sustainability over time—all within the course of a semester. Students in various engineering LCs could engage in significant design projects in which they work in teams to create a mechanical device that will solve a practical problem. Students could then gather information about the effectiveness of the design, test possible alternative designs, and consider other factors that influence design (e.g., cost, availability of resources, and efficiency in manufacturing).

Fink (2003) provides an overview of types of application activities—including thinking abilities, developing skills, and managing complex projects—but he also stresses the importance of providing students with feedback on their practice efforts. Chapter 7 provides strategies for providing students with feedback on learning.

Similar to SLCs, PLCs and LOs must provide deliberate attention to both practice and the community itself. These communities allow members to explore new ideas, current practices, and evidence of success that allow them to improve their practices. These LCs can offer a positive change from isolated professional development exercises by promoting an environment that fosters collaborative inquiry into practice, encourages greater risk taking, and focuses on current problems of practice.

Strategic and Reflective Thinking

Strategic and reflective thinking is the last cognitive component in the Moseley et al. (2005) holistic model. Ultimately, for SLCs we hope that students engage in self-aware and reflective thinking that will promote a learning cycle beyond graduation. Strategic and reflective thinking helps learners shape future performance based on understanding of their own learning.

There are several ways that LCs can encourage strategic and reflective thinking. Targeted assignments can focus on specific and articulated learning outcomes along with criteria for judging quality. Thus, they provide students with opportunities for reflective self-awareness and supportive feedback. For example, a horticulture/English LC asked students to review advertisements in seed catalogs from the previous century and today. Students then developed both a written paper and a poster or PowerPoint presentation that provided a comparison of the two advertisements. The students had a rubric that explained the criteria for effective oral and written communication. The rubric helped them to guide the development of their work and to provide a tool for self-reflection and targeted feedback on the quality of the work. This example also demonstrates the value of offering students a variety of self-assessment modes that allow students to examine their thinking by reading their own work, critiquing their own oral presentation, and comparing their progress on the learning criteria as compared to other samples of student work.

LCs offer a rich environment for helping students learn effective metacognitive strategies—helping students learn how to learn. Some LCs focus on effective strategies that help students become better learners. For example,

many introductory seminars provide sessions on effective studying techniques, effective time management strategies, or available academic assistance
services. They might also have students present techniques used to learn and
to study for or take a test.

Some LCs might administer a learning style inventory to students and
then offer specific ideas or techniques for effective learning based on an
individual's approach to learning. For several discipline-based LCs, the use
of an electronic portfolio early in students' careers offers a powerful tool that
can help support students' learning. When students are asked to review their
own work and summarize how it represents a particular learning outcome or
competency, they can see how learning activities apply to a broader, long-
term learning goal. A portfolio can encourage students to reflect on their
own learning and to identify strategies for enhancing their learning by asking: What am I learning and how can I apply it to my future career? What
else do I need to learn? What can I do to improve my learning in areas that
are challenging?

LCs can help learners know how to inquire about and construct knowledge in a specific field or discipline. Students in disciplinary LCs should be
asked to formulate questions and then to begin work on how to answer those
questions. As students begin this process, they search for relevant information and then analyze the information to determine how it supports their
understanding of a question or problem. Here, students begin to practice
the ways of knowing within a discipline and receive constructive feedback
from faculty along the way.

One example of this practice can be seen in a horticulture LC that asks
students to conduct research on a current problem or issue in horticulture
practice. Students could work with librarians to find out ways of finding and
evaluating information sources. The students could then develop a research
paper and share a draft with a resource faculty member from the horticulture
department who has a specialty in the topical area. The resource faculty
member could offer students suggestions for other sources, strategies for
finding and evaluating information, and corrections to inaccurate understanding of content information.

Another strategy for developing reflective thinking is to empower students to become self-directed learners. Several LCs use electronic portfolios
in which students organize artifacts and reflection summaries to demonstrate
how they achieve intended learning outcomes that can be applied in a number of different ways. One LC faculty member helps first-year students
understand the need to be self-directed learners through a powerful learning

example. The faculty member brings in a kilowatt meter, which most students would recognize as a tool that measures electricity use in a home or business. The teacher then invites students to stand up and share with the class what they know about a kilowatt meter. After a few uncomfortable minutes of silence, the teacher then invites the students to share what they need to learn and how they might learn those things. The students jump into this conversation with lots of energy and enthusiasm once they realize that they bring limited knowledge to the problem.

The Rest of the Story

Look back at the scenario at the beginning of the chapter. Robert and Wanda are preparing for a FLC that will think about ways to promote active learning. They might find value in using the integrated teaching and learning model as a framework for describing the type of learning experiences that the LC seeks to promote. The group might also use the dimension of "strategic and reflective thinking" (see Figure 4.1) as a way to solicit example practices from LC participants that could be shared with peers as best practices.

Conclusion

Like the jazz metaphor at the start of the chapter, the intention of this chapter has been to introduce a holistic framework that might be useful in helping to blend various educational techniques and theories, rather than to provide a prescriptive framework that should be rigidly applied to all LCs. While the holistic framework in this chapter represents one tool for blending different styles and approaches, there are other possible frameworks that could also inform the design and implementation of LCs. Note, however, that great teaching and learning requires attention to specific techniques and theories that best align with intended learning outcomes.

For Reflection

As you create your own meaning from ideas in this chapter, begin to think about a specific LC at your institution (or at an institution you know about if you are in a governmental or other noninstitutional role) and how it can inform your work or interests. Use that LC to answer the following questions and help you reflect on practical implications of the material in this chapter:

- On which of the communities-of-practice components that make for powerful LCs—meaning, practice, community, and identity—do you and/or the LC designers spend the most time?
- How would the time spent on these components change if your LC were more learning centered?
- What assumptions or frameworks do you use to understand learning?
- What is the overall philosophy of educational practice in your organization and how does it influence you?
- What ideas from this chapter challenge your assumptions about learning and the ways that you structure learning experiences?
- How could you benefit by reflecting more frequently on various learning theories and how they apply to your work?
- Take a moment to think about a powerful learning experience in your life. It may be a memory of a favorite teacher. Perhaps you recall the moment you discovered a passion for learning more about a specific problem or subject. Maybe it was a time when you worked with your colleagues to identify a new way of approaching your work. Next, think about what factors supported your powerful learning experience. It may have been the amount of encouragement from others that helped sustain the level of excitement and effort or exposure to new strategies that challenged your thinking.

Now that you have read and reflected on this chapter, you should be able to complete the following items on the Powerful LC Planning Form in Appendix C:

- Section III: #1. "How will you build community?"
- Section III: #2. "How will you develop a culture for learning?"
- Section III: #3. "What norms do you want members to follow and how will you ensure accountability?"
- Section III: #4. "What resources are needed for your LC to be successful?"

5

ACHIEVING OPTIMAL STUDENT SUCCESS THROUGH POWERFUL SLCs, PLCs, AND LOs

What's the Story?

Dr. Ram Singh teaches in the School of Law at Public State University. His department has received an interdisciplinary initiative grant. Dr. Singh reaches out to Dr. Eve Rose in the School of Medicine to coordinate an interdisciplinary event addressing health and ethics. Dr. Rose also introduces Dr. Singh to the head of the nursing program, and a business professor who specializes in health administration. The four of them organize a one-day symposium that is open to any students or faculty interested in law, medicine, pharmacology, nursing, and/ or health administration.

At the conference, participants are divided into groups of three or four people. Each group is carefully designed to maximize diversity, especially across the different disciplines. Dr. Rose asks the participants to introduce themselves to their group one at a time. Individuals share their name, their major, and what first drew them to their major and/or the symposium. Then Dr. Singh presents each group with a complex ethical scenario and a set of questions that calls on expertise from each of the disciplines.

Discussion is lively. At the end of the symposium many participants still want to engage; some go out for food together to continue their discussions. On their way out, Dr. Singh and Dr. Rose overhear a medical student tell a law student, "Wow, I can't believe how hard the law is. There is so much information to learn. I don't know if I could do it." The other student replies, "Are you kidding? You're studying medicine. There is so much to learn about the body and disease, let alone practice medicine."

Dr. Singh and Dr. Rose smile. They are pleased with this first symposium and can't wait to see how they can improve it.

In what ways does this symposium represent an exemplary LC?

> Intelligence, it seems, is readiness for any human situation; it is
> the power, wherever one goes, of being able to see, in any set
> of circumstances, the best response which a human being can
> make to those circumstances.
>
> —Meiklejohn (1932), p. 8

As alluded to in "History of LC Development" in Appendix G, available in the e-edition of this book and at www.styluspub.com/resrcs/other/PLC.pdf, Meiklejohn believes that deep learning and interdisciplinary connections occur best in a student learning community (SLC). Furthermore, he and his colleagues formed an effective professional learning community (PLC) to bring about such an SLC. Many view the Experimental College he and his associates established at the University of Wisconsin–Madison in 1927 to be the forerunner of today's most effective learning organizations (LOs) in which everyone works together to help create optimal student success. Thus, Meiklejohn's work in forming the Experimental College not only demonstrates the importance of SLCs, but also reminds us that a core part of every powerful SLC is the formation of efficient and effective PLCs and LOs to plan, implement, and maintain them.

This necessary interplay of SLCs, PLCs, and LOs is as true today as it was at the time of the Experimental College. This chapter examines more specifically current applications of SLCs, PLCs, and LOs in postsecondary education. It offers resources for design and development of each type of LC by (a) providing background; (b) presenting data from the 100-Institution Survey; (c) identifying exemplars—excellent models of practices, programs, and/or institutions; and (d) reporting suggestions for development from the LC literature.

Developing Powerful SLCs

As demonstrated in chapter 1, a multitude of SLC membership subtypes can be profitably used within any program, college, or university. In building SLCs, students can be configured into groups or cohorts according to any of the four SLC membership subtypes: curricular groups, student type, external (including residential), and course/class.

Students are likely to participate in multiple SLCs during their schooling and may even experience them concurrently. For example, a student could experience all four types simultaneously in the same term or semester by enrolling in linked courses (curricular group); participating in a program for students from migrant worker families (student type); volunteering to tutor for a service-learning project (external); and taking part in within-class LC work, such as Jigsaw (course/class). This overlap is especially likely if the institution is functioning as a true and powerful LO. Some institutions or programs may actively structure SLCs that blend and combine SLC sub-types, such as when residential (external) SLCs are designed to coincide with curricular or student-type cohorts.

There is profound variety and interplay among and across SLC member-ship types. The following three sections use data from both the LC literature and the 100-Institution Survey to describe common, helpful, and/or stimu-lating applications of each of these SLC subtypes in more detail. The discus-sion provides exemplary models and suggestions to serve as inspiration, rather than offer an exhaustive list of how all SLCs ought to function.

The best LCs do not simply follow a formula used by others. Rather, most successful LCs draw on evidence-based best practices and models and then creatively tailor them—crafting, shaping, adapting, and modifying them—to optimally meet the unique needs of their particular goals, mem-bers/target populations, contexts, and institutional cultures.

A good example of such creativity that integrates not only across dispa-rate disciplines in an effective manner but also across different types of insti-tutions is provided by one of the authors. In the fall of 2011, Professor Denise Hill taught both the face-to-face Introduction to Health Law class at Drake University Law School and the online Legal and Ethical Issues in Healthcare course in the Master of Health Administration (MHA) program at Des Moines University. Both courses utilized SLC teams that were assigned for the term. Having a common instructor versed in LCs presented a unique opportunity to utilize SLCs to promote collaborative and integrative learning across courses, professions, and institutions.

The resulting "Partnership Projects" utilized a comprehensive health law scenario involving three clients (hospital administrator, physician, and patient). Each MHA SLC was assigned a client to role-play. A corresponding attorney was assigned to each Law SLC. There were general facts available to all participants and then clients each had individual "secret facts" only they knew.

Law SLCs conducted client intake by interviewing their assigned client teams and conducted discovery with other client SLC teams. The Law SLCs considered the case in light of facts learned, relevant laws, regulations, cases, and other relevant materials provided as part of the case (bylaws, medical policies and procedures, credentialing reports, hospital board minutes, and contracts). The law student teams then drafted a legal memo outlining their legal recommendations for their client SLC. The client MHA SLCs reviewed the advice provided by their attorney teams and responded with a written ethical analysis of the recommendations, an explanation of what actions the client would ultimately take, and other changes the client should make to avoid future liability. The project was repeated the following term using both online and face-to-face MHA courses.

Student feedback regarding the partnership projects was very positive. It indicated that the projects provided a better understanding of the role of attorneys and clients, how to work effectively together, how the experience supported course learning objectives, and how in most cases it enhanced the overall SLC team relationships for the term.

Relevant 100-Institution Survey Revelations

The 100-Institution Survey had three items specifically on development/ characteristics of their SLCs: (a) Why and how did your institution create student LCs? (b) What do you consider to be unique or innovative about your student LCs? and (c) What do you think are the most important aspects of your student LCs, that is, what makes them effective/powerful?

The "why and how" question elicited data that were interesting—for example, generally LCs were developed in order to increase student retention, academic success, engagement, and deeper learning—but not that useful in practical terms, so they are not summarized here. Initially, our intent had been to relate data provided by all three questions to pertinent information about each institution's LCs from the institution's website. However, information on LC web pages often was not definitive enough, whereas in other cases it was very descriptive and definitive. (In several cases, no mention of LCs could be found on the institutional website, which might indicate that some institutions no longer have any formal SLCs.) Institutional website addresses, separately for SLCs and for PLCs, are provided in Appendix L, which is available in the e-edition of this book and at www.styluspub .com/resrcs/other/PLC.pdf for readers who would like to make their own judgments.

Regarding the questions on uniqueness/innovation and effectiveness, we have organized the factors identified in the responses into broad thematic categories, as summarized in Tables 5.1 and 5.2. Some responses addressed multiple factors and thus fit into more than one category. The intent behind categorizing the uniqueness/innovation identified by each institution was

TABLE 5.1

In what ways are your SLCs unique or innovative?

Factors Reported as Unique or Innovative	Frequency	Percentage
1. Remarkable emphasis on curricular *integration/ interdisciplinary* courses	23	28%
2. *Faculty-driven*, unparalleled full-time faculty commitment to LCs	19	23%
3. *Assessment-driven*, unique commitment to data making a difference	12	15%
4. Major focus on learning from *experiences* in the surrounding community	10	12%
5. SLCs with a *special targeted focus* or for a *particular student group*	10	12%
6. Emphasis on *blending* academic affairs and student affairs SLC *efforts*	9	11%
7. Especially *active peer and faculty mentoring* within SLCs	9	11%
8. *Requiring participation* in SLCs in order to register and/ or graduate	7	9%
9. Students/participating faculty *involved beyond the freshman year*	5	6%
10. Enhanced *counselor involvement*	4	5%
11. The *variety of LC models and types* of SLCs creatively used	4	5%
12. *Focus on* student research, creating knowledge, *creative investigation*	2	2.5%
13. *Grouped by majors or themes* in a creative way	2	2.5%
14. *Intensive outreach focus* to inform about SLCs and/or bring people in	2	2.5%
15. Special *training provided to LC coordinators* and participating *faculty*	2	2.5%
16. Factors that were each mentioned by only one person as being unique	53	65%
Survey respondents who did not respond to this question	2	2.5%
Total respondents to the 100-Institution Survey	81	100%

TABLE 5.2
What makes your SLCs effective/powerful?

Factors Reported as Effective or Powerful	Frequency	Percentage
1. *True community* where there is maximum sharing and learning from each other	34	42%
2. Intentional aligned agendas, curricular *integration*, and making connections	32	40%
3. Enthusiastic faculty SLC *commitment* and strategic trained peer involvement	27	33%
4. Intentional "value added" and impact data/*collaboration in interpreting it*	20	25%
5. *Institution-wide support* for SLCs at all levels; also movers and shakers	17	21%
6. Faculty participants believe in, *know, and support the students* in every way	7	9%
7. LC *program quality*, with breadth and meaningful themes emphasized	7	9%
8. Emphasis on *deep learning and student engagement*	5	6%
9. *Shared vision and goals*, and high expectations for the LCs	5	6%
10. Factors that were each mentioned by only one person as being important	43	53%
Survey respondents who did not respond to this question	5	6%
Total respondents to the 100-Institution Survey	81	100%

not to diminish the authenticity of such uniqueness/innovation. Rather, these categories can serve as inspiration; they represent areas of exploration that stimulate one's own innovations.

Regarding Table 5.1 here and Figure E.1 in Appendix E, which provides more detail, 15 different factors pertaining to innovation or uniqueness were identified by multiple respondents. It seems clear that almost every institution was successful in depicting its SLCs as meaningfully unique or innovative in some way. One indication of this was that it proved difficult to categorize the responses. Even within the 23 institutional responses that were assigned to the first factor of integration/interdisciplinary, there was remarkable diversity, and differences within that category were meaningful.

After the classification process was completed, 53 distinctive factors mentioned by only one respondent remained. See a list of those factors at the end of Figure E.1.

Respondents appear to have had an easier time identifying factors that contribute to creating a powerful and effective LC. As can be seen in Table 5.2 and Figure E.2, nine primary factors were emphasized by multiple respondents regarding effectiveness. (This time after the classification process was completed, 43 distinct factors mentioned by only one respondent as contributing to LCs being effective/powerful remained; see the end of Figure E.2.)

With the exception of the "strategic trained peer involvement" component of Factor 3 in Table 5.2, the nine primary factors said to be related to whether an LC is effective/powerful are emphasized throughout this text; most are specifically discussed within meaningful contexts in chapters 3–5.

Given that the strategic trained peer involvement component of Factor 3 in Table 5.2 may be less clear-cut to readers and is not emphasized elsewhere, we briefly discuss it here. Faculty involved in the most powerful SLCs are oriented about effective facilitation and are committed to working well together on integrating across courses and disciplines.[1] However, a number of the most effective LC programs also utilize well-trained student mentors. These student mentors are often past SLC participants and are excited about contributing to the success of the SLC. Some institutions—such as Brigham Young University (BYU); Eastern New Mexico University; Iowa State University (ISU), which pays its student mentors; and Pace University—have gone so far as to require that every formal SLC have an assigned student mentor.

At BYU and elsewhere, SLC faculty and student mentors have seen positive results in actively seeking out and developing academic relationships with LC members. BYU has also experimented with requiring the participation of all first-year students in one or more "mentored courses" and placing a registration hold on those students who do not have such "bundled" courses on their schedule. Other institutions[2] have also experienced positive results through requiring first-year students to participate in LCs, but student participation in the most highly rated LCs has generally been voluntary; what is needed depends on the particular institution.

As described at http://cms.cerritos.edu/lcp, the LC program at Cerritos College has a program coordinator who oversees student development and success. The program coordinator promotes and encourages participation in success workshops, face-to-face counseling, and/or online counseling to help participating students integrate into the college culture and learn how to work in a collaborative environment as a valued member of a team. In other words, the coordinator emphasizes well-designed and ongoing student outcomes assessment, personal attention, and community interaction processes effective in stimulating active, integrative, deep, and reflective learning.

Exemplary SLCs of Different Types and Pertinent Suggestions

Sixteen institutions were mentioned by multiple survey respondents (not including themselves) as having exemplary SLCs: Ball State University, Dallas County Community College, Delta College, Evergreen State College, Iowa State University, Kingsborough Community College, LaGuardia Community College, Miami University of Ohio, Seattle Central Community College, Skagit Valley Community College, Syracuse University, University of Maryland, University of Missouri, University of South Carolina, Valencia Community College, and Wagner College. Thirty-two other institutions were each mentioned by one respondent at a different institution as having exemplary SLCs. For any reader desiring to learn about the SLCs at a particular 100-Institution Survey institution, a listing of websites with information about the SLCs is provided in Appendix L (available in the e-edition of this book and at www.styluspub.com/resrcs/other/PLC.pdf) for all 100 institutions invited to participate in the survey.

Additional information for SLCs from the 100-Institution Survey participants may also be helpful to other practitioners. Appendix M (available in the e-edition of this book and at www.styluspub.com/resrcs/other/PLC.pdf) contains examples of different types of learning community support materials that were either identified or submitted by participants in the survey as materials they believed would be helpful to other institutions. It should be noted, however, as mentioned in the introduction to that appendix, we did not attempt to evaluate the effectiveness of any of those materials using the guidelines/criteria presented in our book.

The following sections discuss different primary types of SLCs. For each type we identify particular institutions that we feel are exemplary in some respect, based on our survey responses, institutional website information, and the LC literature.

Curricular Cohorts

Most early SLCs were created to provide the students with a way to connect socially. Student services usually created these early SLCs. Later research, such as that of A. L. Brown and Campione (1996), started to examine content and curriculum and how SLCs could enhance student learning. Brown and Campione's SLC model was titled "Fostering a Community of Learners" (FCL). A developmental perspective helps student learning both horizontally (within the stated curricula) and vertically (across disciplines). FCL's concentration is promotion of diversity in talents and interests within an identified content area. Most learning within this community happens cyclically based on identified themes.

Lampert, Rittenhouse, and Crumbaugh (1996) concentrate on deep inquiry learning within their structure of SLCs. This type of SLC presents a problem within the content of the course to the entire student body. Students are given approximately 20 minutes to work individually on creating a probable solution. Next, students participate in a discussion presenting ideas or models to resolve the problems posed. The intent is to increase student ability to propose sound arguments using common course language and methods. Lampert et al. follow in-class discussions and note important content or methods suggested by students. When appropriate, they add to the classroom discourse to support deeper learning.

Visher, Schneider, Wathington, and Collado (2010) identified integrative instructional practices to increase student learning. In a review of three community colleges, they identified synchronized topics and assignments, shared assignments, team teaching, and thematic instruction. Each structure provides the instructor new roles in classroom and instructional configuration.

We have selected several institutions that represent exemplary models of SLCs organized around curricular cohorts, each of which is described next.

- **Hillsborough Community College.** This college links a developmental reading course with a student success course, as shown in Figure 5.1. Synchronized topics and assigned readings help to make intentional connections between disciplines. This venue requires a

FIGURE 5.1
Linking developmental reading course with a student success course.

combined syllabus and assignment calendar to aid students in identification of common vocabulary, similar or opposing use of terminology, and transfer of information.

The intent of this community college is to share textbooks, assignments, and cross-departmental learning sessions (Visher et al., 2010) in each community. The design of the SLC aids in transfer of knowledge within the major and success courses as students increase reading skills. Although the recommendation to take developmental and student success courses occurred concurrently, the data show that students made few connections between the courses initially. The connections allow students to use information presented in both classes and function at a higher level of cognition. A reorganization of curricula to incorporate shared texts and assignments led to increased student understanding and transfer of knowledge.

- **Merced Community College (MCC).** The aforementioned synchronized assignments are not the only curricular consideration used by community colleges. MCC uses thematic connections in the development of its SLCs. Figure 5.2 identifies possibilities for linked courses to enhance learning connections (Tinto, 1995). The emphasis in this California-based community college is to create different SLCs that have unique themes and with parallel syllabi (Visher et al., 2010). This LC structure reveals intentional design to help students experience transfer of information between core course work.

One thematic choice indicated by MCC was "ethno-mathematics." The idea was to demonstrate diverse views and relationships historically held by varying ethnicities. When learning about Mayan mathematical systems in math class, students also read and wrote about Mayan use of mathematical systems during English and reading courses. Research in communication-intensive courses demonstrated that integration reinforced methods taught within the math courses. Another integrative approach used by MCC was cross-disciplinary team teaching. The MCC model focused on student reading and

FIGURE 5.2
Possibilities of linked courses to enhance learning connections.

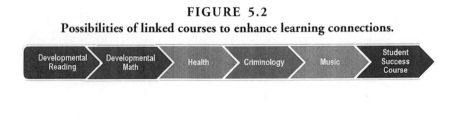

writing skills, particularly on structuring the presentation of hard-to-grasp grammar concepts. The following excerpt explains how team teaching was used to help students understand the concept of illustration (using examples to explain an idea):

> [The students] meet Tuesday and Thursday with [my teaching partner] and they meet every day with me. It was clear by Wednesday that they understood illustration. They had three days with me, they had two days with him, so I was able on Thursday and Friday to introduce verbs and have two extra days on that—whereas if this was a stand-alone class, I wouldn't have been able do that because I would have to give my attention to both the reading and the writing. (Visher et al., 2010, p. 49)

- **Kingsborough Community College.** Another institution of higher learning that uses thematic SLCs is Kingsborough Community College. Kingsborough has been refining the use of SLCs for 16 years. Visher et al. (2010) identify Kingsborough's SLCs as some of the most effective college LCs to date. The base of its LCs includes general education courses or student major requirements. The college couples core courses within program areas (Figure 5.3). These two core courses are then combined with either an integrative seminar or student success course. Each course in the triad incorporates an agreed-upon theme. The structure used by Kingsborough shows student outcomes of increased social interaction and greater breadth of knowledge.

FIGURE 5.3
Sample coupling of core courses within program areas.

Visher et al. (2010) summarize student attitudes about SLCs that incorporate integrative course work: "In general, students in Kingsborough's LCs reported forming stronger relationships with each other than they did with their peers in stand-alone classes" (p. 40). The structure of an integrative seminar provides students with deeper learning, both personal and relevant. Furthermore, students work one-on-one with faculty in addition to participating in small groups. The active learning sessions build connections among course content, real-world experiences, and students' personal lives and learning needs.

Kingsborough's success in establishing LCs that support student learning has been so great that it has been offering summer workshops since 2005. Faculty and administrators across the nation attend in the hope of building more successful LCs. According to the results from our 100-Institution Survey, Kingsborough's summer workshops focus on various themes. The contents include the nuts and bolts of integrating course curricula and assignments while creating a dynamic and active climate for learning.

In a follow-up conversation, Marcia Babbitt, co-coordinator of Opening Doors LCs, and Marissa Schlesinger, associate director of academic affairs, both pointed out that they have an "Advanced LC Program" as well as two other types of SLCs (see www.kbcc.cuny .edu/LC/Pages/LearningCommunities.aspx):

Kingsborough Community College has a long history of LCs and we are very proud of all three of our distinct programs. Our Intensive ESL LC program began in 1995 and enrolls over 100 students each semester. These students have been shown to test out of ESL faster than their non-LC counterparts, which is why all full-time, entering ESL students are now required to enroll in these LCs. Our Advanced LC Program began in 2007 and enrolls approximately 250 students each semester in LCs aligned with their major. Recent MDRC data show that these LCs are especially valuable for our large population of transfer students. Our freshman LC program, Opening Doors, began in 2003 and currently enrolls approximately 1,000 students each year in theme-based, integrative LCs. Random assignment study of Opening Doors demonstrates that our LC students complete more courses and credits in their first semester than their non-LC counterparts, and graduate at higher rates as well.

A few institutions, such as Kingsborough as well as BYU and Eastern New Mexico University, have obtained excellent results by requiring LC participation. However, based on the literature and personal experience it is generally not a good idea except in certain environments with students who are receptive. Comments from a couple of survey respondents also support this conclusion: "Be as inclusive as possible, but don't make things mandatory." "When I came, the residence hall lease agreement *required* that students *must* take a LC; I immediately did away with this requirement."

Residential and Student-Type/Concern Cohorts

Lenning and Ebbers (1999) discussed exemplary residential SLC (living-learning community, or LLC) programs at Earlham College and the following universities: Maryland, Michigan, Michigan State, Missouri, Truman State, Stanford, and Yale. They identified these institutions as having well-designed LLCs based on the conceptual and design principles identified earlier. Evidence suggests that these residential SLCs have a significant positive effect on student learning. Based on the results of the 100-Institution Survey, examination of institutional websites, and reports in the literature (e.g., Peckskamp & McLaughlin, 2010), we now add Ball State University, Bowling Green State University, University of Iowa, Syracuse University, University of Illinois, and Wagner College. The latter two exemplars are addressed in more detail subsequently.

At Bowling Green, students (and faculty) for a number of the LLCs are involved in the same LLC all four years. In addition, some LLCs allow commuter students as members (e.g., Abraham Baldwin Agricultural College, Fresno Pacific University, and St. Louis University) or have created proxy LLCs for commuter students (e.g., Cabrini College, Indiana University–Purdue University Fort Wayne, and University of Central Arkansas).

Even when LLCs have similar educational goals and results, they can be quite different in how they operate.[3] For example, Jones and Lawrie (2010) compared the Leaders Emerging and Developing Program at Syracuse to the dramatically different Freshman Connections Program at Ball State. In the Syracuse program, LLC students who have similar academic or other interests live together on a residence hall floor. The institution also has curricular LCs in which students enroll in the same linked classes. In the Ball State program, students are grouped together in the residence halls according to the core classes they selected during summer registration, rather than by interest. In addition, faculty and academic advisors come into the residence halls to interact with the students in various ways. Jones and Lawrie thus demonstrate that programs "drastically different in structure can share similar educational success" (p. 99).

- **University of Illinois, Urbana–Champaign.** Providing a small liberal arts college learning environment at a large research-based institution is a goal of many universities. Schein (2005) successfully created this atmosphere at the University of Illinois, Urbana–Champaign. In his article "The Zen of Unit One: Residential Learning Communities Can Foster Liberal Learning at Large Universities," Schein outlines his community construction and the success he found.

An important consideration for residential cohorts is how to link academic and student affairs so that the cognitive and personal spheres are working as one. The residence halls for Unit One were reworked to include an intellectual component. Schein (2005) suggested that residence halls be a place for cocurricular activities where safety in sharing intellect is as evident as constructing a social network.

This involves faculty participation outside the classroom in noncredit programming. Unit One uses adjunct professors, teaching assistants, and full-time faculty to teach noncurricular or topical seminars. The intention of a mixed selection of personnel is to focus courses on student learning rather than teaching of specific content. Students are provided with avenues to explore, inquire, and participate in open exchange of ideas.

- **Wagner College.** Wagner College uses thematic residential communities that address specified course work. Residential facilitators help students to make connections. Curricular connections include taking common courses together in addition to attending meetings at the residence hall facilitated by the residential LC facilitator.

Based on Wagner's website in March 2012 (www.wagner.edu/academics/FYPcourses#LC_1), an example of linked course work at Wagner is the combination of a theater and art course to explore the theme of "Leashed and Unleashed Animals in Art" and "Encountering Others in the Old and New World." This second LC "focuses on cultural encounters across two bodies of water, the Mediterranean Sea and the Atlantic Ocean. It examines the conflict and trade between Christians, Muslims, and Jews during the

Middle Ages and between Europeans and indigenous peoples of the 'New World' as the former began to explore and colonize it."

Several institutions have emphasized students participating in LCs all four years of their undergraduate careers (e.g., Bowling Green, as mentioned earlier; Dominican University; and University of Texas at Arlington),[4] as opposed to the traditional practice of designing LCs solely for first-year students. Wagner College has created a plan that uses three distinct types of LCs to assist students' face-to-face interaction during different years of their learning: the First Year Experience, taken within the first 30 hours of an academic program; Intermediate LCs, taken anytime in the second or third year of study; and a Senior Program.

According to Wagner's website (www.wagner.edu/experiential_learning/FYP) the First Year Program makes available experiential learning opportunities by providing small-group field experiences that connect with courses linked through assigned LCs. This provides students an opportunity to have some of the same experiences, discuss happenings in the field, and then relate learning in class.

The Intermediate LCs emphasize the linkage between social and interdisciplinary academic topics. The intent is to introduce and support a variety of perspectives through "learning by doing." The focus in these LCs is effective communication through research and presentation.

The Senior Program is structured like the First Year Experience. The intent of the community is to create a place where students make connections based on four years of learning and experiences. They then share them with small and large groups.

Although studies of residential LCs are readily found in the Washington Center report, S. F. Smith and Rodgers (2005) look at Wagner's residential LC from a new student affairs perspective. Their study explores the implementation of educational best practice theory from career service, counseling, financial aid, judicial affairs, health center, and residential life staff members. Three faculty members collaborated with the staff to help transform the university culture into a student-centered institution. Quotes from residential life and student affairs explain their commitment to involvement in the SLC. The assistant director of Greek Life states:

> We firmly believe, due to the research, that students who are involved are more satisfied with their university and we have a greater chance of retaining them. And so we feel like we do what we can to not only get them involved but keep them involved in things that they want to do personally and professionally. (S. F. Smith & Rodgers, 2005, p. 478)

The Student Services and Affairs Office comments:

> Students need to be engaged in meaningful experiences . . . and part of the process that we have is not only to create those meaningful experiences for them, but to help them translate those experiences into learning that they can understand and use. And the more we can engage them in meaningful kinds of activities, the more our students learn. (S. F. Smith & Rodgers, 2005, p. 478)

Course/Class as a Cohort

Most of the survey respondents addressed SLCs primarily at program levels but did not address the individual class as an LC. However, individual professors can do much to promote the learning benefits of LCs within their own classes regardless of whether their institution has program-level LCs or not. The following are suggestions for cultivating powerful course/class LCs.

J. Anderson (1995) presents a comprehensive model for the total classroom as an LC. He focuses on developing effective problem-solving and human relations skills in students and on the instructor becoming primarily a facilitator. He emphasizes the *R*'s of reflection, responsibility, relationship, and respect. He also stresses the importance of tying into the students' past experiences—as well as providing them with new experiences that develop their knowledge, understanding, and skills—and helping them make use of all five of their senses to support their learning. Church (2008) cites recent research that such total class community is developed through identity, familiarity, warmth and beauty, and trust. This model has implications for colleges and universities even though it was initially directed at elementary-secondary institutions.

To foster these qualities, class time must be dedicated to community development early on in the term/semester. As Chickering and Gamson (1987) note, teachers/facilitators must[5]

1. Create activities that promote contact between students and faculty.
2. Design opportunities to develop reciprocity and cooperation among students.
3. Encourage active learning environments to promote transfer.
4. Give prompt constructive feedback to help refinement and reflection.
5. Construct events that emphasize time on task.
6. Create a venue that presumes high expectations are shared and agreed upon.

7. Respect diversity/talents of faculty and students regardless of individual ways of learning.

As illustrated by Table 5.3, certain colleges and universities have emphasized some of these principles in the implementation of their LCs.

In addition to such principles, it is important to learn students' names, provide opportunities for experiential learning, and use within-class LCs. Identifying what social and intellectual development experiences students bring to their college/university experience continues to be crucial. Knowing one's students is as important as knowing one's content.

The great variety of classroom practices across many institutions makes it too difficult to single out specific exemplary institutions pertaining to "within class" LCs. The following discussion highlights suggestions for creating effective cohorts within the classroom. Classroom cohorts have a different look and feel. Instructional practice varies as well. This type of cohort reflects teacher decision making based on homogeneous and heterogeneous grouping. Types of within-class groupings and definitions and examples for the LC typology in chapter 1 are presented in Appendix I. For a recent resource that provides helpful guidelines for effectively implementing such within-class groups at the college level, see Millis (2010).

Let us now take a different focus on classroom cohorts that we trust will also be helpful. Strack and Deutsch (2004) and Sloman (1996) present the idea of a fast learning system. The system depends on recognizing interconnections among logical, verbal, and symbolic representations to assist in making judgments.

This system provides an effective methodology for remembering information. Because of the compatibility between the fast learning system and explicit attitudes SLCs (Rydell & McConnell, 2006), monitoring teacher power and role is important. One of the instructor's main roles is to identify the purpose in creating SLCs within the classroom. The instructor also bears the responsibility of restructuring groups for desired learning outcomes as well as maximum student participation and/or engagement.

There are several ways of structuring groups and creating cohorts. Groups or cohorts can be based on topic—what is to be mastered in terms of either content skills or process skills. They can also be based on purpose—making connections either across or between fields of study. Figure 5.4 provides a visual model of this decision-making process. The first decision to make is whether the cohort will be based on topic or purpose; the left side of Figure 5.4 follows the decision process for cohorts based on topic, and the

TABLE 5.3
Implementation of Chickering and Gamson's
principles of good practice for learning.

Principle	Example	School
Encourages contact between students and faculty	Freshman seminar taught by senior faculty	St. Joseph's College
	Undergraduate students joined as junior research colleagues	Massachusetts Institute of Technology
	Creation of resource groups to help students/groups include a faculty member, peer, and two community resources	Sinclair Community College
Develops reciprocity and cooperation among students	Learning groups (5–7 students) created within large lecture classes	Stony Brook's Federated Learning Communities
	Learning cohorts who take the same block of courses at the same time	Stony Brook's Federated Learning Communities
Encourages active learning	Team projects	Brown University
	Student-created syllabi or labs	State University of New York at Cortland
	Cooperative job programs	University of Michigan
Gives prompt feedback	Entering student assessment	Bronx Community College
	Frequent advising regarding general abilities and analytical thinking	Alverno College
Emphasizes time on task	Mastery learning	Matteo Ricci College
	Contract learning	Seattle University
	Computer-assisted instruction	Empire State College
Communicates high expectations	University workshops for underprepared students	University of Wisconsin
	Honors program for underprepared minorities	University of California, Berkeley
Respects diverse talents and ways of learning	Individualized structure programs	University of California, Irvine
	Meeting diverse learning styles	University of Massachusetts–Boston

FIGURE 5.4
Decision making pertaining to LCs.

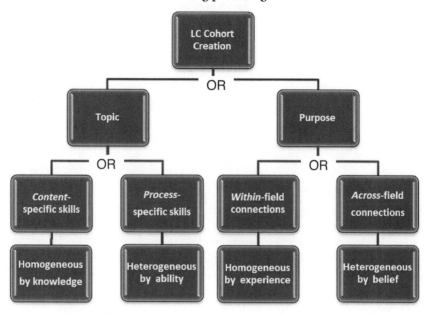

right side follows the process based on purpose. The second decision for cohorts based on topic is what skills are to be learned or developed. Skills may be content specific (increasing understanding of concepts, vocabulary, theories, etc.) or process specific (developing abilities such as research methods, analysis, or critical inquiry). Content-specific topics lend themselves to cohorts with content-based skills (understanding) that are homogeneous, whereas process-specific topics lend themselves to cohorts with more process-based skills (ability) that are heterogeneous. The second decision for cohorts based on purpose is whether connections are to be made within the field or across fields.

Content-specific topics require use of common logical and verbal examples in discussions and tasks. By grouping students into homogeneous cohorts based on similar levels of understanding, members will already possess similar levels of logic and verbal complexity. Together, they can build on the foundations of that common understanding in discussions and activities to stimulate greater depth of understanding and engagement. Thus, homogeneous cohorts provide students an opportunity to share and engage information at their highest level of academic functioning. However, if the group members have different levels of understanding, less knowledgeable students may feel confused or left behind, while more knowledgeable students may feel less stimulated by the level of discussion and cease to develop any further.

By contrast, heterogeneous cohorts work well for process-based skills, which depend more on practice than level of mental engagement. Students with stronger abilities gain metalevel insights by having to analyze their process in order to teach students with weaker skills. Weaker-skilled students gain in turn from the more intimate assistance of a peer. The interdependence of these student cohorts also builds a bridge between learners. Students in heterogeneous groupings are found to develop friendships and support systems within courses (Tinto, 2003), and intellectual and psychological development grow due to the mismatch of skills (King & Kitchener, 1994a, 1994b).

Making connections within a field of study benefits from homogeneous groupings based on common experiences. DuFour (2004) notes that homogeneous learning formats enable deeper learning by removing barriers to success. Again, the common language and logic that comes from shared and/or similar experiences within the field allows members to approach activities with greater depth and precision. By contrast, members of heterogeneous cohorts need to consider information and perspectives from peers who may have different cultural, theoretical, or disciplinary knowledge. Heterogeneous cohorts create communities of learners that can strengthen all voices within the group.

Different disciplines or fields of study are rooted in distinct belief systems and methodologies. They each view information from different perspectives, approach problems with different tools, and provide a variety of answers to solve the same problem. Interactions in heterogeneous cohorts with members from different disciplines and belief systems encourage members to look with new eyes. Zhao and Kuh (2004) found that heterogeneous groups with disequilibrium of experiences, beliefs, and personal perspectives build opportunities to recognize that there can be many "right" answers to solving a problem. Such interactions provide new contexts, develop new schema, and create open-minded, forward-thinking individuals (Bransford, Brown, & Cocking, 1999a).

Other Cohort Arrangements

The "academic program" SLCs introduced in chapter 1 are in many ways a combination of the three types of cohorts that we have discussed. For another example of an alternative cohort, see the discussion in Appendix D about the nonselective "Organizational Management" program SLCs at Roberts Wesleyan College. Superb results have been obtained with both face-to-face and online versions of the program, at dozens of colleges and universities across the country. These are without a doubt exemplary powerful SLCs.

It should also be mentioned that some institutions have an amazing variety of successful/powerful SLCs, presumably because of grassroots stimulation. Exemplary in this respect are Iowa State University (see the following websites: www.inside.iastate.edu/2011/0519/lc.php and www.lc.iastate.edu) and Syracuse University (see Peckskamp & McLaughlin, 2010, and http://lc.syr.edu).

Additional Suggestions for Building Powerful SLCs

A number of suggestions for building powerful SLCs of different types, some of which are applicable across all types of SLCs, have been implied or stated directly in the previous section. Let us now focus on additional general suggestions that may be helpful.

Identification of Social and Personality Development

Bandura's theory of social development and Lave's situational learning theory provide support for creating curricula that embed context and culture within instructional design. Bandura's theory suggests a consistent flow to and from individual and environment. Professors and peers have opportunities to support and dissect meaning by identifying student belief systems and cultural experiences instead of having a surface view of responses and suggestions.

One way to support this deeper creation of meaning and respect for others' perspectives is to help students identify personal attributes that aid their learning while supporting their use of environmental factors or traits that could cause stress. Knowing what traits will add to or detract from groups—small or large—is key to improving student learning. It helps to foster social intelligence and enables students to participate in LCs more effectively. Awareness of differences among members can enhance communication, foster appreciation for individual learning styles, and create opportunities to find like-minded thinkers able to provide help one can understand to foster social intelligence as well as enable students to participate in LCs.

Many personality tests and other tools exist to differentiate personal orientations to the world, such as Myers-Briggs and Keirsey Temperament

Sorter. Use of such tools in LCs can help members become more aware of what they can contribute and how unique members affect one another. For example, Etools4Education provides access to an online version of such a personality test. This organization chooses to use the True Colors Personality Test (see www.online-distance-learning-education.com/personality-test.html and www.truecolorscareer.com/quiz.asp). The personality test divides people into four color groups: gold, blue, green, and orange. Students use pictures, key words, and statements to help identify "their" color. For example, Table 5.4 lists behaviors for "gold" personalities and Table 5.5 lists those for "orange."

There are many traits that could cause people with gold personalities to be assets as well as a detriment in group function. People with gold personalities are used to planning, and they can create a group that sets goals and identifies when tasks are accomplished successfully. However, if another person in the group has orange personality traits, and through his or her lack of

TABLE 5.4
Likes and dislikes of gold personalities.

Behaviors That Frustrate Gold Personalities	*Behaviors of Gold Personalities That Frustrate Others*
• Being irresponsible	• Controlling
• Not having a plan	• Being bossy
• Not being disciplined	• Working long hours
• Being lazy	• Being obsessive
• Taking high risks	• Being judgmental
• Engaging in illegal behaviors	• Planning for everything

TABLE 5.5
Likes and dislikes of orange personalities.

Behaviors That Frustrate Orange Personalities	*Behaviors of Orange Personalities That Frustrate Others*
• Obeying rules and laws	• Ignoring rules
• Following the same routine	• Being undisciplined
• Meeting deadlines	• Not having a plan
• Doing paperwork	• Being quick tempered
• Not being adventurous	• Thinking aloud
• Adhering to too much structure	• Engaging in impulse buying

planning appears to deviate from the initial plan, the climate could become negative very quickly. Knowing whom one is working with and how to communicate with them sets the stage for clear and complete communication, aiding in learning and successful dialogue.

Building trust between the professor and student in conjunction with student-to-student trust is another strategy that promotes the bonding needed for academic success. Trust-building activities also assist in creating a learning environment that produces learners who are risk takers, inquirers, and problem solvers.

Development of Deep Learning Within a Community

Scardamalia and Bereiter (1994) identify four characteristics that define an SLC at the high school and college levels, and activities such as "Walk Across the Room" (see Figure 5.5) support all four of those characteristics. The

FIGURE 5.5
Walk Across the Room.

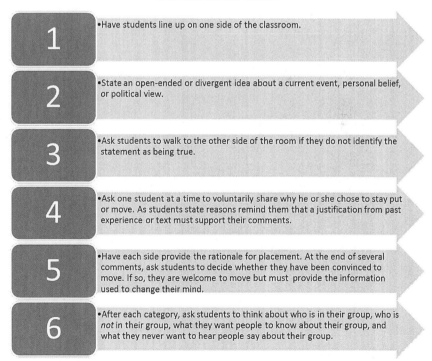

1 • Have students line up on one side of the classroom.

2 • State an open-ended or divergent idea about a current event, personal belief, or political view.

3 • Ask students to walk to the other side of the room if they do not identify the statement as being true.

4 • Ask one student at a time to voluntarily share why he or she chose to stay put or move. As students state reasons remind them that a justification from past experience or text must support their comments.

5 • Have each side provide the rationale for placement. At the end of several comments, ask students to decide whether they have been convinced to move. If so, they are welcome to move but must provide the information used to change their mind.

6 • After each category, ask students to think about who is in their group, who is *not* in their group, what they want people to know about their group, and what they never want to hear people say about their group.

characteristics are that each LC structure should include (a) creation of a culture in which there is diversity of expertise, (b) identification of common objectives, (c) a variety of ways to share learning, and (d) a community focus on learning how to learn. These authors also provide a checklist to aid the construction of SLCs.

Through the proposal of a divergent idea and opportunities to justify beliefs, the "Walk Across the Room" activity creates an open dialogue in the classroom while empowering student thought, inquiry, and verbal exchange. Participation in the activity produces an environment of honesty and respect leading to trust building. Categories should move from relatively safe and nonconfrontational to more challenging and uncomfortable ones. The intent of this exercise is to introduce students to a trust-building activity by providing a rationale behind people's thinking and reactions. Starting off with a statement such as "The best flavor of ice cream is chocolate" allows students to play with this format before bringing in deeper statements.

Comparable activities for virtual delivery formats can be developed. Chapter 3 discussed how face-to-face, virtual, and hybrid LCs are alike and different. For delivery formats as they particularly apply to powerful SLCs, see Appendix J.

Developing Powerful PLCs

As discussed in chapter 1, educational PLCs are professional groups (usually of faculty, staff, or both) organized into small study, planning, and implementation groups in order to collaborate on strategies to achieve optimum student learning. For some faculty, that might include changing their focus from how they teach to how students learn.

PLCs can go by many names. Based on projects in the Carnegie Academy for the Scholarship of Teaching and Learning,[6] Huber and Hutchings (2005) discuss implementation of a PLC vision—originally envisioned by Dan Bernstein at the University of Kansas—that calls on talented college teachers to share their insights as part of a "teaching commons." According to the authors, many times, talented teachers find ingenious solutions to problems in learning, but they may not reflect on their discoveries or share their solutions with others, both of which are important PLC learning activities. Thus, Huber and Hutchings envision the teaching commons as a space for such sharing to occur:

> It is not, of course, a physical place but rather an intellectual space. . . .
> The teaching commons that is now being built by growing numbers of

faculty engaged in such work makes real breakthroughs in teaching and learning more likely than ever before. In such a space, conversation about teaching and learning—informed by evidence and grounded in practice— can become the norm rather than the exception. Disciplines can engage in active trading of ideas about pedagogy. (pp. 31–32)

The authors map out the value of this teaching commons (which others have called a "learning commons") and what it should look like. In addition, they suggest various incentives that can contribute to the creation and implementation of such entities.

Tsai, Laffey, and Hanuscin (2010) studied teachers participating in the practice of PLCs. Their data indicate positive member benefits and engagement for every PLC. However, each PLC was also found to be different from the others in some way. The authors conclude that a PLC may be expected to change over time as membership and practices change. These results might also suggest that part of the LC's power lies in its adaptability to uniquely reflect the complex medley of its context, members, and institutional culture.

Faculty LCs (FLCs) constitute an especially important subcategory of PLCs. For a detailed conceptual discussion specific to FLCs, see materials developed by Miami University of Ohio at www.units.muohio.edu/flc/what is.php.[7] These materials encourage the FLC program director to determine in advance whether the FLC is a cohort-based or topic-based FLC and to limit groups to 8–12 members.

Powerful PLCs in education have many benefits—to the institution, to the educational professionals who participate in them, as well as to those students whose learning is the focus of the PLC's efforts. Gannon-Leary and Fontainha (2007) identified the following direct benefits of such PLCs:

- Enhanced learning environment
- Synergies created
- Capabilities extended to higher level
- Knowledge and learning shared
- Insights gained from one another
- Knowledge deepened
- Innovation and expertise developed
- Cyclical, fluid knowledge developed
- Feeling of connection developed
- Ongoing interactions maintained
- Members assimilated into the group (pp. 6–7)

Despite the benefits, many institutions do not have institution-wide PLCs or they are not powerful. Regarding most PLCs operating today, Servage (2008) complains that "presently, PLCs focus their efforts on the means of teaching and not its ends" (p. 65). It should be emphasized that in our view PLCs are never powerful unless both the means and ends are a focus.

The following sections examine what the 100-Institution Survey reveals about what institutions are doing in relation to PLCs and highlight a few exemplary, powerful PLCs that serve as models of both means and ends. These model PLCs demonstrate important benefits to professional learning and development as well as student learning and success.

Relevant 100-Institution Survey Revelations

Although directed at SLC coordinators, the 100-Institution Survey that we conducted for this book does include an item on PLCs: "Does your institution have a formal institution-wide **PLC** that focuses on student learning? If so, please tell me about it." Figure 5.6 summarizes answers to this question for the 81 institutions responding to the survey.

FIGURE 5.6
Does your institution have a formal institution-wide *PLC* that focuses on student learning?

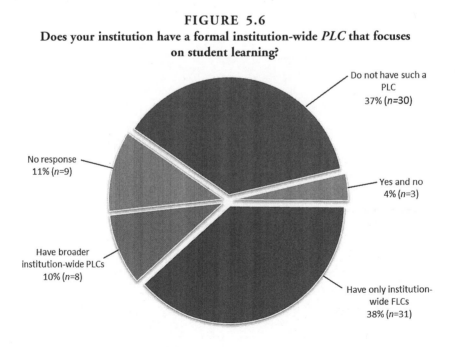

Do not have such a PLC 37% (*n*=30)

No response 11% (*n*=9)

Yes and no 4% (*n*=3)

Have broader institution-wide PLCs 10% (*n*=8)

Have only institution-wide FLCs 38% (*n*=31)

Of the 37% of respondents reporting that they do not have any institution-wide PLC, a couple said developing such PLCs was a goal and several reported formal or informal PLCs not institution-wide in scope. For example: "The whole is only as great as its parts, and although there are pockets of excellence it is not institution-wide." "We only have informal faculty circles discussing improvement of student learning; *none* of them are formal entities that have been charged to come up with proposals and ideas."

A couple of the respondents, one from a public community college and one from a small private college, appeared to the interviewer to have strong institution-wide PLCs, but the respondents seemed not to recognize it. Presumably, to them SLCs are the only "real" LCs.

Of the 4% of respondents reporting "yes *and* no," one referred to a "Center for Teaching and Learning" to assist faculty. Another stated: "We sort of do, through our Summer Reading Group, which for example recently read *Brain Rules* and participated together in workshops on learning."

Of the 38% of respondents who reported that their institutions had institution-wide FLCs, we have selected a number of exemplary ones; they are discussed separately in the following section. FLCs were often initiated and/or coordinated by centers for teaching and learning. Other FLCs apparently were not connected to a center in this way, as indicated by this response: "Lots of things pertaining to faculty member interactions apply here; formal and informal FLCs across campus are numerous."

Based on the survey, faculty participation may or may not be attached to incentives. In some cases, faculty participants receive stipends. For example, "Yes, we have had faculty teaching circles for about 10 years, and are now putting them online. We pay $300 per faculty member for participation in a faculty teaching and learning circle, plus provide lunch if they meet on campus." (Also see the description for Florida Atlantic University in the section "Exemplary Institutional FLCs.") In other cases, stipends are not provided (e.g., see the description for Wagner College in that section).

Of the eight reported broader PLCs that focus on student learning, seven involve faculty, staff, and administrators meeting regularly to discuss student learning on campus. The eighth PLC also includes students and members from the surrounding local community.

Exemplary Institutional PLCs With Broader Membership

We have selected two institutions that represent exemplary examples of an institution with broader membership. As emphasized by Huber and Hutchings (2005), "Students need to be part of the discussion about learning"

(p. 118). Having students involved in PLCs along with faculty, staff, and administrators encourages student ideas and input at an earlier, more formative stage and allows professional ideas about teaching/learning improvement to be easily and naturally tested on students in a timely manner.

1. **Western Washington State University (WWU).** This institution includes students as well as community members in its PLCs. In her response to the survey, Dr. Carmen Werder, director of the Teaching-Learning Academy and Writing Instruction Support and Learning Commons explains:

> Yes, our Teaching-Learning Academy (TLA) functions as both a PLC and an SLC. I serve as director and coordinate the dialogue groups that include faculty, staff, students, and the community. We also have a teaching writing community that I coordinate as director of Writing Instruction Support, but we . . . stay connected virtually only. We also have a teaching writing community that I coordinate as director of Writing Instruction Support (WIS) that features an annual multiple-day working retreat, a writing research fellows program (that pairs students with faculty studying writing instruction), as well as periodic development sessions with students, and we stay connected virtually.

The academy that Dr. Werder refers to provides teaching and learning resources and services that are complementary to what is provided by WWU's Center for Instructional Innovation & Assessment (CIIA). CIIA has an Innovative Teaching Showcase that is described as follows on the university's website (http://pandora.cii.wwu.edu/cii/showcase/default.asp):

> An online publication created by the Center for Instructional Innovation and Assessment (CIIA) as a way to highlight and share exceptional teaching practices by Western Washington University faculty. Each year, several instructors are nominated to participate, and then work extensively with the CIIA to create this in-depth resource. The Showcase is published on this website at the end of each academic year.

The CIIA also sponsors an effective FLC that is described as follows at www.wwu.edu/depts/facultygur: "The Faculty GUR Group was formed to bring together faculty from different departments across the university in a learning community that will seek to enhance each participant's general education by relying on each other's domain of expertise." CIIA offers many learning resources, including teaching tips, a listing of recommended books, and links to four teaching center websites at other institutions:

- Center for Instruction, Research, & Technology at Indiana State University (www.indstate.edu/cirt1)
- Center for Faculty Excellence at University of North Carolina at Chapel Hill (http://cfe.unc.edu)
- Schreyer Institute for Teaching Excellence at Pennsylvania State University (www.schreyerinstitute.psu.edu)
- Maricopa Center for Learning and Instruction at Maricopa Community College (www.mcli.dist.maricopa.edu)

The CIIA has also made available links to possible model FLCs at other universities for use by faculty members and FLCs at WWU:

- Georgia Southern University Center for Excellence in Teaching (http://academics.georgiasouthern.edu/cet/programs/flc.htm)
- University of Georgia Center for Teaching and Learning (www.isd .uga.edu/flc)
- Kent State University "Critical and Transformative Practices in Professional Learning Communities," *Teacher Education Quarterly* (www.kent.edu/fpdc/learning-and-teaching/index.cfm)
- Miami University of Ohio Center for the Enhancement of Learning, Teaching, and University Assessment (www.units.muohio.edu/celt)
- University of Miami (Miller School of Medicine) Educational Development Office (http://edo.med.miami.edu)
- Michigan State University Office of Faculty and Organizational Development (www1.provost.msu.edu/facdev/FLC/about.asp)
- University of Notre Dame Kaneb Center for Teaching and Learning (http://kaneb.nd.edu/programs/flc/index.html)
- Virginia Commonwealth University Center for Teaching Excellence (www.vcu.edu/cte/programs/faculty_learning_communities.htm)
- Western Carolina University Coulter Faculty Commons (www.wcu .edu/7062.asp)

2. **Iowa State University.** Another good example of a PLC with broader membership (which may at times include student involvement) is provided by the Learning Enhancement Action/Resource Network (LEA/RN) at ISU. Dr. Barbara Licklider, professor of educational leadership and policy studies, initiated and coordinated LEA/RN for many years in cooperation with the Center for Excellence in Learning and Teaching (CELT).

LEA/RN consists of faculty and staff learning teams—often involving student input and participation at appropriate times—within various colleges and departments across the campus. These teams have been discussing, studying, and promoting effective student learning and LCs since the mid-1990s. CELT also does ongoing faculty development that sometimes uses teaching and learning circles.

Exemplary Institutional Faculty, Staff, and Administrator PLCs

The following four institutions represent excellence in their faculty, staff, and administrator PLCs:

1. **Cabrillo College.** In responding to our survey, Dr. Victoria Banales, English instructor and basic skills coordinator, stated: "Cabrillo has a Faculty Experiential Learning Institute (FELI) that provides workshops, curriculum enrichment, technical training, or practicums several times each year. In addition, faculty and staff involved in LCs are in ongoing dialogue about how to maximize student learning."

The college's website (www.cabrillo.edu/services/aces/ACES_Five_Year_Action_Plan.pdf) states the mission of one of those faculty-staff PLCs, called the Basic Skills and LCs Advisory Council (BSLCAC):

> To provide students a community in a pedagogically rich environment to enhance the skills they need to be successful in college courses required for their career and/or transfer goals. To provide faculty and staff a community of practice that studies and experiments with pedagogies and curricula that are successful in meeting the needs of these students.

FLCs at Cabrillo are also exemplary. They are designed to support the college's growing SLCs and are described on the college's website (www.cabrillo.edu/services/aces/Learning_Community_Guidelines_v.2.pdf) as follows::

> Faculty members will meet/communicate in person, through e-mail, or by phone approximately once a week during the semester in which the LC is being offered. The main focus of the meetings is to discuss student progress and conduct early interventions. In addition, faculty will align courses, discuss challenges and successes, problem solve, plan upcoming class activities, integrate assignments, etc. It is expected that the majority of the meetings will be conducted in person with all cohort faculty members present. Faculty will document their attendance at cohort meetings via sign-up

sheets; Cohort Leads will collect the documentation and submit monthly attendance reports (three per semester) to the Learning Communities coordinator. (p. 1)

2. **St. Lawrence University.** Dr. Cathy Crosby-Currie, former associate dean of the first year and associate professor of psychology, responded to our survey as follows:

St. Lawrence is an institution at which discussions about teaching and learning never stop. These conversations are going on in several different venues. We have had multiple grant projects over the years from Teagle and the American Association of Colleges and Universities that involve faculty/staff LCs around issues like engaged pedagogy/learning, increasing diversity education, and addressing challenges of the sophomore year. We also have a University Assessment Committee that encourages and coordinates our student learning assessment. Finally, our Associate Dean for Academic Affairs has responsibility for our Center for Teaching and Learning and is the co-chair of our Faculty Teaching and Scholarship Committee, both of which offer various opportunities for faculty and staff development including a multi-day "college" for faculty and staff at the end of each academic year.

3. **The University of Iowa.** Dr. Andrew Beckett, University College assistant dean of first-year programs, responded to our survey for the University of Iowa. He stated: "Since 2006 the university has utilized a Student Success Team. Consisting of faculty and staff volunteers from various departments, the cross-functional group seeks innovative ways of helping students succeed in their college careers." This Student Success Team is described on the university's website (http://provost.uiowa.edu/work/strategic-initiatives/docs/tfreports/SITF_Undergrad.pdf) as follows:

Through the Student Success Team, we have begun a movement of seeing student success as everyone's role, but are still in the beginning stages of this effort. We need to expect more of our students, and more of ourselves, in order to see an overall improvement in the quality of a UI education. (p. 25)

4. **University of Maryland at College Park.** Greig Stewart, executive director, College Park Scholars, stated the following in response to our survey question about PLCs:

All LLCs (Honors, Scholars, Global Communities, CIVICUS, Writers' House, Beyond the Classroom, International House, etc.) are overseen by Provost's Advisory Committee on Living-Learning and Special Programs, which includes faculty, administrators and staff. The following URL (http://provost.umd.edu/living_learning_programs.cfm) takes one to an announcement on enhancing living-learning programs. The bottom paragraph speaks to "strategic oversight," that is, the establishment of the advisory committee. By positioning the oversight of LLCs in the Office of the Provost, it underscores the university's commitment to excellence in undergraduate learning. It also ensures that when discretionary dollars are available in the provost's office, those dollars may be funneled into enhancements or additions to LLCs.

Exemplary Institutional FLCs

The following eight institutions represent excellence in their faculty PLCs (often called FLCs).

1. **Bowling Green State University.** Dr. Patrick Vrooman is director of the Partners in Context and Community Learning Center, a professional development LLC for education majors interested in urban education. Although the focus of his PLC (and of many of the PLCs discussed here) is much broader than first-year programs, Dr. Vrooman stated that "the first-year programs require fairly intensive faculty involvement that extends across the university within the discipline and results in a university-wide LC." Nine Bowling Green FLCs are described for the 2010–11 school year at www.bgsu.edu/ctl/page30860.html. One of them focuses on service-learning and is described on the university's website (www.bgsu.edu/offices/service-learning/newsletter/10-22-2010/page87936.html) as follows:

> The Office of Service-Learning in collaboration with the Center for Teaching and Learning initiated the Faculty Learning Communities as a way to promote the institutionalization of service-learning courses in every department, to encourage interdisciplinary dialogue, and to advance the objectives of BGSU's core curriculum.

2. **Chandler-Gilbert Community College.** Yvonne Reineke of the Department of English offers the following response to our survey question: (1) "The division chairs hold retreats, off and on, called Writing, Reflection and Renewal"; (2) "Development Committee efforts in the area of critical

thinking"; and (3) "During the last year we have developed a Faculty Network for Excellence in Mentoring New Faculty."

3. **Dominican University.** Jodi Cressman, director of the Borra Center for Teaching & Learning Excellence (CTLE), stated the following in our survey:

> Yes, the CTLE Faculty Commons provides a library with resources on teaching and learning and common space on a continuing basis for informal conversations about teaching/scholarship, browsing the library holdings and reading, and reflection or work on teaching. The space is also used periodically for university-wide workshops, presentations, seminars, etc. on teaching and learning innovations and effectiveness.

Visit www.dom.edu/fdrs/bctle/index.html for the college's current-year listing of seminars for faculty pertaining to improving student learning.

4. **Florida Atlantic University.** Jennifer Bebergal, director for student retention in the Center for Teaching and Learning (www.fau.edu/ctl) stated:

> For the last three years we have had 8 to 12 FLCs each year on a variety of topics related to teaching and learning. Faculty members receive a stipend for leading such a PLC. Members must be actively involved, and each professional LC must develop some kind of product and do a showcase.

For current-year FLCs at the university, see www.fau.edu/ctl/Faculty_Learning_Communities.php.

5. **Miami University of Ohio.** Tresa Barlage, associate director of residence life, responded to our PLC survey question as follows: "We have many formal FLCs around many topics (including student learning) and they are coordinated by our Center for Enhancement of Learning, Teaching and Assessment."

In addition, Miami University of Ohio has taken the lead nationally on scholarship and presenting workshops pertaining to development of FLCs (e.g., see www.units.muohio.edu/celt/faculty/flcs/miami, www.units.muohio.edu/flc/whatis.php, and www.units.muohio.edu/flc/30_components/index.php). The report of a Middle Tennessee State University faculty member who attended a Miami FLC workshop (see www.mtsu.edu/ltanditc/SourceLink_F08-for-screen.pdf) indicates the impact that these FLCs have:

> *Ron Kates, English*—Last fall, I joined a group of MTSU faculty and staff who came together to investigate faculty learning communities (FLCs)

after having been inspired in a workshop led by Dr. Milt Cox of Miami University of Ohio. Generally, an FLC is an academic group with a purpose. It is composed of 6 to 12 faculty members and requires a commitment to meet, work, collaborate with colleagues on the FLC and disseminate the outcomes of the group's work to the academic community. For several months, we researched FLC structures and outcomes from nearly three dozen schools of varying sizes, locations, and demographic make-ups, and spoke to faculty about their experiences. Finally . . . the group reached consensus: FLCs could have a transformative impact on teaching and learning at MTSU by engaging faculty in professionally and personally beneficial interactions with peers across campus.

6. **Skagit Valley College.** Jennifer Handley—English instructor, general education coordinator (main campus), and chair, District General Education Committee—responded to our PLC question as follows:

We have an advisory committee that works closely with the General Education coordinators to suggest the kinds of faculty support that are needed. This support may come in the form of annual orientation sessions for LC faculty, workshops offered through the Center for Learning and Teaching, and districtwide retreats. In addition, new faculty members are encouraged to collaborate with more experienced LC faculty to propose new courses.

7. **University of North Dakota.** Tami Carmichael, associate professor of humanities and integrated studies, stated in response to the PLC question in our survey:

The Office of Instructional Development is dedicated to enhancing the quality of teaching and learning at the University of North Dakota. Through its various activities, programs, and resources OID promotes campuswide conversations about teaching, fosters innovation in curriculum and instruction, recognizes excellence, and encourages the continuing development of faculty as teachers. This office coordinates the Alice T. Clark Scholars Mentoring Program, an orientation and collegial support program for faculty new to UND. Its purposes are to assist faculty in developing professional and personal networks; increase faculty awareness of campus culture and resources; [and] support the professional development of faculty as teachers and scholars.
    A second-year program is offered for those who successfully complete the first-year program. Funded by the UND Foundation, the program is named in honor of retired Vice President for Academic Affairs Alice T.

Clark. It is administered through the Office of Instructional Development. . . . The program consists of two components:

    a. A one-on-one mentoring relationship with an experienced faculty member

    b. A yearlong series of monthly cohort meetings in which participants get a chance to meet and talk with key campus figures and to discuss topics of common interest and value to new faculty. (An out-of-town fall retreat allows for more extended conversations and group socializing.)

I [Carmichael] would like to emphasize that I do not work with the Office of Instructional Development. The director is Dr. Anne Kelsch. I only speak about the excellent programs they offer as someone who has witnessed and benefited from them. For more information, see the website at http://webapp.und.edu/dept/oid/.

8. **Wagner College.** Dr. Anne Love, associate provost for assessment, stated:

Wagner College has "scholarship circles" for faculty to come together monthly to discuss ongoing scholarship, encourage one another's work, and offer feedback in writing. Faculty members apply to be included in a circle each year, so that they can start focusing on a project prior to the start of the meetings. There is no compensation for involvement.

Exemplary PLCs Across Institutions

Effective PLCs that focus on student learning and success and the development of supportive LCs also exist across and between colleges and universities. These across-institutional PLCs can function on a national basis, such as the consortia on LCs created by the Washington Center for Improving the Quality of Undergraduate Education or the American Educational Research Association Special Interest Group on Learning Science and Advanced Technologies for Learning. Or they can function on a regional basis, such as the Atlantic Center for LCs or the Dialogues in Methods of Education (D.I.M.E.) (for a description of the latter see www.mste.uiuc.edu/dime/). Some across-institution PLCs are even worldwide, such as the International Society for the Scholarship of Teaching and Learning. Often across-institution PLC members meet electronically as well as face-to-face.

Individual educators can, and often do, belong to a number of different LCs, and this number is increasing with the continuing development of many strictly online PLCs. Duncan-Howell (2010) identified and discussed three online communities for teachers and concluded that such online PLCs have much potential as an ongoing source of professional development for teachers. Following are six noteworthy online PLCs focusing on student learning in which higher education faculty participate as members:

1. **Inquiry Learning Forum (ILF).** "The Inquiry Learning Forum: Fostering and Sustaining Knowledge Networking to Support a Community of Science and Mathematics Teachers" was a grant sponsored by the National Science Foundation. According to the project website (www.nsf.gov/cise/kdi/tools/lrng_forum.html), the initiative

> is an online community of K-12 math and science teachers who work together to create, improve, and share classrooms centered on the learner. The ILF promotes inquiry-based learning, which encourages students to ask questions, to be curious about the world around them, to make discoveries, and to test those discoveries rigorously in a quest for new understanding. This process is guided by teachers.

2. **Math Forum.** The collaborative communities in Math Forum appear to have been one of the initial virtual PLCs. Shumar (2009) has taken a social theory approach to studying the impact of Math Forum's collaborative communities on the professional development of teachers and other participants. He notes that "the collaborative community building work that Math Forum teachers do online allows them to not only form a learning community but allows them to overcome tensions around mathematical identity formation which are important for advancing one's thinking as a math teacher" (p. 269).

3. **MERLOT.** The Multimedia Educational Resource for Learning and Online Teaching (http://merlot.org) is an online learning organization that has been in existence since 1997. It has well over 100,000 members from a wide range of disciplines who are interested in evidence-based teaching and learning. Members participate online in one or more of a couple dozen different curricular discipline communities offered on the site. They network with other members and interact with guest experts in their own and other disciplines. Members can also browse a wide selection of over 36,000 curriculum materials, learning support resources, and diverse learning exercises to use with their students.

4. **Math and Science Partnership Network.** "MSPnet (http://mspnet.org) was created to serve multiple, nested communities composed of university faculty, K-12 educators, administrators, and professional developers who

are engaged in efforts to improve math and science education . . . launched in January 2004 . . . funded by the National Science Foundation . . . [and has served] over 5,000 members" (Falk & Drayton, 2009, p. 17).

5. **Tapped In.** Tapped In (http://tappedin.org), launched in the mid-1990s, offers teachers and organizations virtual buildings and meeting rooms where groups can use an advanced technological environment and a suite of interactive tools to communicate and collaborate. The vision of the creators of Tapped In was to invite educational professionals "to be tenants in the TI environment and use it to help accomplish their own TPD (Teacher Professional Development) agendas. . . . Their hope was that it would be used by many different organizations and constituencies for their own purposes; consequently, the site itself is content free" (Falk & Drayton, 2009, p. 18).

6. **WIDE World.** "WIDE (Wide-scale Interactive Development for Educators) World at the Harvard Graduate School of Education offers research-based online and onsite professional development (PD) programs to help educators achieve systemic and sustainable educational changes by improving student learning, teaching and leadership. Since 1999, WIDE has instructed and coached over 19,000 educators from nearly 100 countries from six continents, growing over 700% of course enrollment in five years (2003–2008)" (Joo, n.d.).

The development and popularizing of social networking online communities—Facebook, MySpace, and LinkedIn—may in the long term make defined networks such as the ones that we have described less relevant. Here each person creates her or his own self-defined interest community. Regarding this development, Drayton, Obuchowski, and Falk (2009) predict:

> Personally centered networks will push the future of online community experience even further, as interacting individuals will create their own metasites that are not limited by community boundaries. They will rely on RSS feeds, subscription functionalities, and sophisticated notification systems to track their interests, groups, and friends across site boundaries. Further, they will track this information through integrated technologies that include and may combine laptop, PDA, phone, TV, and so on. (p. 213)

Suggestions for Building Powerful PLCs

This section traces suggestions for building powerful PLCs based on the LC literature. These suggestions come from several streams of research. The first is the extensive, well-documented research on PLCs at the elementary-secondary level that we believe contains knowledge and ideas that are transferable to higher education. At the beginning of this project, a thorough search in a local university library revealed that the majority of recent books on LCs focus on PLCs, but that *every single one* of those books is targeted *solely* at the elementary-secondary education level. PLCs and their designs and impacts have been a prominent focus at the elementary-secondary school level since the turn of the century. For example, Hord (1997), DuFour (2004) (also see DuFour, Eaker, & DuFour, 2005), and Murphy and Lick (2005) were the prominent pioneers in stimulating implementation of face-to-face PLCs within elementary-secondary schools. Similarly, Falk and Drayton (2009) have offered recommendations for online PLCs that extend beyond individual elementary-secondary institutions and districts. Thus, PLCs at the elementary-secondary level of education provide strong, longitudinal evidence and knowledge about successful PLCs, and we should be able to generalize from these PLCs (as well as from PLCs in business and industry) to create adaptations and suggestions for optimal formation and use of PLCs focused on postsecondary education.

A second stream of research was stimulated by the extensive scholarly work pertaining to FLCs conducted at Miami University in Ohio in recent years. Since Miami began its research, journal articles and conference presentations pertaining to higher education FLCs and PLCs are becoming more common. For instance, under the direction of Milton Cox, who initially coordinated a project on FLCs funded by the Fund for the Improvement of Postsecondary Education (FIPSE), the university has sponsored an annual Faculty Learning Community Developers' and Facilitators' Summer Institute and conference that began in approximately 2000 (see www.units.mu ohio.edu/flc). The Summer Institute was responsible for an edited Jossey-Bass *New Directions in Teaching and Learning* monograph on FLCs (Cox & Richlin, 2004) and in 2009 initiated publication of the semiannual and peer-reviewed *Learning Communities Journal,* which focuses on this topic. There have always been various faculty, staff, and joint committees on postsecondary education campuses charged with improving some aspect of student life. However, most of these committees have traditionally focused on matters other than how to improve student learning outcomes. In addition, they—including curriculum committees—have usually thought in segmented ways and not viewed their central focus to be on optimizing student learning and development. Effective sharing and community reflection on both pertinent research and members' experiences in teaching and learning are key to powerful PLCs. Discussions must be lively and substantive exchanges. Participation by a variety of members must be encouraged and open-minded, deep listening to all perspectives must be stressed. After such individual and group reflection and sharing, the group needs to arrive at agreed-upon conclusions about the lessons learned, potential barriers to watch out for and avoid, and how those lessons should be applied in the future.

Such deliberations also require effective leadership, coordination, and planning, another key to helping PLCs become powerful. This will in turn require an institutional reward system that encourages serious and enthusiastic LC participation and involvement in the scholarship of teaching and learning. Rewards for such participation and scholarship could include oral or written recognition (either personal or public), release time, and reimbursement of expenses or some other kind of financial reward such as a stipend.

The most important incentive to include for active involvement in such activities by faculty is for the involvement to contribute significantly to faculty promotion/tenure. As Huber and Hutchings (2005) emphasize, that means "we must push forward with new genres and forms to document the work of teaching and learning" (p. 118). They also stress another important key for powerful PLCs: the development of an institutional infrastructure that will provide all needed support for quality PLCs and pedagogy.

It should be acknowledged that virtual PLCs have requirements for success that do not apply for face-to-face PLCs. Falk and Drayton (2009) discuss factors to consider when virtual PLCs are created, facilitated, and sustained:

> The increased capabilities to combine features that optimize content retrieval, content creation, and collaboration, and to customize users' experience according to their preferences, history, and community affiliations, have created new possibilities that must be taken into account when creating LCs for professional development. . . . There are four dimensions that strongly influence decisions on the nature of the architectural design, content, the suite of tools, expectations for dissemination, and leadership structures in any community for professional development. All of these decisions will in turn shape the nature of the participants' experience. These dimensions are: 1. The nature of the community; . . . 2. The nature of the professional development experience; . . . 3. The nature of the audience and of the products; . . . 4. The focus of leadership and facilitation. (p. 21)

Falk and Drayton (2009) also observe that it is common for virtual PLC members to begin the relationship face-to-face with other members they know or met in the past. For example, they may meet at a conference or summer institute and get into follow-up dialogue online, and it can involve such things as sharing draft documents and asking for confidential feedback.

In addition, Cox (2004) separately discussed 30 components of a PLC; see the Miami University of Ohio website at www.units.muohio.edu/flc/ 30_components/index.php. Effective functioning of all 30 components pertaining to any PLC is important for a PLC to be powerful in its effect on student learning and success. Cox divided them into the following nine categories: mission and purpose, curriculum, administration, connections, affiliated participants, meetings and activities, scholarly process, assessment, and enablers/rewards. In addition, Cox identified, alongside each of the 30 components, whether the component is primarily the responsibility of an FLC facilitator, the FLC program director, or both of them.

Jacobs and Yendol-Hoppey (2010) studied a PLC of prospective teacher field supervisors and discovered that deep dialogue about "multiple levels of shared dilemmas and the use of dialogic tools to foster critical reflection" that were modeled by the facilitator led to the supervisors moving "from simply transformative learning to transformative action" (p. 114). For more information about such tools, see Levine (2010). For an extensive bibliography pertaining to all types of FLCs that was compiled at Miami University of Ohio, see www.units.muohio.edu/flc/bibliography.php.

Cox and Richlin's (2004) monograph deals with a number of applied topics that are important: institutional considerations in developing an FLC program, development of facilitators for FLCs, facilitation of FLCs, management of multiple FLCs, assessment of FLCs, technology in support of FLCs, development of diversity with FLCs, development of the scholarship of teaching and learning through FLCs, midcareer and senior FLCs, and FLCs for preparing new or future faculty. See Ortquist-Ahrens and Torosyan (2009) for additional details on the roles of the FLC facilitator, and the Southwest Educational Development Laboratory report at www.sedl.org/ pubs/change45/6.html for the importance of and procedures for assessing institutional and participant readiness for PLCs.

Miami University of Ohio provides an extremely useful set of recommendations for creating and implementing FLCs at www.units.muohio.edu/ flc/recommendations.php. The following topics are covered: initiation, initial planning, application, selection, prestige, trust and safety, legacy, activities, scholarship of teaching, assessment, sharing, leadership, the role of FLC project director, compensation and rewards, and overcoming obstacles.

Developing Powerful LOs

As discussed in chapter 1, in LOs the entire institution (or a primary structural entity therein) demonstrates a clear and intentional organization-wide culture of learning supported by both the formal leadership and a preponderance of members throughout the institution. LOs can be organized to maximize learning for all members pertaining to one or more dimensions of knowledge. To reiterate, this book focuses on only one such dimension: that pertaining to knowledge and understanding of how to optimize student learning.

Relevant 100-Institution Survey Revelations

The 100-Institution Survey question pertaining to LOs was as follows: "A Learning Organization is an institution where everyone throughout the institution is focusing continually on innovations to improve learning. Does this describe your institution?" Figure 5.7 summarizes responses to this question.

Of the 28% of respondents reporting that their institution is not an LO, a number of them acknowledged that only small pockets within the

FIGURE 5.7
Is your institution a true *learning organization*?

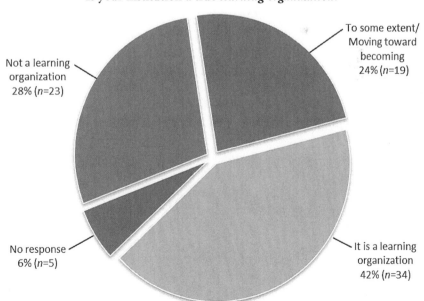

To some extent/
Moving toward
becoming
24% (*n*=19)

Not a learning
organization
28% (*n*=23)

No response
6% (*n*=5)

It is a learning
organization
42% (*n*=34)

institution are continually focusing on improvement of student learning. For example, one respondent stated, "Organizationally we like to think so, but in actuality there are only core pockets." Another stated, "We wish this were true, but instead we are silos. But we are pretty good."

A number of the respondents expressed a desire for their institution to become a true LO: "We aspire to be there, but currently have only pockets of such activity throughout the faculty." "We would like to move there; a few faculty members are talking about this."

One respondent referred to the state of the economy being a factor: "In such challenging economic times, I would think such institutions are rare." Another respondent suggested that a change in campus culture currently taking place might or might not lead toward such a desired state.

Twenty-four percent of respondents reported that their institution is an LO to some extent or moving toward becoming one, and similar comments predominated, such as: "We do, but still have a long way to go, especially faculty." "Somewhat; significant people have such a focus." "Yes, but it takes different forms in different parts of the university." "I would say it is happening in pockets; there is not one single effort across the campus." "On our 'best days' we could be described in this way."

Several of these respondents described developments at their institutions that may be helpful to other institutions: "Certain segments within the university can be described like this; for example, we have a Council for Student Success that meets regularly." "We bring in speakers to support the internalization of such a campuswide philosophy and awareness of the latest trends in higher education." "Through our campuswide LC/LLC initiative, we hope to improve learning through communal living—breaking the university up into 'villages' of small, themed learning labs."

Of the 42% of respondents claiming that their institution is definitely an LO, many assumed that all educational institutions had to be "learning organizations." Unfortunately, they were not directly asked to provide evidence or to explain why they responded as they did. Most merely answered "yes" and did not give any reason, but a few of the respondents provided unsolicited rationales that may or may not support our observation: "Absolutely; there is a master plan for the campus." "Yes, we are always rethinking." "Yes, given that we are a public institution continually trying to find innovative options."

However, a number of the respondents did provide rationales suggesting that the institution is a true LO: "I think I would define what happens here as widespread examining data and brainstorming ideas to make college life and success better for students." "Exactly! Our university has been innovating since its beginnings. Faculty and staff here are on the cutting edge of pedagogical innovation—to the point that we simply are sometimes too busy doing too many things!" "Absolutely! The grand challenge is interdisciplinary." Other responses providing such a helpful rationale are quoted, and the institutions identified with permission, in the following section.

Exemplary LOs

For some survey respondents, the question on "learning organization," in which it was defined as "*everyone* throughout the institution *focusing continually* on innovations to improve learning," seemed unrealistic or impossible. Therefore, we decided that this definition (which we had based on Peter Senge's LO concept) is perhaps too much of an ideal, especially for large research universities with their semiautonomous colleges. Consequently, we now define LO in terms of there being a preponderance of people throughout the organization—as opposed to "everyone"—thinking and acting this way (see the definition for LO in the introduction and the abbreviated definition in chapter 1). Using that definition, we selected a few colleges and universities as exemplary LOs.

It should be emphasized, however, that institutions should be continually striving toward the ideal that Senge initially enunciated even though in practical terms it is not completely attainable. By staying focused on "everyone," the successful LO recognizes and encourages the important roles and contributions of *all* community members, including ones who might often get overlooked or ignored. For instance, at the most basic levels, it is easier to learn in a clean and safe environment, yet often custodial staff and security staff do not get included in conversations about student learning and retention. Support staff members such as custodians, security, food service providers, housekeepers, and secretaries can and do serve in the larger institutional community's goal of maximizing students' success and retention—through the quality of their interactions with students and the quality of their services for students. We considered statements made by survey respondents and also looked at institutions not in our survey sample, carefully examining the website for each institution that seemed to show promise. We then used a compare-and-contrast procedure to decide which institutions should be suggested as exemplary "learning organizations" for others to examine and possibly emulate. The top 10 are listed here in alphabetical order:

1. **Alverno College.** The college's website (www.alverno.edu/aboutalverno/missionhistory) states: "We have built a community of learning, in

which all functions of the College support our students in meeting explicit expectations." This statement is put into operational terms by the following description at http://depts.alverno.edu/ere/community_of_inquiry/commun ity_of_inquiry.htm:

> Taking collective responsibility across a program for achieving student learning outcomes is facilitated by approaches that build a community of inquiry. Such an inquiry needs to simultaneously generate and draw on the common educational purposes. At Alverno, the outcome-oriented ability-based curriculum, with its emphasis on supporting experiential and reflective learning through performance assessment, provides a common conceptual framework for inquiry. . . .
>
> The faculty's collaborative inquiry into learning outcomes within and across the disciplines was a key step in initially developing the ability-based curriculum and has remained vital to improving and updating it. This kind of inquiry itself has a strong experiential and deliberative base, carried out in different groupings within the institutional community. Sharing what they are learning about learning as they constantly modify their practice in the context of a common program is one way that educators increase their knowledge about how and what learning endures. Effective collaboration across the curriculum requires faculty discourse that includes close analysis of practice, conscious reflections on the frameworks of practice and their critique in relation to student learning outcomes.

2. **Collin County Community College.** Dr. Tracy McKenzie, professor of sociology and chair of the LCs program, stated: "Absolutely; there is an environment and culture here that encourages innovative teaching. For example, in 2009, the college introduced a new program to help veterans transition from battlefields and bases to classrooms and civilian life. That spring four core classes—Government 2301, Speech 1211, U.S. History 1302 and Psychology 1301—were offered to only veterans."

Various places on the college's website at www.collin.edu provide other examples suggesting the conclusion that there is an environment and culture throughout the institution that encourages innovative teaching that will maximize student learning and success, including:

- "In LCs courses, professors team teach and connect the concepts of their disciplines under a common theme or question."
- A consortium led by Collin College has been selected for a $19,998,974 grant, part of nearly $500 million in federal grants targeted for training and workforce development to help unemployed

workers who are changing careers. More than 200 community colleges around the country applied and 32 were selected by the US Department of Labor in coordination with the US Department of Education.

- Collin College's nursing program announced that the National League of Nursing has named it a Center of Excellence in Nursing Education. Collin College's nursing program is Texas' first and only Center of Excellence in Nursing Education. Of the more than 1,800 nursing programs in the country, only 19 have been named a Center of Excellence.

- The faculty includes three US Professors of the Year, a Texas Professor of the Year, and five Minnie Stevens Piper Professors.

3. **Indiana University–Purdue University Fort Wayne.** Gregory Anderson, associate director of First-Year Experience, stated in response to our survey question: "Yes, and key players who are innovative." Illustrative of this point are the following statements from him and quotes from the university's website:

- Dr. Richard Light, a Harvard professor and author, writes in *Making the Most of College*, "Students who are able to integrate the in-class and outside-of-class parts of their lives can reap great benefits." Of course, the greatest benefit is graduating with a college degree. Since IPFW agrees with Light's research, faculty members include ten activities into their LCs through a community hour; therefore, students cannot register for classes during this hour. Faculty plan cocurricular or academic activities (going to a special lecture or watching a movie), and they plan extra-curricular or more fun activities (have a class dinner or attending an IPFW event).

- The instructors pick a time to meet for one hour when the campus calendar has no other campus activity, and this occurs ten times within the semester. Ten times each semester the students get connected to the University, the faculty and each other in a special way during a time when there are no other scheduled distractions.

- Each faculty member receives $150 to buy food, etc. and promote good ideas for the community hour, for example, two recreation centers on campus are made available for such activities during these scheduled hours.

- Even though this is largely a commuter campus, 85% to 90% of the students say it is a great idea.

4. **Iowa State University.** Douglas Grunewald, codirector of LCs at the university, stated: "Many people throughout the institution are committed to the continuous improvement of the university." More of his responses to questions in our survey pertaining to SLCs support that generalization:

> We created LCs by allowing them to develop at the grassroots level in a decentralized manner. After a few years of experimentation we provided a centralized structure that included providing funding for individual programs. We continued to provide central services and support when it was practical (i.e., training, marketing) while leaving the details to the individual coordinators who were running each LC.
>
> We intentionally implemented an organizational structure which created an equal partnership between Student Affairs and Academic Affairs. We did much assessment to demonstrate the success of the program and developed a Request for Proposal process that required each LC to document learning outcomes. Every LC utilizes peer mentors—undergraduate students who support the program in a variety of ways based on their individual outcomes. These paid student staff positions also provide excellent leadership development for the mentors.
>
> Most LCs are discipline-based, focused on first-year students, have an assessment plan, utilize peer mentors, and are organized by highly dedicated faculty and staff. The Registrar's Office does an outstanding job of putting students together in classes. The Department of English is actively involved in numerous linked classes. Some LCs have residence clusters which add a positive living/learning dimension to the programs. We also have an excellent website that provides valuable resources to our staff. It is easy for students to sign up for an LC and there is no additional cost to participate.

A listing of ISU's LC statistics (www.lc.iastate.edu/LC_15yr_success .html) demonstrates impressive positive effects of ISU's LC efforts on student learning outcomes and campuswide perceptions at the university. These data demonstrate that widespread internalization of positive attitudes toward active learning methods and effective SLCs has over time permeated throughout the total university—including administration, support staff, faculty, and students—and resulted in a related and identifiable campus culture supportive of such ideas and approaches to learning.

It should be mentioned that during the mid-nineties, one of the authors of this book was involved in getting SLCs off the ground campuswide at ISU, and another coordinated assessment of LCs at the university for several years until 2010. As a result, they both acknowledge from personal knowledge as well as the aforementioned data that this research university is a legitimate LO as it pertains to the development of SLCs and policies across the institution intended to maximize student learning, success, and retention.

5. **Kingsborough Community College.** Note the following quote from a February 2011 article titled "Changing the Odds for Students: Spotlight on Kingsborough College" found at www.forumfyi.org/files/RB21%20 CB26%20Issue%20Brief%20v3.pdf on the Kingsborough website:

> When Regina Peruggi became President of Kingsborough Community College in 2004, the school's graduation rate hovered at just under 25 percent, mirroring that of similar institutions nationwide. Kingsborough had a dedicated faculty and staff, and a range of supports were available on campus. Many isolated interventions had been tried. But after years of bare-bones budgets and underprepared students, college leaders, in their own words, became lulled into believing they were doing the best they could, given the circumstances. . . . When Peruggi came on board, she and her leadership team engaged faculty, staff and students; questioned long-held assumptions; and made reversing business as usual a top priority. Her leadership fostered the redesign of whole divisions and the creation of new services. Classroom practices shifted. The college revamped admissions and advising, and centralized enrollment services—moves that changed institutional culture and integrated disparate best practices into a more cohesive whole. The entire institution became focused on student success, and no part remained unchanged.

6. **Syracuse University.** A recent book edited by Peckskamp and McLaughlin (2010) discusses a number of innovative and successful SLCs across the campus of Syracuse University and suggests there is an institution-wide culture focusing on maximizing student learning success that is indicative of a true LO. Reinforcing this perception is the following statement highlighted on the university's website at www.syr.edu:

> Scholarship in Action is the bold vision that propels Syracuse University—a vision for education that's not static or for its own sake, but breaks out of the traditional "ivory tower." It drives us to forge innovative and sustained partnerships across our local and global communities. And that

makes SU a place where students become leaders, scholars become collaborators, and the community is continually energized by new ideas.

7. **The Evergreen State College.** From 1972 to 1975, starting one year after it opened, Evergreen was one of seven members of the Consortium on Follow-Up Evaluation at Nontraditional Colleges that was coordinated by the senior author of this book. At that time there was a definite focus throughout the institution on innovation to achieve maximum student learning and success. The college has been intimately involved since the late 1980s in applying what has been learned about positively impacting student learning and success through its acclaimed Washington Center for Improving the Quality of Undergraduate Education, which is still the acknowledged leader of the nationwide LC movement. The institution-wide culture emphasizing such innovation has enabled Evergreen to state on its website at www.evergreen.edu/about/changelives.htm that Loren Pope, the famous writer about education who formerly was education editor at the *New York Times*, included Evergreen in his book titled *Colleges That Change Lives.* Evergreen was the only public institution included in Pope's earlier editions, and one of only two public institutions in his last (2006) edition. Pope (2006) highlights two factors common for all of the 40 colleges and universities selected for inclusion in his book:

> These schools share two essential elements, a familial sense of communal enterprise that gets students heavily involved in cooperative rather than competitive learning, and a faculty of scholars devoted to helping young people develop their powers, mentors who often become their valued friends. (p. 2)

Elsewhere on Evergreen's website, a concrete description of how faculty throughout Evergreen teach collaboratively is provided for prospective students. As described at www.evergreen.edu/about/curriculumoverview.htm, faculty team teach in groups of from two to four and focus on what they call "shared learning."

8. **Villanova University.** Nancy Kelley, director of academic LCs, stated in response to the LO question on our survey: "Our lunch room—we all eat at the same place—is a 'grist mill' for generating ideas, sharing victories and frustrations, brainstorming on how to improve learning, etc." This response fits with the following excerpt from www1.villanova.edu/villanova/media/fastfacts.html:

The strength of the Villanova experience comes in part from the University's welcoming community. All members are bonded together by a shared responsibility to uphold the ideals of St. Augustine and let the principles of truth, unity, and love guide their lives. The Villanova community helps students grow intellectually, professionally, and spiritually, and challenges them to reach their full potential.

Villanova's academic experience . . . forms an environment in which students and professors are partners in learning. Every member of the Villanova community is dedicated to providing a personalized experience that fosters every student's intellectual and spiritual well-being.

These statements suggest that there is an institution-wide culture that encourages faculty and staff at all levels to innovate and contribute as appropriate to students' learning and success and that such attitudes are internalized throughout the institution.

9. **Wagner College.** Dr. Anne Love, referred to previously, stated on our survey:

Yes. Each level of LC has a small group of faculty who coordinate the administrative aspects of the programs, and they engage in ongoing program development. As concerns or new ideas are raised they are explored, and improvements/modifications proposed and adopted. Surveys of students at each level of LC provide much of the information about program improvement.

Although her focus was strictly on LCs, Wagner's LCs are institution-wide, pertain to all four years of college, and serve as the core of the Wagner Plan described at www.wagner.edu/academics/wagnerplan as follows:

Wagner College has developed a curriculum that unites deep learning and practical application. The Wagner Plan incorporates our longstanding commitment to the liberal arts, experiential learning and interdisciplinary education with our geographical location and enduring bond with New York City.

Beginning their very first semester at Wagner, students not only study issues and learn critical-thinking, writing and problem-solving skills, but they also see and practice what they are learning. This "practical" side of liberal education is clearly seen in our Learning Communities and Reflective Tutorials and in the investment faculty make in connecting students with the world outside the classroom.

All of the above suggests an institution-wide culture that involves the *entire* campus community in ongoing efforts to maximize deep learning and success for all students. So does Wagner's leadership of the Atlantic Center for Learning Communities (www.wagner.edu/aclc), a consortium that "supports institutions in the region who are developing LC initiatives."

10. **West Valley College.** Figure 5.8 presents a strategic goal approved by the College Council at West Valley College on March 8, 2007. This goal provides another exemplary example of what a college or university could perhaps become as a bona fide LO. It continued as a strategic goal after Dr. Lori Gaskin became president of the college in 2009. Unfortunately, when contacted about this goal in November 2011, West Valley officials reported that because of severe cutbacks in funding from the state of California, it is no longer in line with what they are striving to achieve.

Suggestions for Building Powerful LOs

LOs have received little attention in postsecondary education. This is true even though such a focus has been prevalent at the elementary/secondary education level over the last decade. For example, Sergiovanni (2000) states the following:

> Community is at the heart of a school's lifeworld. It provides the substance for finding and making meaning and the framework for culture building. Think of community as a powerful antioxidant that can protect the schools lifeworld, ensuring that means will serve ends rather than determine them. . . . Schools can be understood as
>
> - Learning communities where students and other members of the school community are committed to thinking, growing, and inquiring and where learning is an attitude as well as an activity, a way of life as well as a process
> - Collegial communities where members are connected to each other for mutual benefit and to pursue common goals by a sense of felt interdependence and mutual obligation
> - Caring communities where members make a total commitment to each other and where the characteristics that define their relationships are moral in character
> - Inclusive communities where economic, religious, cultural, ethnic, family and other differences are brought together into a mutually respectful whole
> - Inquiring communities where principals and teachers commit themselves to a spirit of collective inquiry as they reflect on their practice and search for solutions to the problems they face.

FIGURE 5.8
Strategic goal of West Valley College, 2007.

1. Learning Community. We will shape a learning community which blends the traditional focus on content with the development of additional skills that learners need to contribute successfully to our contemporary, multi-cultural society by:
- Effectively developing a sense of community
- Encouraging collaboration
- Making all members of the college community active partners with shared responsibility in the learning experience
- Developing appropriate skills to promote lifelong learning
- Supporting collaborative learning and problem solving within the classroom, across the college and throughout the district

We will continue to support student success by:
- Developing, evaluating, and improving our educational programs and services
- Assisting students in setting their educational goals and evaluating progress toward them
- Utilizing continual assessment to improve the student learning experience

We will promote ongoing professional and personal growth by:
- Providing orientation for all full- and part-time employees
- Providing opportunities, resources, and mentoring

2. Diversity & Inclusion. We will foster an increasingly diverse and inclusive learning community by:
- Communicating and building better relationships with the communities we serve
- Decreasing systemic financial, geographic, academic, physical, personal and cultural barriers to make the campus more accessible and inviting
- Attracting, hiring, retaining, and supporting a highly qualified, multi-faceted staff
- Preparing and encouraging students to contribute successfully to our contemporary, multi-cultural society

3. Collaborative Leadership. We will work collaboratively, as active partners in the learning community, on behalf of the common good of the College and District. We will take responsibility, both individually and collectively, to engage in shared decision-making by:
- Improving and sustaining an environment of mutual respect, confidence, support and trust
- Communicating, interacting and building teams within and across constituencies
- Ensuring timely, effective communication
- Making intentional, conscientious, thoughtful, and timely decisions

4. Physical Resources. We will proactively and innovatively support the learning community with physical resources (buildings, grounds, learning stations, instructional space, and equipment) by:
- Making the campus more accessible, inviting, safe, and physically attractive to a diverse population
- Maintaining, reconfiguring, and developing classrooms, laboratories and other facilities to promote collaborative learning
- Sharing our physical resources more effectively

FIGURE 5.8 (Continued)

> • Using technologies that help us transcend the limitations of the physical environment by thinking of the community as the classroom
> • Promoting the College campus as a resource to the community and viewing the community as a resource for the College
>
> **5. Fiscal Innovation.** We will proactively and innovatively fund our learning community by:
> • Engaging in strategic financial planning
> • Securing appropriate alternative sources of funding
> • Allocating resources through fiscal policies, priorities, and processes that support institutional goals

Note. From www.westvalley.edu/mission.html in November 2010.

Three characteristics are important in gauging the extent to which a school forms a community: the extent to which members share common interpersonal bonds, the extent to which members share an identity with a common place (for example, my class, my space, my school), and the extent to which members share a commitment to values, norms and beliefs. (pp. 59–60)

Ideally, for the powerful potential of LCs to be achieved in postsecondary education, the entire institution needs to be involved—including faculty, staff, and students as well as others, such as governing boards, alumni, and friends of the institution. They must be organized—separately and in concert—to think about, plan for, and contribute to implementation of SLCs and optimum student learning.

To be powerful, LOs must be true LCs in and of themselves. They must play a crucial role in planning, implementation, and maintenance of LCs throughout the campus and cyberspace so that they can affect our society in a maximally positive manner. Everyone must become involved in creating a total new culture and vision for the institution in which optimizing student learning is the focus throughout. The total institution must become a true "learning organization," as must subunits within the organization, such as the various academic departments, the admissions department, the financial aid department, the facilities and maintenance department, and student affairs.

The key to development of such an institution-wide culture and practice is charismatic and motivating leadership that inspires institution-wide loyalty and trust, provides needed incentives, and helps everyone throughout the institution feel supported and involved. As stated on infed's website (www.infed.org/thinkers/senge.htm) in October 2011, "Learning organizations require a new view of leadership. . . . In a learning organization, leaders are designers, stewards and teachers." See the website for in-depth discussion of each characteristic.

Furthermore, for this revolution in student learning to occur, each LO must include a variety of powerful PLCs across the institution that are continually considering how SLCs and student learning can be optimized. Across-institution support from other institutions with similar goals may also be helpful. For example, there are consortiums designed for that specific purpose, such as the Consortium for Innovative Environments in Learning (see www.cielearn.org/initiatives.htm).

The Miami University of Ohio FIPSE project provides another example of across-institution support. The project was designed to help six prominent universities adapt Miami's FLC model to transform their campuses into an effective campuswide culture for learning (see www.units.muohio.edu/flc/other_info/fipseinfo.php). Miami paired Senge's five components of an LO that will foster close relationships campuswide (systems thinking, personal mastery, mental models, building a shared vision, and team learning) with corresponding institutional changes that are needed to become an LO (see www.units.muohio.edu/flc/other_info/becoming.php). These changes are presented in Figure 5.9.

J. S. Brown's (1997) five core values for all LOs should also be considered:

> (1) All members of the organization are learners; (2) Learning is natural, healthy, and something that we all seek—making fewer hierarchical distinctions of teachers and learners; (3) Consider the learner as a complex system who is affected by many experiences over a lifetime; (4) Focus on the group of learners, not individual learners, by utilizing approaches to learning that are powerful for all kinds of learners; and (5) Set as the highest priority for institutional strength the designing of structures that require cross-discipline learning. (pp. 8–9)

The Southwest Educational Development Laboratory's emphasis on assessing readiness (see www.sedl.org/pubs/change45/6.html) before proceeding with LC development, referred to in the section "Suggestions for

FIGURE 5.9
Institutional changes needed to become an LO.

Creation and recovery of a common language and processes across departments and divisions; setting and honoring institutional missions, goals, actions, and rewards
Support for faculty to continue as experts in their disciplines, yet broaden their scholarship beyond discovery to include integration, application, and teaching, particularly multidisciplinary perspectives
Change from a culture of autonomy and rewards for individual work to one of community building; rewards for faculty contributions to institutional goals and solutions of problems
Sharing of departmental and disciplinary visions across disciplines; identifying joint approaches to issues such as implementing student learning communities, improving student learning, integration of technology, creation of an intellectual community
Colleges and universities with "learning communities for teaching and research with colleagues and students"

Note. From www.units.muohio.edu/flc/other_info/becoming.php.

Building Powerful PLCs," applies here also. All of the effort will be for naught if the institution is not ready to begin implementing such change.

Although targeted at elementary-secondary educators, perhaps the best vision of what a true LO in higher education can become, if one generalizes, is provided by Spady and Schwahn (2010). Figures 5.10 and 5.11 present the true community that they envision.

They also refer to five essential defining components of an LO and devote chapters to them as follows: (a) its collegial culture of professionalism (chapter 2), (b) its transformational philosophy and rationale (chapter 3), (c) its life-performance learner outcomes (chapter 4), (d) its empowering learning system (chapters 5 and 6), and (e) its aligned support structure (chapter 7).

Spady and Schwahn (2010) state the following about what they have called "empowering LCs":

Perhaps the biggest paradigm stretch for your people will come . . . where we explain the whys, whats, and hows of deriving life performance learner

FIGURE 5.10
Spady and Schwahn's view of transformational change.

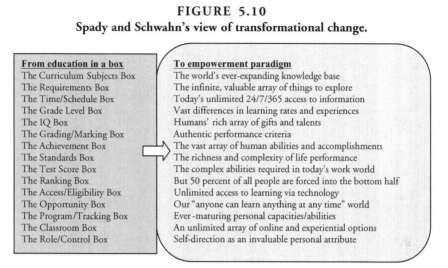

From education in a box	To empowerment paradigm
The Curriculum Subjects Box	The world's ever-expanding knowledge base
The Requirements Box	The infinite, valuable array of things to explore
The Time/Schedule Box	Today's unlimited 24/7/365 access to information
The Grade Level Box	Vast differences in learning rates and experiences
The IQ Box	Humans' rich array of gifts and talents
The Grading/Marking Box	Authentic performance criteria
The Achievement Box	The vast array of human abilities and accomplishments
The Standards Box	The richness and complexity of life performance
The Test Score Box	The complex abilities required in today's work world
The Ranking Box	But 50 percent of all people are forced into the bottom half
The Access/Eligibility Box	Unlimited access to learning via technology
The Opportunity Box	Our "anyone can learn anything at any time" world
The Program/Tracking Box	Ever-maturing personal capacities/abilities
The Classroom Box	An unlimited array of online and experiential options
The Role/Control Box	Self-direction as an invaluable personal attribute

Note. Excerpted from Spady and Schwahn (2010, p. 11).

outcomes. We'll be showing exciting examples from across the world that really symbolize learning transformation and empowerment in future-focused form. And on its heels comes the heavy-lifting parts of your change process: implementing an empowering learning system . . . and building an aligned support structure . . . Expect to see what the terms "systemic" and "restructuring" really mean from a paradigm change perspective, and what the essence of a true "LC" is—in action. (p. 21)

Is it possible for higher education institutions in general to become true LOs in the manner that Spady and Schwahn have envisioned for elementary-secondary education institutions? Only time will tell. In the introduction to a very recent study, Holyoke, Sturko, Wood, and Wu (2012) emphasized that both educational researchers and college/university faculty are skeptical that higher education institutions can become "learning organizations." Those authors' study results do suggest, however, that there is more openness to implementing such a concept at private four-year colleges and universities than at any other types of postsecondary institutions. Furthermore, their data suggest that the best place to begin is to have institutional academic departments work toward becoming such LOs.

FIGURE 5.11
Spady and Schwahn's view of paradigm change.

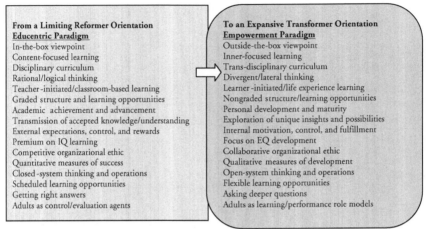

From a Limiting Reformer Orientation	To an Expansive Transformer Orientation
Educentric Paradigm	**Empowerment Paradigm**
In-the-box viewpoint	Outside-the-box viewpoint
Content-focused learning	Inner-focused learning
Disciplinary curriculum	Trans-disciplinary curriculum
Rational/logical thinking	Divergent/lateral thinking
Teacher-initiated/classroom-based learning	Learner-initiated/life experience learning
Graded structure and learning opportunities	Nongraded structure/learning opportunities
Academic achievement and advancement	Personal development and maturity
Transmission of accepted knowledge/understanding	Exploration of unique insights and possibilities
External expectations, control, and rewards	Internal motivation, control, and fulfillment
Premium on IQ learning	Focus on EQ development
Competitive organizational ethic	Collaborative organizational ethic
Quantitative measures of success	Qualitative measures of development
Closed-system thinking and operations	Open-system thinking and operations
Scheduled learning opportunities	Flexible learning opportunities
Getting right answers	Asking deeper questions
Adults as control/evaluation agents	Adults as learning/performance role models

Note. Excerpted from Spady and Schwahn (2010, p. 15).

The Rest of the Story

Look back at the scenario at the beginning of the chapter. Dr. Singh and Dr. Rose developed an exceptionally effective LC that includes students as well as diverse faculty and staff. They expanded participation beyond their two schools and used heterogeneous groups to create deep learning from various perspectives. Dr. Rose and Dr. Singh created "real-life" scenarios that required various perspectives to be considered. Furthermore, the LC discussion really brought out commonalities across the disciplines and the value of a true interdisciplinary approach. As in many lively LCs, the interaction continues outside the formal setting—a pre-med and a pre-law student are both amazed at what the other must accomplish in his or her discipline. To take these LCs one step further, these professors could integrate the symposium as part of linking courses within the pre-med and pre-law programs. This would create a cumulative effect in interdisciplinary LCs.

Conclusion

SLCs are created for a variety of purposes, but the intent is singular: student learning. Although the framework for deep learning and student community building is important, the main purpose of LCs—to promote strategic and reflective learners who are intellectually and socially adept within society—

must never be forgotten. Curricular, classroom, residential, and student-type/concern cohorts help to assist student learning whether focusing on developmental needs or honors' students. The collaboration—between and within disciplines and departments—helps to solidify SLCs on college campuses. Finally, choice in format should be considered. As every learner has his or her learning style, so do institutions of learning.

The intentional combination of each format will help students and faculty support the highest level of learning. Consideration of the SLC's foundation, purpose, and format will provide answers to the following three questions: (a) How well do we promote student success? (b) How many students do our efforts reach in meaningful ways? and (c) What is our evidence?

For SLCs to achieve optimum positive effects, the entire institution and important units therein need to be organized separately and in concert. Each LO must include a variety of PLCs—made up of faculty, staff, or both—that are continually considering how SLCs and student learning can be optimized. All must be involved in creating a total new culture and vision for the institution in which optimizing student learning is the focus throughout so that an institution functions as a true LO.

For Reflection

As you create your own meaning from ideas in this chapter, begin to think about a specific LC at your institution (or at an institution you know about if you are in a governmental or other noninstitutional role) and how it can inform your work or interests. Use that LC to answer the following questions and help you reflect on practical implications of the material in this chapter:

- Which of the discussed SLC formats appealed to you? What was their foundation and purpose?
- How do those formats contribute to deep learning and student community building for the particular group of students served by your LC? What is the learning style of your institution?
- What intentional combination of each format will help students and faculty support the highest level of learning?
- Does this format combination apply equally to other student groups at your institution?
- Does your institution have talented college teachers who have found ingenious solutions to problems in learning but have not reflected on

or shared those solutions with others on a regular and continual basis? How can this situation best be corrected? What specific steps would be required?

- What legitimate PLCs are operating at your institution? How powerful are they? Which of them are FLCs and which have a broader membership? Should any of them become broader in their membership? If so, which ones?

- Based on the examples and guidelines provided in this chapter, what will it take to make each kind of PLC at your institution optimally powerful?

- Which characteristics of your institution would qualify it to be a legitimate LO as described in this chapter? Which characteristics of your institution would prevent it from being classified as a true LO?

- Is your institution a bona fide LO? If so, how can it become a powerful LO? If not, what would need to happen for it to earn that status?

Now that you have read and reflected on this chapter, you should be able to complete the following items on the Powerful LC Planning Form in Appendix C:

- Section I: #2. "Why are you doing this?"
- Section I: #3. "What are your overarching goals?"
- Section I: #4. "Purpose Statement."
- Section I: #5. "Who are the stakeholders?"
- Section I: #6. "What resources (or sources of resources) are available to support the LC?"
- Section II: #1. "What will the LC look like?"
- Section II: #2. "How will you select members for your LC?"
- Section II: #3. "What are the overarching goals of the LC?"
- Section III: #1. "How will you build community?"
- Section III: #2. "How will you develop a culture for learning?"
- Section III: #3. "What norms do you want members to follow and how will you ensure accountability?"
- Section III: #4. "What resources are needed for your LC to be successful?"

Notes

1. For example, at SUNY Potsdam, SLC faculty meet weekly to integrate their SLC courses; at a number of other institutions, faculty team teach (one survey respondent stated an opinion that the use of team teaching is critical if you want to have a powerful LC).

2. For example, Catholic University of America; Charleston College, which has only full-time faculty involved (like at University of Alabama–Birmingham and University of Oregon, as well as others) and three days of special faculty training each May; Eastern New Mexico University; Harper College, which requires SLC participation for graduation; Kennesaw State University, which requires all entering students with less than 15 credit hours to participate; Medaille College, which emphasizes collaborative SLC projects out in metropolitan Buffalo, New York; Portland State University, which requires all entering students except honors students to participate; Skagit Community College, which requires every student to take at least one coordinated studies course in order to graduate.

3. They can also be different in terms of such matters as whether there is an extra cost for participation in an LLC. For example, students at the University of Illinois pay an extra fee over and above the regular residence hall cost to participate in an LLC.

4. Stonehill College designed all its SLCs for second-year students, none for first-year students. The University of Iowa has a variety of specially designed/distinctive LLCs for transfer students and separately for returning students, in addition to an array of LLCs for first-year students.

5. Each of these principles is supported by best-practice research.

6. Information about the projects is available at http://carnegiefoundation.org/scholarship-teaching-learning.

7. Note that the concept of FLCs used at Miami University of Ohio limits faculty participants to transdisciplinary faculty but broadens participation to include professional staff and nonteaching graduate students as well.

6

CREATING LEGAL AND
ETHICAL LCs

Without commonly shared and widely entrenched moral values and obligations, neither the law, nor democratic government, or even the market economy will function properly.

—Havel (2000, p. 401)

In the authors' experience,[1] learning communities (LCs) must establish commonly shared values (ethics) and mutual obligations (rule of law) to function effectively. Given that LCs arise in a variety of contexts and involve a multitude of stakeholders, a number of legal and ethical issues naturally occur. For example, as members of an LC engage in closely held discussions, concerns about privacy, academic freedom, constitutional freedom of speech, defamation, and outright discrimination may all arise. Therefore, sponsoring organizations must plan for potential legal and ethical issues as they develop, redesign, and implement LCs.

The LC literature is largely silent about legal and ethical considerations facing LCs. Likewise, when respondents to the 100-Institution Survey were asked about the top legal or ethical issues encountered by LCs, most had not thought about it and could not readily identify any. Several commented that this was an important consideration and eventually came up with issues to share, including allegations of discrimination against people who wish to participate in an LC, physical and financial barriers to access, ethical challenges in social media, copyright and ownership of intellectual property, the importance and drawbacks of member privacy, selection of appropriate LC content (does not involve overly sensitive topics or marginalize specific populations), and liability concerns associated with service-learning.

Other respondents, including one who was an attorney, suggested that most legal and ethical issues experienced by LCs are not separate and distinct from those encountered in general higher education. While we do not dispute that these issues are similar to those present in other educational settings, we assert that there are different points of emphasis when legal and ethical issues arise in the LC context. If ignored, these issues can expose LC members, coordinators, and sponsoring institutions to significant legal liability. On that basis, we take the position that LCs must be prepared to specifically address legal and ethical issues that could arise in the LC environment.

This chapter discusses key legal and ethical issues pertaining to LCs in higher education.[2] However, the information presented here may well prove useful to stakeholders in all areas of education, regardless of whether the community is face-to-face, virtual, or hybrid. This chapter is not meant to provide an exhaustive exploration of legal and ethical issues in education, but rather to highlight and focus on particular issues that may affect LCs more predominantly and uniquely. For example, while cheating, plagiarism, and copyright violations are significant areas of concern in education that could affect LCs, most institutions already have policies in place that can adequately be applied to meet the needs of the LC. Similarly, most institutions require contracts to be drafted and/or approved by legal counsel for the institution, so only peripheral LC contract issues are addressed herein.

Although there is overlap, such LC issues fit into three general categories: (a) membership and access; (b) relationships; and (c) integrity, privacy, and liability. A practice-based scenario is provided for each category. Appendix F provides corresponding charts that list major laws and a summary of LC recommendations for the primary legal and ethical issues in each category.

Membership and Access

What's the Story?

Don is a 45-year-old junior transfer student from Area Community College (ACC) and is a Hmong refugee. He wishes to join three of the LCs at Public University (PU) to get to know other students and ensure his academic success in this larger university learning environment.

- LC-1 is a residential living-learning community where all freshmen and most transfer students live together to acclimate to the campus. Don wishes to join so that he too can get to know other students and acclimate to the campus. He is notified that he is ineligible because a college policy restricts living in the dorm to students who are under 26 years of age.

- LC-2 is a targeted LC designed to provide academic support (free tutors, interpreters, and mentors) to "disadvantaged" students. The membership criteria include academic status (<2.5 GPA), financial need (under 200% of poverty on the Federal Student Financial Aid form), limited English proficiency (low TOEFL test score and/or English as a second language), and disability status (documented in accordance with the Americans with Disabilities Act). Don wishes to participate because he has a hearing impairment, he is not yet confident about his ability to understand English, and he basically does not have any income or assets except for financial aid. He had previously qualified for similar LCs at ACC that enabled him to attain a 3.0 GPA. Don is turned down because his GPA is above the 2.5 maximum specified.
- LC-3 is an honors engineering LC. Don is excited because he was a successful civil engineer in his native country. There are no set selection criteria for this LC. Instead, current members consider each applicant's academic performance and engineering experience on a case-by-case basis. Don gets a letter telling him that he should reapply in the future after he has a PU academic record and has demonstrated "local" engineering experience. Don knows that Mark, a 20-year-old ACC transfer student with a similar GPA, was accepted even though his only practical engineering experience was shadowing a prominent local engineer for a month. Mark tells Don in confidence that LC members did not think he would "fit in well with the group" and that "third world engineering is inferior."

LC Membership Issues

Generally, anytime there is membership in a group, allegations of illegal discrimination or unethical barriers to access may eventually arise. LCs are no exception. In fact, they may be under heightened scrutiny given that these communities are organized, officially sanctioned or affiliated with the sponsoring academic organization, and generally utilize institutional resources. This is particularly true for public institutions, which are primarily financed using taxpayer dollars, and institutions that receive federal financial assistance such as financial aid.

Therefore, powerful LCs should specifically address the membership selection process, potential discrimination, and barriers to access in their risk management process. Best practice suggests involving university legal counsel throughout the LC development process to ensure that the LC's designated purpose, membership criteria, and selection process do not illegally discriminate. Such practice also provides meaningful access in compliance with all legal and ethical mandates. Advisors can make linkages with relevant institutional policies to ensure that LC processes coordinate effectively with any institutional requirements.

The importance of having a carefully crafted and transparent purpose statement, membership criteria, and selection process for ensuring that an LC is operating in a fair, ethical, and legal manner must be stressed. How membership criteria and processes are defined and utilized by an LC is often the linchpin of legal discrimination and access claims. The following subsections highlight the most common areas of discrimination in academia, illustrate how these discrimination concerns may arise in the LC context, and discuss recommended risk management strategies that can improve the outcome when there are claims of discrimination against an LC.

Common Areas of Discrimination

Many academic and professional codes of ethics conclude that discrimination is not ethical, and these ethical standards are upheld by the law. The Higher Education Opportunity Act of 2008 stresses that *all* students be "treated equally and fairly." The Civil Rights Act of 1964, the Age Discrimination in Employment Act of 1967, the Americans with Disabilities Act of 1990 (ADA), and other laws ban discrimination against "protected classes" of individuals covered by these laws and provide for extensive civil penalties. Under these laws, institutions are prohibited from using federal funds, directly or indirectly, to discriminate on the basis of race, religion, color, national origin, gender, age, genetic information, veteran/military status, disability, or other areas covered by law.[3] Several state and local jurisdictions have constitutional provisions, human rights laws, executive orders, and judicial case law that also explicitly prohibit discrimination based on sexual orientation, sexual identity (e.g., transgender), and other classifications.

From a legal perspective, discrimination is a primary area of concern anytime membership is involved. Therefore, LC membership criteria and selection processes that exclude (or are restricted to) members from some legally protected classes (race, skin color, religion, national origin) without a compelling reason will be treated with strict scrutiny, which leaves organizations vulnerable to claims of illegal discrimination. For example, if LC membership is restricted to a single race—even if it is for a legitimate nondiscriminatory purpose—a person from the excluded race could allege discrimination.

Some other protected classes are also illegal to discriminate against but are considered under different levels of judicial scrutiny. Decisions based on gender and marital status are under intermediate scrutiny and must involve an important nondiscriminatory purpose to be legal. Finally, while it is illegal to discriminate based on age, disability, wealth, political preference, political affiliation, or status as an ex-felon, the organization must demonstrate only a legitimate reasonable nondiscriminatory purpose to have the action upheld. For example, an LC cannot require physical or mental history forms to screen out people with physical or mental disabilities. However, an LC can have eligibility requirements based on essential functions or safety risks if those requirements relate directly to the purpose of the LC and are applied to all members.

Allegations of discrimination can expose the institution, LC coordinator/instructor, and LC members to having civil rights complaints or lawsuits filed against them. Administrative and case law shows how agencies and courts will scrutinize the designated purpose for the community, the membership criteria outlined, and the selection process used to ensure that membership actions were narrowly tailored[4] to achieve the stated important objective, particularly if the academic institution involved is publicly funded.

If the LC selection process is clear and was set up with an eye toward potential allegations of discrimination, it is more likely to be upheld by the courts. Thus, having a clear purpose, criteria, and transparent selection process is the best way to withstand attack by individuals who were denied membership. One 100-Institution Survey respondent noted, "Our General Counsel emphasized the importance of being transparent with parents and students about all the LC selection criteria and the selection process." During the development process, it is crucial that criteria selected are a valid measure of traits needed to achieve the designated purpose.

Affirmative Action and Targeted LCs

Some laws not only prohibit discrimination but require affirmative steps to support access to institutional programs and services for individuals from a protected class. (These requirements are addressed further in the section "LC Access Issues.") Affirmative action provisions in the Equal Employment Opportunity Act of 1972 require institutions of higher learning to make good-faith efforts to ensure equal opportunity and to eliminate barriers to equal treatment for employees and job applicants who are from a group of people historically affected by discrimination. Given that many affirmative action requirements relate to employment and professional LCs (PLCs) generally include employed faculty and staff, affirmative action objectives should be part of the PLC development process. This obligation may extend to graduate fellowships and teaching assistantships and likely LC peer coordinators in student LCs (SLCs) if these individuals are considered employees.

Lenning and Ebbers (1999) expanded the general typography of LC categories to include "student-type learning communities" designed to meet the needs of specific populations of students rather than to meet general education or interdisciplinary goals. Accordingly, these targeted "student-type" LCs can be an effective and efficient means for organizations to provide support to members from classes of people historically affected by discrimination. For example, organizations can design SLCs or PLCs to promote recruitment and retention of minority students, faculty, and staff.

Another example is targeting faculty or students with disabilities or limited English proficiency (LEP), or students from a minority background who have specific cultural or developmental needs. Sometimes individuals who are not from a protected class, such as transfer students or students from low-income families, also benefit from a targeted approach. For more information on the rationale and background for these types of focused LCs, see Tinto (1998).

Although the targeted approach is a powerful use of the LC model, the distinctions can give rise to claims of unfair selection and discrimination by nonmembers who would like to participate but are not from the targeted class. For example, if an SLC is designated for minority students needing special academic assistance, and there is a nonminority student who feels that he or she needs similar academic assistance (or that selected students have an unfair academic advantage), that student may claim to be discriminated against and denied equal access to university resources solely on the basis of race or national origin.

One respondent in the 100-Institution Survey who clearly thought through such issues was Tae Nosaka, university LCs coordinator at Colorado State University and assistant director of the university's "Key Communities." The Key Communities—which focus on low-income students and students from particular cultural backgrounds and have a strict requirement that members meet during the first two years of college—have been found to definitely instill academic success in members. However, Nosaka questions whether it is ethical or legal to put a predominance of low-income students and students from particular cultural backgrounds in the same group. The LC developers consulted an attorney in setting up their selection process and likely it is sound from a legal perspective, but this is an open question that sponsoring organizations should consider.

There are state laws, such as California's Proposition 209, that ban the preferential use of race in college and university admissions decisions. Courts have taken a similar position, invalidating preferential use of protected classifications in admissions and financial aid decisions because they were discrimination in violation of Title VI of the Civil Rights Act of 1964.[5] In the *Gratz v. Bollinger* case, the US Supreme Court clarified that the strictest level of judicial scrutiny (narrowly applied to support a compelling governmental interest) should be used to analyze the use of protected classifications (539 U.S. 326, 27 [2003]). This is a difficult legal burden to meet.

Does this mean that targeted LCs are not permissible? Not necessarily. The admissions policy in the *Gratz* case did not pass constitutional strict scrutiny because the formula used made race a *decisive factor* that favored otherwise less qualified applicants. However, the court suggested that the formula could have been upheld as a means of promoting diversity if the formula used race as a tiebreaker among equally qualified applicants.

In *Grutter v. Bollinger*, 539 U.S. 306 (2003), the US Supreme Court upheld a carefully crafted admissions selection policy because it was sufficiently flexible and modestly considered race as part of the broader institutional goal of a diverse student body.[6] The court reasoned that "attaining a diverse student body is at the heart of [a university's] proper institutional mission" in determining that pursuit of a diverse student body was sufficiently compelling to overcome strict constitutional scrutiny because of the unique educational obligation to expose students "to widely diverse people, cultures, ideas, and viewpoints" and to "all segments of American society, including people of all races and ethnicities" (*Id.* at 329–332).

A court would likely extend similar reasoning to the LC setting because diversity is crucial to the group's success. If LC membership is too homogeneous and/or there is not equitable minority representation or perspectives, the group will likely have a limited impact on learning. Further, the goals and activities of such an LC may unintentionally overlook the views or impact of decisions on minority students. This would support use of interest surveys or other assessment tools that consider race, gender, ethnicity, age, or other factors when assigning members to specific LCs to promote optimum group diversity.

Much like the processes upheld in the *Grutter* and *Gratz* cases, a flexible and carefully crafted selection process designed to promote a powerful LC's compelling interest in a diverse learning environment could justify consideration of race or other protected classifications as one of several factors used in assigning equally qualified individuals to the LC. However, consideration of race or other similar factors should not be used in a preferential or decisive manner. Furthermore, the assignment process will be best received if an LC uses a holistic approach instead of equating diversity with membership in legally protected classes. Each person should be evaluated on an individual basis considering a wide variety of relevant factors such as personal and professional experiences, special abilities, or geography—instead of exclusively focusing on race or other protected classifications.[7]

Evenhanded Application of Standards

Occasionally the issue will not be that the membership selection criteria are inherently discriminatory, but that the criteria were not applied evenhandedly among potential members—that similarly situated individuals were treated differently without sufficient justification. An example would be an SLC for international students that accepts only members who come from third world countries.

In the PLC context, consider an LC sponsored by the provost to address the impact of workload on integrative teaching. One criterion is a letter of support from the dean. On its face this would appear to be a reasonable and neutral requirement. However, what if the dean routinely writes letters of support for any interested faculty members but tells one faculty member that he will not write a letter because she is too vocal about workload concerns during college faculty meetings? This differential treatment likely violates equal protection rights under the Fifth Amendment of the US Constitution because the decision appears to be impermissibly based on the person's expression of free speech protected under the First Amendment.

One respondent to the 100-Institution Survey discussed how failure to enforce SLC criteria fairly can undermine the purpose of the LC. This person gave the example of arbitrarily allowing upper-class students in LCs that are supposed to be limited to first-year students. The presence of upper-classmen will likely be a disruption to the SLC.

Disparate Impact

Complaints about discrimination do not always focus on the selection process; rather, they may center on how the resulting membership produced unfair or uneven representation of the protected group of individuals. For example, if there is a prestigious PLC that does not include any interested minority faculty or staff, there could be an allegation of disparate impact. Minority faculty members who were denied participation could claim that this limited their rank, promotion, and tenure opportunities or equal employment opportunities.

Although there is a legal basis for disparate impact discrimination claims, these cases are challenging to prove. There are also ethical considerations related to diversity and access. Thus, sponsoring institutions should be mindful of the potential for disparate impact in the design of LCs so as to meet their legal and ethical obligations.

Concerns About Unethical Selection

Some selection processes do not involve legally prohibited discrimination but are instead *perceived* to be unethical. In the learning organization (LO) or PLC context, claims of an unethical disparate impact might arise if faculty from one college or department in a university is underrepresented in comparison with other colleges or departments. This sometimes occurs when there is overrepresentation of faculty from an area of the institution that is perceived to be prominent. Although this would not be illegal, it may decrease the level of trust among members. Further, members who represent underserved areas of the organization may be resistant to fully engaging in the LC process. It also may call into question the LC's credibility if it is dismissed as being biased toward the overrepresented area.

By contrast, the 100-Institution Survey response from Colorado State University discusses how "the selection process can be tricky if all students are required to participate; it is important to give students options." Respondents from Hobart and William Smith Colleges echo a similar theme, emphasizing the value of "flexibility, autonomy and not limiting freedom." Further, if particular students do not wish to participate, could they negatively impact or even sabotage the LC? LCs should consider whether mandating participation is appropriate and provide an opportunity to opt out, even if this option is not one that is "advertised." Allowing students the autonomy to choose may be less of an option in cases in which the LC is an essential part of a class or is required for cohorts such as freshman LCs.

Transparent and Evidence-Based Selection

Ultimately, accommodation may not be possible for everyone who wishes to be involved in an LC. Limited resources or other logistics may require size or other restrictions that impact membership access. This could easily occur in the context of prestigious "honors" LCs designed for academically talented students, such as the highly regarded College Park Scholars program (and Honors College) at the University of Maryland.

To illustrate, students (or their parents) who are not selected for these types of prestigious "honors" LCs could claim that they should be included because they are "gifted" and "academically talented." The possibility of such a claim makes clear the importance of having carefully crafted written selection criteria. For example, terms such as *honors, gifted, advanced placement*, or *academically talented* should be clearly defined and include measurable standards such as GPA, registration in set courses, and/or other relevant descriptions. Selection rubrics can assist with measures that are important but more subjective, such as "work" or "leadership" experience.

Furthermore, explaining to students and parents about genuine capacity issues, the selection process followed, and feedback about why the student was not selected may fend off complaints. In some cases, students may be able to use provided feedback to order their affairs and improve their chances of being selected for the LC in the future. This sentiment is echoed by the following comment by a survey respondent from Saint Louis University: "Our general counsel emphasized the importance of being transparent with parents and students about all the LC selection criteria and the selection process. It is important students, and parents of students who are dependents, be informed about the LC student capacity and why they did not get selected."

Involving the institutional legal counsel and/or an attorney experienced in dealing with discrimination laws (particularly one who actively counsels academic clients) throughout the LC development process is well worth the cost. This risk management practice was stressed by several respondents of the 100-Institution Survey who reported the crucial role that legal counsel played in LC selection criteria and procedures.

LC Access Issues

LCs can present a variety of legal and ethical access concerns. In any LCs, "access" pertains to more than just membership or availability. It includes questions about the availability of those LCs, their tools, the potential benefits, and how widely and effectively publicized the selection process is. Differences in technology and other restrictions should be considered in planning for these communications. Remember, if the message does not reach targeted individuals or is not conveyed in a clear manner, in essence their access has been adversely affected.

Disability-Based Discrimination and Accommodation

In some cases, the individual needs of an LC member (or other stakeholder) may require taking steps to ensure that there is meaningful access to the community and its activities. Section 504 of the ADA requires reasonable accommodations to ensure that people with disabilities have meaningful access to facilities, programs, telecommunications, and other service areas. The ADA, the Rehabilitation Act of 1973, and pertinent state disability laws cover educational institutions both as employers and in their relationship with students and the public. Therefore, this protection extends to members of SLCs and PLCs, their spouses, and other family members.

The ADA does not provide a list of covered impairments but broadly defines *disability* as "a physical or mental impairment that substantially limits one or more major life activities."[8] In the Americans with Disabilities Act Amendments Act of 2010 (ADAAA) Congress clarified its original intention that this definition of *disability* is to be broadly construed under the ADA. Among the major life activities listed in the ADAAA that were historically not considered life activities are sleeping; reproducing; eating; normal cell growth; and digestive, bowel, and bladder functioning. ADAAA regulations provide examples of covered disabilities including diabetes, epilepsy, serious depression, bipolar disorder, multiple sclerosis, and other impairments unduly excluded by the ADA in the past. Therefore, the ADAAA requires LCs to prepare for larger numbers of accommodation requests, many of which relate to increasingly complex impairments and accommodations.

Recognizing and Responding to Requests for Accommodation

LC coordinators are often the primary contact for members (or applicants) with covered disabilities, so they need to have a general understanding of the ADA and how these issues should be addressed by the LC. Coordinators should be trained to recognize when there is a disability that may require accommodation, how to follow relevant institutional policies and procedures, and whom to work with (human resources, disability services, and/or legal counsel) to determine when and how the ADA applies.

Assuming that there is a documented disability in need of accommodation, those parties often work with the affected individual to develop a plan of reasonable accommodation designed to address the student's needs while protecting that person's confidentiality. Even if the ADA does not apply when an accommodation is requested, ethics dictates wherever practicable that the coordinator still work with the member to address concerns and explore potential solutions confidentially and in a timely manner. This responsiveness will promote continued access and success for the LC.

Table 6.1 outlines key questions and considerations that an LC coordinator should address with the institution when an accommodation is

TABLE 6.1
Key questions and considerations on accommodation.

ADA Factors	Key Questions to Ask	Considerations and Actions
Notice triggers duties	1. Was there a formal request to the LC? 2. Was there an informal talk with the LC coordinator regarding the disability? 3. Was a disability observed?	**YES to ANY:** The LC has received notice of potential disability and should be prepared to offer accommodations.
The ADA covers "disabilities"	1. Does the LC member have a physical and/or mental impairment? 2. Does that impairment substantially limit one or more major life activities? 3. Is there medical documentation verifying the disability or is the person regarded as having it?	**YES to ALL:** It is likely that the member has an ADA-covered disability. The LC should be prepared to offer accommodations. *(Regardless whether ADA-covered, be responsive to request and try to address need if possible)*
Requested accommodations necessary for access	1. Does the disability restrict access to important LC services and activities? 2. Does the requested accommodation address the underlying disability access concern?	**YES to ALL:** The request is necessary and should be accommodated.
Accommodation reasonable	1. Does the accommodation pose a direct threat to the health and safety of others? 2. Does the accommodation require substantial change to essential elements of the LC curriculum/ manner of providing services? 3. Does the accommodation pose undue financial or administrative burden?	**NO to ALL:** The request is reasonable and should be accommodated. **YES to ANY:** The request may not be reasonable. Further analysis is necessary. If not reasonable, alternative accommodations should be found.

requested. They apply to both SLCs and PLCs, but the emphasis is on SLCs given that PLCs are generally addressed in relevant institutional employment policies.

Targeted LCs can be a cost-effective and meaningful way to accommodate the needs of interested students. As an illustration, students who have Asperger's syndrome are increasingly requesting that universities furnish personal coaches to help them interpret and follow syllabi requirements and communicate with professors (Morrison, Sansosti, & Hadley, 2009). For many institutions this request may pose an undue financial burden and may not be a reasonable accommodation, but an LC model could effectively serve the same purpose at a lower cost while providing the added benefit of peer interaction.

Universal Design Requirements

Section 508 of the Rehabilitation Act[9] requires that courses provide access to all electronic instructional materials. Further, the latest iteration of the Higher Education Opportunity Act requires postsecondary institutions to apply "universal design principles" in designing their curricula. These requirements apply whether or not there are students with disabilities in the class (SLC) because organizations must now be proactive in their efforts to eliminate barriers and ensure broad usability for students and instructors with disabilities.

Under universal design, the goal for all levels of the educational system (including face-to-face and online delivery formats) is to move from one that responds to individual requests for accommodation to one that is intentionally designed to ensure ready access in advance of individual need. This is similar to the way public accommodation provisions in the ADA have transformed the built environment into one that is automatically expected to provide broad public access (i.e., designated handicapped parking spots, ramps, elevators, or electronic doors). The Center for Universal Design in Education at the University of Washington provides resources to help educators apply universal design to all aspects of the postsecondary setting.[10]

Consider, for example, an out-of-state online SLC member who is legally blind. He has asked to have course materials (the text, instructor PowerPoint lectures, and LC discussion boards) provided in a format that meets National Instructional Materials Accessibility Standards (NIMAS) so that assistive technology can be used to easily transfer materials into specialized formats such as Braille, audio, large print, and electronic text. Under the traditional approach to accommodation, assistance to the student would begin once he notified the coordinator or made an official accommodation request.

Given that the coordinator might not have experience dealing with ADA accommodation requests, she might scramble to figure out whom to contact and what to do. She would then have to try to retrofit course materials after the fact. Allowing the student to use a different book is not realistic given that all LC materials and the discussion board follow it. Perhaps the institution would offer to hire a person to read LC materials; however, in a virtual LC it might take additional time to locate an individual available to take on that role. Because PowerPoint slides are presently not compatible with most assistive technology, the instructor and/or coordinator must reformat them into compatible digital text formatting as well as possibly record the lectures.

Most challenging would be trying to help the student actively participate on the LC discussion board. Typically, LC members use their own formatting approach to posting on the board. Further, it is an asynchronous and ongoing board, so a reader would not be a good fit. All of these steps would take considerable time, during which the member would have severely limited access to the LC. This would undoubtedly leave the student several weeks behind the rest of the members, putting him at a significant academic and social disadvantage—denying him meaningful access to the activities of the LC, in violation of the ADA.

Under a universal design approach, NIMAS compatibility would have been a consideration during the text selection process for the LC. Therefore, when the LC started, the student already would have been able to use assistive technology to transfer the book into the desired formats. The instructor would have drafted the lecture PowerPoint slides using semantic markup–capable digital text formatting and have logistics in place to easily transfer the lecture from PowerPoint to NIMAS-compatible software.

Finally, the coordinator would have oriented all members about their shared responsibility to ensure LC accessibility and how to draft written communications in an NIMAS-compatible format. Members may have received a universal design style sheet for use throughout the LC. This expectation would have been incorporated into the syllabus and initial ground rules—focusing on general system accessibility rather than on the needs of a particular student. Assuming that the instructor and team members use the proper formatting, the student should be able to utilize assistive technology to read the lectures and posts and to participate actively in the discussion board along with other LC members.

Access for People With LEP

LEP—limited ability to speak or understand English—is another area where LC members may experience barriers to meaningful access and/or discrimination. Failure to accommodate a person who has LEP is a form of national origin discrimination under the Civil Rights Act of 1964.[11] Accordingly, the Departmental Directive Administrative Communications System emphasizes the agency's commitment to

> making its services and programs available to LEP persons as part of its mission "to promote student achievement and preparation for global competitiveness by fostering educational excellence and ensuring equal access." . . . Based on this commitment, the Education Department makes designated publications available in languages other than English and provides interpretation services to persons who are not proficient in English.

This requirement extends to "federally conducted programs and activities," including recipients of federal student aid. Although some states have laws and constitutional provisions establishing English as the official language of their state, these provisions do not eliminate the Executive Order 13166 obligation for recipients of federal funds to accommodate to individuals with LEP.

The January 12, 2004, "Guidance to Federal Financial Assistance Recipients Regarding Title VI, Prohibition Against National Origin Discrimination Affecting Limited English Proficient Persons" was designed to assist organizations in meeting this requirement. It outlines four factors to weigh in determining whether or not an institution is obligated to arrange and pay for an interpreter or translation for individuals with LEP.[12] Each sponsoring institution should balance the factors and have their own LEP compliance plan. However, in almost all cases these accommodations will be required for colleges and universities receiving federal student aid.

Therefore, LCs must be prepared to accommodate and incur the costs of providing required communication assistance to members or other stakeholders with LEP. Interpretation and/or translation of LC group discussions—particularly asynchronous virtual discussion boards—may be particularly challenging for coordinators to accommodate because they are generally ongoing throughout the term. Accordingly, LCs should become familiar with LEP technical assistance resources designed to help organizations meet their legal and ethical obligations to accommodate individuals with LEP. One helpful resource for LCs is the language access assessment and planning tool at www.lep.gov/resources/2011_Language_Access_Asses sment_and_Planning_Tool.pdf.

Financial Barriers to LC Access

Several respondents to the 100-Institution Survey expressed concerns about the ethical impact that finances could have on LC access. The respondent from Western Washington State University, Dr. Carmen Werder, stated: "I think there's an ethical, and perhaps even legal, issue when only some students are offered the opportunity to participate in LCs or can afford to pay the extra fees required to participate. This means not all students have full access."

In itself, socioeconomic status is not a legally protected classification and access is not guaranteed. For example, the ADA specifically notes that environmental, cultural, and economic disadvantages are not covered disabilities. Therefore, LC participation fees and other LC expenses are legally permissible. From an ethical perspective, LCs need to weigh the impact that finances have on members and stakeholders when decisions have financial implications against the need or benefit that will be realized for the LC if included.

Another respondent asked, "If you use technology in teaching, how can you, as a faculty member, guarantee that students from lower socioeconomic status have access to the required equipment and/or software? If these students do not have access, does this not create an equity issue?" SLCs can establish minimum technology requirements for members, just as students are required to purchase specific books and minimum technology access for a class. In some cases, financial aid or institutional grants may be available to assist students with access. In other situations, the LC could work with the institution to seek funding to assist students with financial constraints to access the necessary technology.

Answers to the broader ethical issue of how financial constraints impact access to LC activities and services are less clear. When making decisions in these types of situations, the LC coordinator needs to judiciously weigh the purpose and membership makeup of the LC against the purpose, benefit, and cost of the proposed technology. The coordinator needs to communicate with the group and/or individual members to gauge their responsiveness to the proposed activities and related expenses. This can help the coordinator assess the overall group buy-in and prevent members from prematurely quitting or mentally disengaging from the LC out of embarrassment, frustration, or because they just cannot afford the mandatory fees.

The coordinator also needs to explore available resources and creative solutions. For example, could these costs be anticipated sufficiently in advance to be included in any LC budget proposals? Would a fund-raiser be appropriate? If the technology is needed for a limited purpose, could institutional technology or the library purchase it and then lend it to the affected members? Or could members work as partners and share the equipment?

There would be similar concerns about the fee-based LC activities such as service activities or trips. In those cases, would it be reasonable to pursue LC experiences if not all members could afford to take part? Alternatively, would it be ethical to prevent other LC members from participating in those learning experiences because some members would not have the financial means to participate? LC coordinators need to strategize how they will address these resource-based ethical decisions.

The Rest of the Story

LC-1: While unfortunate for Don, the decision is legally and ethically defensible. Age discrimination is illegal; however, it is legal for organizations to use age as a criterion if there is a reasonable basis for making age a distinction. Age restrictions for residing in campus dorms are reasonable for the interest and protection of all students. PU is not singling out Don; no students over 26 can live in the dorm and he is 45. It would also seem to be an ethical decision. Although LC-1 could accept members who do not live in the dorm, that decision might undermine the purpose of setting it up as a living-learning community. Furthermore, if all of the other members live together but Don lives elsewhere, he could feel isolated, which could overcome the beneficence of participating in the group. Freshmen and other transfer students could use Don's situation as an example to support their contention that they should not have to live in the LC-1 dorm. Another ethical response might be to develop a separate nonresidential LC targeted at transfer or adult learners for students such as Don.

LC-2: In this case the LC coordinator used GPA as the basis for denial. This is an objective measure and Don did not qualify under that standard. Assuming this was applied evenly to all applicants and there is a reason for not letting in students with a GPA equal to or greater than 2.5, this would likely be considered legal. We do not have enough information regarding how the criteria (GPA < 2.5, financial need, LEP, disability status) were defined and whether there was a reason to prioritize GPA. However, sometimes it is necessary to limit membership because of limited resources. The LC should make sure that the purpose, criteria, and rationale for the criteria are clearly described and provide that information to Don and others who are not accepted. The university is legally obligated to accommodate Don's LEP and hearing impairment if it is aware of it, and the discussion with the LC coordinator could be considered notice to PU. However, the law does not dictate how an institution will meet that requirement. Accordingly, the university does not have to allow students who do not meet reasonable established criteria to join an LC unless that LC is the designated way that the institution provides accommodations to similarly situated students.

Using a single factor to determine eligibility without balancing the other compelling criteria (all of which applied to Don) would appear counter to the purpose of the LC—supporting underserved students. From an ethical perspective, this approach is denying access to students who could benefit most from such resources while including many students with a GPA below 2.5 who clearly are not underserved. If there are no resource restrictions, perhaps students meeting any of the four criteria or a certain number of criteria should be eligible instead.

LC-3: This selection process was unethical, poorly designed, and lacked transparency. Current LC members inconsistently applied ill-defined and discriminatory criteria to select new members. Don was denied membership and Mark was accepted. Don and Mark had similar grades from the same community college, but Don had substantial experience as a working engineer and did not get admitted, whereas Mark had no real engineering experience and was admitted. This, coupled with the alleged comments about not fitting in and third world engineering being inferior, suggests that there was a discriminatory motive in violation of federal discrimination laws and the equal protection clause of the Constitution. Given that the LC coordinator is an agent of PU and that there was not proper institutional oversight, Don would be well positioned to bring a lawsuit against PU and LC members for violating his rights.

Relationships

What's the Story

Cam is the student peer coordinator for an LC at Area Community College (ACC). Most of the group members bonded quickly; in fact, Cam worries that they are so in sync that they are not exploring options, thinking critically, or interacting with the larger campus. The exception is Leslie, a member who is a few years older and a little quirky. Last month members of the LC told Cam that Leslie refused to contribute to their assigned team project and will not respond to calls or e-mails. Cam tells them to proceed on the project without her. Days before the due date, Leslie e-mails the group to find out what they need from her. They tell her the project is done, and she becomes upset.

Cam agrees to meet Leslie for coffee off campus to discuss the situation. She tells Cam that there was a death in her family and that she feels members are acting childishly by not letting her contribute to the project now. Leslie resents being forced to participate in a "cliquish" team that does not like her or want to hear her ideas. She tearfully explains that she was neglected as a child and that she feels the same alienation when LC members shun her. When Leslie confesses that she has been thinking about hurting herself, Cam tries to reassure her and gives her a hug. He tells her she can call anytime and gives her his cell number. Leslie starts calling several times a day and often stops by his room uninvited. Cam starts screening his calls and avoiding the dorm so he will not have to deal with her—she always seems to be there whenever he has to be there. Other LC members are frustrated that Cam let Leslie off the hook on the project. They note that he never seems to be around, and when he is, she always seems to be present. They feel he favors Leslie, and one person speculates that perhaps they are "involved." The LC members decide as a group that they need not put as much effort into the LC assignments because Cam does not seem to care anyway.

One day when Leslie follows him to the library after class, Cam feels like she is stalking him. He tells her abruptly that he cannot help her anymore and she should get professional help. Leslie screams, "You and that evil group will be sorry for hurting me!" Cam is freaked out and goes to the LC faculty advisor. She tells him that Leslie's file contains numerous mental health records and that in the faculty lounge they call her "Loco Leslie." "Don't worry," she says with a laugh. "Leslie is harmless to a big guy like you. If you want an academic career you'll need a thicker skin." Cam can no longer handle the situation and quits his LC peer coordinator job.

Promoting Positive, Healthy Relationships Within the Community

LCs are founded on mutual trust and respect among members. Powerful LCs recognize the impact that power dynamics and other relational issues can have on group cohesion and learning in both virtual and face-to-face SLCs. B. Anderson and Simpson (2007) note:

> Online teaching environments amplify the ethical issues faced by instructors and students. . . . The existence of power relations between instructors and student and between students themselves in face-to-face educational contexts is widely acknowledged. Such relations distort educational opportunities for students, ensuring differential outcomes that reinforce social hierarchies. . . . Power relations such as those formed in face-to-face classes are also enacted as part of the online environment. . . . [Thus] the moral issues teachers face as they work with their [online] students are the same as those met in the face-to-face classroom. (pp. 132–133)

Although these issues are more apparent in the SLC context, social hierarchies and power dynamics also exist among faculty members and can be a similar distraction for a PLC. To counteract these concerns and maximize learning across LC settings, all participants in the learning process should be expected to model professional and ethical behavior in their interactions with others. Hanson (1995) states:

> Everyday classroom life is saturated with moral meaning. . . . Even the most routine aspects of teaching convey moral messages to students . . . that may have as important an impact on them as the formal curriculum itself. . . . It is crucial to heed from a moral point of view what takes place in the routine affairs of the school and classroom. Those affairs can strongly influence students' character and personal disposition. . . . Teachers, through their everyday conduct and practice, can create environments in which students can "catch" positive ways of regarding and treating other people and their efforts. (p. 59)

In that regard, ensuring that relationships and interactions meet specific moral and ethical standards is particularly important for LCs. Ideally, the LC itself is designed to foster trust and promote effective group interactions to promote designated learning objectives. However, this effort and the resulting relationships give rise to several specific legal and ethical issues. Just as the LC coordinator takes the lead in bringing about "social presence" and bonding among group members, the coordinator is also the person responsible for leading the group in determining and setting ethical and legal boundaries for group interactions. On its website, The Association of Independent Liberal Arts Colleges for Teacher Education (n.d.) summarizes ethical standards for LCs as follows:

> An exceptional . . . institution views teaching as a moral activity . . . rooted in moral and ethical positions that are influenced by multiple views. The institution is one that creates an intellectually safe environment that promotes dignity and respect for all people within the academic community. The institutional ethos is communicated through its people, policies, and programs.

Thus, the coordinator should ensure that all participant rights, responsibilities, and consequences be made absolutely clear. Each LC needs clear written expectations regarding boundaries, interactions, and legal ethical standards. These written expectations can be in the form of ground rules or statements in syllabi, or on learning management systems. They should cross-reference relevant university policies and include a process and chain of command for reporting concerns.

The coordinator can start this important dialogue by providing members with an initial list of expectations and then engage members in their development and/or approval. Rules should place an emphasis on common interpersonal ethical values about how to treat others (e.g., respecting and appreciating others and what they have to contribute). Throughout the LC encounter, coordinators must use a host of tools to promote group cohesiveness; acceptance; and, ultimately, compliance with these expectations.

Once finalized, written expectations must be actively communicated to all members, whether in person or through virtual means. (Examples of common issues and appropriate responses could be provided through presentation, role plays, videos, or other illustrative content.) Members should have an opportunity to ask clarifying questions; add additional rules; and, where possible, mutually agree to them. This interactive dialogue provides notice to all participants about their rights and responsibilities and is an opportunity to generate member buy-in. Some communities may choose to document this assent by having members sign a written acknowledgment, take a quiz, or sign a contract. Expectations should routinely be reevaluated with a process for amending, adding, or removing rules. When changes are made, members must be notified in an effective and timely manner—usually in writing, to document notice.

Even after members come to agreement on mutual expectations, community relationships may still break down if they are not encouraged, facilitated, and supported on an ongoing basis. The LC coordinator is responsible for monitoring and enforcing these expectations, because failure to do so can impact participant buy-in and relationships. Furthermore, in some situations, failure to report or seek appropriate assistance from the institution can lead to accreditation concerns and/or criminal and civil liability. Coordinators must be vigilant about situations that dictate reporting and institutional involvement. From a legal standpoint, having these written expectations and policies in place can be a strong defense if an action is brought against the coordinator, the institution, or other members as long as they are communicated, enforced, and applied fairly. Thus, it is crucial to train coordinators to monitor and fairly enforce rules and policies, to recognize issues, and to know how to involve the institution. Although establishing agreed-upon norms and standards is important for maintaining the integrity and effectiveness of the overall LC, the coordinator must prepare to deal with breakdowns in relationships between LC members, between LC members and individuals outside of the LC, and between the member(s) and the coordinator.

Relationships Between the LC Coordinator and Members

Maintaining SLC Instructor Presence

While SLC teams are a great way to reduce a course instructor's workload and enhance learning in face-to-face and virtual courses, instructors must not place too much reliance on LC group interaction or student coordinators to drive the learning process because it will reduce instructor presence. The postsecondary education literature is clear that regardless of the learning environment (face-to-face, online, or hybrid), instructor presence is vital to learning. As noted by Mandernach, Gonzales, and Garrett (2005), "Learning communities include all participants, student and instructor; the instructor however, sets the climate and ensures that 'a community of learning is people-centered, and through dialog, discussion, and sharing, learners have the opportunity to connect with others.'"

Active instructor participation is particularly important in asynchronous virtual SLCs in which ongoing feedback and interaction can compensate for the lack of real-time contact with the instructor that is generally experienced in the face-to-face setting. The authors have all personally observed the impact that instructor presence (or lack thereof) has on student accountability, and on identification of students who are struggling with content or technology and/or who have stopped actively participating in SLCs. Given that presence is essential to fostering student growth and establishing a positive online learning climate, ethical LC instructors must ensure that they maintain regular substantive contact with members and do not delegate too much.

There is not a federal legal standard regarding the level of instructor presence required for virtual SLCs. However, it is relevant for compliance with the Department of Education's October 31, 2011, Final Program Integrity Rules,[13] which obligate postsecondary institutions to confirm that the federal government is not paying federal student aid tuition for students who are not attending classes. Under these regulations, schools must determine each student's "last date of attendance" when deciding whether students should be considered to have withdrawn and must return federal student aid awards. Determining the "last date of attendance" is particularly challenging for online courses, as nicely summarized in a December 5, 2011, *Virtual School Meanderings* blog post by Michael Barbour:

> The last date of attendance was calculated instead by the last time a student participated in an online discussion or made contact with a faculty

member. . . . Simply clicking in was not enough, the department argued in responses to comments in the final rule, because students could leave their computers after logging into class, or someone else could log in for them. Both would make distance education fraud more likely. Institutions of higher education are responsible to publish, monitor and enforce these requirements and most rely on instructors to carry out these obligations.

Accordingly, the LC instructor and/or coordinator for SLCs in an academic course must have a meaningful way to ensure that student members who received student federal aid actively participate in the LC or report them to the institution for follow-up as a potential withdrawal from the SLC.

Virtual SLCs should also be aware of state laws regarding online education that may define and/or affirmatively require a more specific level of instructor contact in virtual settings. For example, Title V, section 55204 of the California Code requires instructors in distance learning courses to have "regular effective contact" and "regular substantive contact" with students. Accrediting bodies may also look at these issues. For example, one rationale given for the Higher Learning Commission's recent focus on allocation of credits is to ensure institutions "with courses in alternative formats have and follow policies consistent with commonly accepted practice in higher education."[14]

Setting Professional Boundaries

When interacting with students, the LC coordinator can go too far in trying to instill social presence. In some cases, this can be seen as unethical or may even be illegal. One illustration relates to surveillance of student discussion boards in virtual SLCs. Students generally expect (and often welcome) instructors to monitor their interactions with other members. However, Parry (2009) reports a practice "by some professors in online courses of taking part in student e-mail discussions through use of a fake persona. Responses by students and professors when finding out about the practice range from shock and feelings of violation to indifference" (p. A10).

One might justify this approach because the intended purpose is to enhance LC member engagement. Such a utilitarian response could be viewed along the lines of "the ends justify the means." However, enhanced LC discussions would not absolve the coordinator of participating in an activity that many colleagues and students consider patently deceptive. Such participation demonstrates a lack of veracity on the part of the leader who is charged with modeling integrity for the LC. If students learn about this falsehood after the fact, they may feel that the coordinator breached fiduciary duty to the group. This will jeopardize learning because LC members will no longer trust the instructor or may suspect that other LC members are also fictional.

The authors have personally observed more ethical ways to effectively promote active discussion and critical thinking. The most obvious is for the instructor to provide regular probative feedback and use Socratic questioning during the course of the discussion. Another is to assign students to specific roles designed to promote active, thoughtful discussion. This approach is particularly effective when roles are well defined and rotated among LC members. Students have an enhanced sense of responsibility toward the group when they know they themselves will take on that role during the term. Akin and Neal (2007) discussed this strategy:

> Assigning student roles in the discussion is helpful to extending participation length. Students can serve as moderator to their group, . . . serve as partial question designer, . . . play an assigned part in a case study discussion or a role playing exercise, or they can actually assign the parts and act as stage manager for their group. Often some students step up and act as gate keepers, watching the discussion, making sure all aspects have been covered and often producing outline sheets of what has been covered.

Another example of overreaching by SLC coordinators is found in the social networking context. Young (2008) reported:

> A growing number of professors are experimenting with Facebook, Twitter, and other social-networking tools for their courses, but some students greet an invitation to join professors' personal networks with horror, seeing faculty members as intruders in their private online spaces. Recognizing that, some professors have coined the term "creepy tree house" to describe technological innovations by faculty members that make students' skin crawl. . . . There are productive—and non-creepy—ways for professors to use social-networking technologies, but . . . the best approach is to create online forums that students want to join, rather than forcing participation.

For a definition and in-depth discussion of the "creepy tree house," see Jared Stein's (2008) blog post at http://jaredstein.org. LinkedIn and other professional-based social media sites may be a better approach than Facebook and similar social networking sites for LCs because they are less personal in nature and are therefore seen as less intrusive to students. Some professors have promoted LC coordinator blogs as a desirable alternative to using social media such as Facebook and Twitter. One example of an LC effectively using LinkedIn is the TreeHouse Learning Community available at www.linkedin .com/company/treehouse-learning-community.

Although some defend these types of social interaction, we find them ethically problematic within the LC context because of the heightened importance of trust and how these practices may intrude on a student's sense of personal privacy. Similarly, when LC coordinators become too close with the members in an SLC, it can impact their professional relationship with the group. In some cases, it may give members a false sense of security that students will not be held to academic standards, which is counter to the purpose of LCs—learning. Members may also feel so casual and relaxed that they will make inappropriate statements, believing the coordinator will not enforce ground rules, uphold the honor code, or make them face conse- quences for their actions. This perception is more likely to prevail in SLCs in which the coordinator is also a student or is about the same age as the student members. Regardless, the coordinator must be conscientious about professional boundaries and cautious about perceptions when interacting with SLC members.

Sometimes the close relationship is with an individual member. Often these situations start out as mentoring relationships or casual friendships with a member with whom the coordinator has a lot in common. Or they may arise when the coordinator is listening sympathetically to a member who wishes to share his or her concerns about other members, vent frustra- tions about the LC, or discuss personal problems. Such close relationships are bound to negatively affect LC group dynamics because other members might feel that particular members are not being held to the same standards or are favored (real or perceived) by the LC coordinator. This can be particu- larly challenging in situations in which the LC's extra efforts are actually part of an affirmative obligation to accommodate a member with a disability or other need that may not be readily apparent to other members. This is a dilemma because the coordinator cannot explain the circumstances to other members, given legal and ethical privacy restrictions under the ADA, the Family Educational Rights and Privacy Act (FERPA), and/or the Health Insurance Portability and Accountability Act of 1996 (HIPAA).

Consider an SLC member who documents that she has Asperger's syn- drome—an autism spectrum disorder characterized by difficulties in social interaction, repetitive patterns of behavior/interests, and executive function- ing difficulties. This disability makes it difficult for her to function effectively within the LC. She follows the institutional process to request that the LC coordinator assist her in interacting effectively with her fellow community members. However, she is explicit that she does not want other LC members to know about her disability.

This poses a challenging situation for the LC coordinator, who cannot engage the other members in cooperating but does not want the team to think this student is being singled out or given favorable treatment. Thus, in developing a plan of accommodation the coordinator should decide in advance what specific steps or interventions will be utilized and work with the student to determine how that will be played out with the larger team. Perhaps certain assistance could be provided privately to the student, or the coordinator could make general comments to the larger team designed to subtly elicit follow-up from the student.

Because faculty working with SLCs frequently serve as advisors to individual student members, ethics pertaining to faculty advising is also a relevant concern. Helpful guidelines on ethics related to advising are provided at www.nacada.ksu.edu/Clearinghouse/Advisingissues/Advising-Ethics.htm.

Avoiding Intimate Relationships Between LC Coordinators and Student Members

If the close relationship between an LC coordinator and student member becomes (or is perceived to be) intimate, it will harm all LC stakeholders. The American Association of University Professors' (AAUP) policy "Consensual Relations Between Faculty and Students" is relevant to sexual relationships between SLC coordinators and student members. It states:

> Sexual relationships in which one member of the . . . community has supervisory or other evaluative responsibility for the other create the appearance of favoritism, the potential for actual favoritism and the potential for sexual harassment. This is also true of faculty conduct that may reasonably be perceived as inviting or encouraging a sexual relationship. Such relationships can raise serious concerns about the validity of consent, conflict of interest and unfair treatment of others. They may undermine the real or perceived integrity of the evaluation and supervision provided and the trust inherent in such relationships. (2006, p. 247)

Mutual trust and respect between the LC coordinator and members is paramount because the coordinator has a fiduciary duty to each member.

This fiduciary relationship is irrevocably altered if the coordinator becomes intimate with a student member. The resulting harm to a student's reputation as well as his or her emotional, educational, developmental, and physical well-being has been well documented in the literature and mainstream media. Accordingly, it is particularly inappropriate and unethical for an SLC coordinator to have a romantic and/or sexual encounter with a student.

From a legal perspective, there currently is not an overarching law in higher education that outright prohibits sexual relationships between instructors (academic advisors or evaluators) and students unless the student is a minor, a dependent adult, or other special circumstances apply. However, there are other potential legal consequences that will impact the coordinator if such a relationship is pursued. He or she may face substantial disciplinary actions including termination of contract and/or employment. These situations can also impute significant civil (and even criminal) liability to the LC coordinator, LC, and sponsoring organization if the student alleges that there was sexual assault, sexual harassment, emotional distress, exploitation, breach of contract, defamation, or other legal claims—a common occurrence at the conclusion of an intimate relationship in which there is an imbalance of power between the individuals involved.

These relationships are malfeasant for the LC as a whole. The authors have observed that even in situations in which members of a group liked and otherwise respected a faculty leader and/or student, once there was active speculation about the existence of such an intimate relationship, the entire group became engulfed in an emotional atmosphere of suspicion, anger, and mistrust. Whether occurring in an SLC or a PLC, intimate relationships involving members inevitably distract from the focus on learning and impact member productivity and engagement.

In some cases a member might misperceive that his or her relationship with a coordinator is intimate or romantic. Seemingly simple things such as exchanging private phone numbers, inviting individual students off campus or to a dorm room, and spending an inordinate amount of time together can give the impression that there is a deeper personal connection. In some cases it may actually read as a deeply emotional and/or sexual relationship that can negatively impact those in the relationship and/or other members of the LC, regardless of who initiates such a relationship or how it came about. The pressures of the university setting can also contribute to stalking behaviors by students who are having a difficult time adjusting to their academic and/or social settings.

Such situations demonstrate the importance of establishing boundaries between LC coordinators and students. They can be prevented by referring members to counseling or other support services. Coordinators need to know tips for prevention, how to establish boundaries, and how to seek assistance in these types of situations. Osterholm, Horn, and Kritsonis (2007) provide a comprehensive review on how to avoid misunderstandings, preventative measures, and how to draft institutional policies regarding intimate relationships.[15] Coordinators should also be given a list of campus resources to assist in referring student members to support services.

Member-to-Member Relationships

Cultural Awareness

A powerful and ethical LC/LO views diversity from a broad perspective. Leaders establish an inclusive environment that celebrates the unique individual contributions that *all* members can make. In addition, extra steps should be taken to ensure that individuals from different, less mainstream cultural backgrounds feel included in the LC and do not become alienated. To establish an LC environment that values diversity and welcomes individuals from diverse backgrounds, all members must be culturally competent, sensitive, and responsive.

Effective facilitation by the LC coordinator will be important in establishing an environment of mutual respect that accepts, recognizes, and values the individual diversity and contributions of all members. Conversely, poor facilitation can contribute to an environment of distrust, frustration, division, and conflict among members. Members must also be educated so that they know how to be sensitive and respond to cultural differences and understand the impact that culture has on the LC and larger society. Cultural issues could be addressed with members during the orientation process and/ or reflected in ground rules and other key LCs/LOs.[16]

Hyper-Bonding and Groupthink

Member bonding and acceptance are important foundations for a powerful LC. However, these bonds can become unethical and undermine the learning focus of the LC if that connection becomes too intense. In those situations, LC relationships can result in behavior conformity in which the group accepts and reinforces members' negative conduct (Jaffee, Carle, Phillips, & Paltoo, 2008). Hyper-bonding and groupthink are two such group phenomena. Although it is the prevailing term used in practice, there is no common definition of *hyper-bonding* accepted in the literature. For our purposes, hyper-bonding is when there is such a cohesive bond between (some or all) LC members that they feel empowered around their own norms of behavior and that behavior is reinforced within the group (Jaffee, 2004; B. L. Smith, MacGregor, Matthews, & Gabelnick, 2004, p. 102). Domizi (2008) discusses some of the problems that can arise from hyper-bonding:

> The negative phenomenon of "hyper-bonding" among students is receiving increasing attention on learning community electronic listservs (Dixon, 2004). Hyper-bonding can manifest itself in several ways, from one group of students building relationships that exclude other learning community members to an entire learning community isolating itself from other students in the same residence hall or "ganging up" on a professor to protest class structure, assignments, or grading. Findings of this study suggest that the phenomenon of hyper-bonding among learning community students does exist and deserves further exploration. (p. 108)

Janis (1972) first defined *groupthink* as "a mode of thinking that people engage in when they are deeply involved in a cohesive in-group, when the members' strivings for unanimity override their motivation to realistically appraise alternative courses of action" (p. 9). More recently, Dattner (2011) described groupthink in a *Psychology Today* blog post as "a dynamic wherein members of a team see the world through a biased, narrow lens, reach premature conclusions, and make bad decisions."

Groupthink and hyper-bonding can contribute to the following negative outcomes in an LC: group-prompted separation from others, isolation by individuals who may feel left out or judged by the LC, disruptive behavior, less productive and innovative work, antagonism directed toward LC leaders, domination of the group by powerful and/or intimidating LC members, intolerance for diversity, and unduly restrictive group consideration of ideas or people (Hubbell & Hubbell, 2010; Jaffee, 2007; Janis, 1982; Lichtenstein, 2005). Simply forming an LC does not presume that there will be sufficient member bonding to create a powerful LC. Likewise, developing an LC will not necessarily generate hyper-bonding and groupthink—the conditions and climate set in an individual LC (Jaffee, 2007). In his 2011 blog post, Dattner also provided the following strategy that a coordinator could use to prevent groupthink: "take a step back from his or her team, and allow the group to reach its own independent consensus before making a final decision . . . encouraging the members of the group to speak their minds openly so that different perspectives are discussed and debated." Accordingly, the coordinator can consciously work to establish an LC environment that promotes an appropriate balance of member cohesiveness but is designed to counteract negative hyper-bonding and groupthink.[17]

Disruptive, Harassing, or Violent Behavior

As in other learning environments, LCs may encounter behavior that disrupts or undermines learning. LC members have the right to expect that their peers will behave in a civil manner. Thus, coordinators have a corresponding ethical obligation to maintain a productive learning environment free of interference. Feldmann (2001) discusses these issues in terms of "incivility," which is "any action that interferes with a harmonious and cooperative learning atmosphere" (p. 137). Although opinions regarding disruptive behaviors or lack of civility vary widely, most of these behaviors can be categorized as forms of aggressive, defiant, disruptive, or emotional disturbances. Harrell and Hollins (2009) put it well:

> This behavior includes less severe actions such as sleeping in class, tardiness, and talking among peers to more severe actions such as cheating, fighting, verbal or physical abuse, or suicidal threats. Some of the less severe behaviors are tolerated by some faculty members, but not by others. As each [LC coordinator] . . . designs his/her learning environment, attention has to be given to what student behaviors will and will not be considered disruptive. (p. 69)

In a virtual LC, additional complexities and potential problems are introduced. For example, B. Anderson and Simpson (2007) discuss the role of anonymous posting, noting that "posting anonymously can have value. However, allowing anonymous posts also affords the possibility of direct and potentially unidentifiable attacks on other students—rare in our experience but something we have witnessed" (p. 132). Identifying and communicating clear standards of behavior and consequences can be a powerful deterrent to inappropriate and disruptive behavior in an LC. Special notice about those parameters should be included in ground rules, statements in syllabi, or other documents. Some LCs develop contracts of acceptable behavior, which may help prevent disruptive behaviors. Having an established conflict resolution process is also a deterrent to disruptive and inappropriate behavior.

Once agreed-upon standards are established, coordinators must monitor adherence and encourage members to hold each other accountable. As Feldmann (2001) notes:

Faculty erroneously tend to overlook some of the low-level acts of class-room incivility in the hope they will go away. However, failure to address these actions appears to condone them, sending a message that these behaviors, this incivility, can be repeated. . . . [Coordinators should ensure that] behavioral parameters are established, modeled, and maintained.

The instructor and/or coordinators should respectfully confront members who are behaving inappropriately and follow due process if action is needed. Providing documentation, following institutional policies/procedures, and consulting with institutional officials will be crucial anytime a pattern of disruptive behavior is observed. Although most disruptive behavior will not rise to the level of harassment, threat, or violence, it is sometimes a precursor to such behavior. Therefore, documentation of inappropriate and/or disruptive behavior and corrective actions taken will be important if further action is needed later. That documentation may be kept separately and not incorporated into the student's official student file so as to be protected from disclosure.[18]

Sexual harassment is another area of behavior that is inappropriate and harmful to the LC. It is a form of sex discrimination under Title VII of the Civil Rights Act of 1964, which was extended to sexual harassment of students under Title IX of the Educational Amendments of 1972. It includes any physically or verbally offensive action involving sexuality. Members who bring legal actions alleging a hostile work environment or sexual harassment are best positioned if they act in a timely manner and follow the institutional and legal processes. Once the coordinator becomes aware of the potential for sexual harassment, he or she must not delay in responding to or ignore the complaint but instead follow the institution's sexual harassment policies and procedures. Every report of sexual harassment must be promptly investigated and any inappropriate behavior swiftly addressed to mitigate liability.

LCs and sponsoring organizations also have an affirmative legal obligation to safeguard individuals (including the person engaging in the behavior) and property. The General Duty clause of the federal Occupational Safety and Health Act of 1970 (OSHA) has been interpreted to require employers to prevent and abate the recognized threat of violence in the workplace. See OSHA's Workplace Violence Fact Sheet (2002), available at www.osha.gov/OshDoc/data_General_Facts/factsheet-workplace-violence.pdf. Several states have laws and policies regarding maintenance of a violence-free work-place—which in most cases would extend to public colleges and universities. Courts have held colleges and universities responsible for failing to respond to complaints or have sufficient security measures in place to protect students, employees, and invited members of the public from violence. Sokolow, Lewis, Keller, and Daly (2008) provide an excellent legal analysis of liability and offer suggestions for prevention and behavioral interventions that can be applied to the LC setting. At the very least, the LC coordinator should receive threat assessment training to recognize potentially threatening situations as well as become knowledgeable about the institution's policies and procedures for notifying and working with designated threat assessment personnel.

In recent years it has become clear that harassment and threatening behavior do not always occur in a face-to-face physical setting. The tragic suicides of young students Tyler Clementi, Megan Meiers, and Phoebe Prince have been tied to online cyberbullying. According to Belsey (2011), "Cyberbullying involves the use of information and communication technologies to support deliberate, repeated, and hostile behaviour by an individual or group, that is intended to harm others." Several states have passed legislation addressing cyberbullying.

There have also been numerous court cases holding individuals responsible for this type of behavior. For example, the court in *Wisniewski v. Board of Education Weedsport Central School District* (2008) specifically noted, "The fact that Aaron's creation and transmission of the IM icon occurred away from school property does not necessarily insulate him from school discipline. We have recognized that off-campus conduct can create a foreseeable risk of substantial disruption within a school" (at p. 39).

Clearly this type of impermissible activity could occur in the LC context. Accordingly, LC coordinators in all delivery formats should be aware of the potential for cyberbullying and/or defamation by members and be prepared to intervene appropriately.

The Rest of the Story

The story of Cam, the student peer coordinator, started off this section. It is apparent that members are not recognizing or respecting boundaries in the LC setting. The majority of the group members appear to have hyper-bonded, resulting in groupthink. In response, Leslie is not contributing to the assignments and is further alienating herself. Cam does not take steps to counteract member hyper-bonding or to address the conflict between Leslie and the group. By not enforcing group rules and not holding Leslie accountable for the project, he loses credibility and instructor presence with the group.

When Cam does try to step in and right the situation, he makes several mistakes. His attempts to be helpful and caring to Leslie (meeting her for coffee off campus, reassuring and hugging her after she tells him about her childhood and her thoughts of suicide, and giving her his cell number) send her mixed messages about boundaries. Then when Leslie misinterprets his intentions and crosses personal boundaries, he tries to avoid her instead of getting help or dealing with the issue. Cam's failure to establish boundaries and avoidance strategy have sent mixed messages to Leslie and the other members. The frequent visits initiated by Leslie have led to speculation that he is personally involved with her. Cam also appears to be unaware that his failure to hold members accountable and lack of presence in the residence hall has led other LC members to disengage and he fails to take affirmative steps to correct the situation.

Finally, it is clear that the LC faculty instructor failed to meet her legal/ethical responsibilities by (a) delegating too much responsibility to Cam as the SLC peer coordinator; (b) not training Cam how to clarify expectations, establish boundaries, and deal with troubled or disruptive students; (c) not encouraging him to contact her for assistance whenever concerns or questions arose; (d) failing to establish and maintain instructor presence with the SLC; (e) downplaying the issues when Cam finally did seek her help; and (f) disclosing a student's mental health status—which sets her up for defamation and breach of privacy claims.

Integrity, Privacy, and Liability

What's the Story?

Mary is SLC coordinator at Private Nursing College (PNC). She plans an optional service-learning project at Friends Residential Care Facility (FRCF) over spring break. The SLC information sheet states, "I guarantee you will have a safe, fun, and rewarding experience if you participate in the service-learning project." On the trip the following situations occur:

- A frail resident breaks her pelvis after slipping on a wet floor mopped by SLC member Matt Jones. Matt explains that the director of maintenance told him to clean up a mess from a sick resident. Staff could not find the "Caution: Wet Floor" sign but told him to go ahead with the cleanup. FRCF's administrator, Angela, is upset when Matt's name comes up on the state's dependent adult abuse registry during a postaccident background check. Angela tells Mary that she expected PNC to do a background check and never would have let the students come if she had known they were not screened. Matt has no idea why he would be listed on the abuse registry and is concerned it will derail his nursing career.
- Avery is an LC member assigned to shadow an FRCF nurse during medication rounds. The nurse forgets a sharps container and leaves the used syringes on the cart, which violates federal blood-borne pathogen and other safety regulations. Because of the nurse's carelessness, Avery gets

stuck by a used needle while she is pushing the cart to the next room. Later, Avery is upset when she learns that she may have been exposed to HIV, hepatitis, or other infectious diseases and now has to go through extensive testing and treatment that is lengthy, painful, and expensive.

- That evening the administrator comes across public postings from SLC members on an online discussion forum about working conditions for nurses. In the postings they identify themselves as PNC students completing a service-learning project at FRCF. One student, Susan, writes about the rewards of working with residents and posts a picture of herself with a smiling FRCF resident. Another student complains about the "dirty parts" of nursing, confessing that she almost threw up the first time she emptied a bedpan. A third student responds, "At least you don't have to glove up so you don't catch crabs and scabies from the horny old dog at the end of the hall!"

- On the drive back to campus, the bus driver swerves unexpectedly and crashes into a side rail. A police officer tells the students that the driver has a .12 blood alcohol content. He notes that the driver never should have been driving because he had already been charged with operating while intoxicated this year, and his commercial driver's license is suspended. Susan received a bloody gash on her forehead during the crash and Mary goes with her to the hospital. Mary calls to tell LC members that Susan is staying in the hospital overnight for observation. She reads the medical record to the LC members, explaining that Susan has a severe cut and concussion so she will be undergoing tests to see if she has any lasting head trauma or brain damage. Mary promises to keep them up to date.

LC Content and Communications

Overpromising or Guaranteeing of Outcomes

In LC communications, the coordinator should be careful not to guarantee or overpromise results to LC stakeholders because this can damage the credibility of both the LC and the coordinator. In such situations, members may lose trust and/or disengage from the LC because they feel misled if promised outcomes are not achieved.

From a legal standpoint, courts are more likely to hold organizations and individuals to a higher standard of performance if a party gave an express guarantee or promise that the other party relied on in deciding whether or not to participate. In legal terms this is called detrimental reliance or promissory estoppel, which means that a court may treat the situation as if there were a contract between the parties even if there was not one. Thus, LC members may allege that the LC made a promise regarding the LC outcomes; that it was foreseeable that individuals would be induced to participate in the LC or optional LC activity based on the coordinator's assurances;

that a member(s) reasonably and detrimentally relied on these promises when selecting participation in the LC over other opportunities; and (d) that injustice can be prevented if the promise is enforced and/or the member(s) reimbursed for damages incurred as a result of failure to meet the promised LC outcome. As a respondent from Florida Atlantic University noted in the 100-Institution Survey, descriptions of LCs in the college catalogue could be legally enforceable. Therefore, caution should be used when statements are made regarding SLCs in catalogs or other public venues.

Exaggerating expected LC outcomes or overpromising outcomes in communications with institutional administration or external grant funders is similarly problematic. Given the role that outcome-based decision making now plays in higher education, failure to meet the stated outcomes could result in permanent loss of administrative support or grant funding. Therefore, coordinators must ensure that all objectives and expectations communicated with stakeholders be realistic, be measurable, and do not give the impression that they are enforceable promises or guarantees.

Promotion of Quality Content

Content and discussions generated during LC interactions are a vital component of LCs. They also give rise to several legal and ethical issues. Such issues were identified by 100-Institution Survey respondents, including the following: certain LC themes or topics could lead to marginalization of some of the student population, it must not be overlooked that one needs permission to publish student work, care must be taken not to include oversensitive topics, and there is the question of who really owns the online course and what ownership means for faculty.

Regardless of the delivery format or setting, all LC content should be designed to support the intended purpose(s) of the LC. As LC instructors and/or coordinators develop materials, activities, and discussion questions, they should deliberately think about how each will contribute to (or detract from) quality, effective communication and learning in support of the LC's stated purpose. Selection of topics is an important consideration.

AAUP's widely accepted "1940 Statement of Principles on Academic Freedom and Tenure" (AAUP 2006) cautions faculty to avoid controversial matters unrelated to the subject being discussed. The focus should be on thought-provoking issues that are designed to promote critical thinking and stimulate active, respectful conversation. Be aware that issues that are inappropriate or offensive in one LC context may be appropriate in another if they support the learning that is the focus of the LC. For example, a course on human sexuality might appropriately include sexual content that would be inappropriate in a geology course.

While controversial or divisive topics may be appropriate, they should be posited in a way that focuses members on mutual understanding and problem solving rather than partisan debate. Consider how the question, "Is abortion murder?" would likely incite contentious debate without contributing to learning, whereas the question, "What are the major arguments given in support of and opposition to laws banning partial birth abortion?" is a probative query that could lead to dialogue that actually contributes to member learning.

In addition to selecting LC discussion topics and activities, the coordinator plays a vital role in quality assurance. Effective review and feedback mechanisms should be in place to hold members accountable for the quality of their content. If a response is superficial, members should be given feedback regarding how they are not meeting standards addressed in the syllabus, LC ground rules, or other LC policies they received in advance. The coordinator may be concerned that this will upset members and cause them to disengage from the LC, but the opposite is generally true. However, if members are permitted to get by with poor-quality responses, it will serve as a disincentive for the rest of the group to put forth the extra effort required for quality work.

Leaders are also expected to demonstrate veracity to promote member growth. As noted by Perlmutter (2011), "I learned then that useful mentors are not relentless cheerleaders but rather truth-tellers—even when their candor hurts." For example, discussion board content should contribute to learning and meet the requirements established to support the LC. An SLC coordinator should not permit members to get by with thoughtless or superfluous discussion board posts or responses. If a member(s) fails to remediate content, the consequence should be a loss of points, removal from the LC, or other accountability steps consistent with LC ground rules and/or policies. In many powerful LCs, accountability is also a shared responsibility with members. This can be a matter of informally holding one another accountable or formal alternation of leadership roles such as weekly peer facilitators.

Just as in other areas of academia, there is constant tension between content that is constitutionally protected by the First Amendment or considered academic freedom under institutional policies and procedures and content that is considered disruptive, obscene, or even threatening that needs to be affirmatively addressed by the LC. Distinguishing between the two is a challenge that LC coordinators will inevitably face. Is there a duty to remove content that a member feels is offensive or would doing so be impermissible censorship and suppression of free speech? Generally, educational institutions can curtail student speech if it falls in areas that are not protected such as threatening or disruptive behavior. In *Wisniewski v. Board of Education Weedsport Central School District* (2008), the court explained:

> Even if Aaron's transmission of an icon depicting and calling for the killing of his teacher could be viewed as an expression of opinion within the meaning of *Tinker*, we conclude that it crosses the boundary of protected speech and constitutes student conduct that poses a reasonably foreseeable risk that the icon would come to the attention of school authorities and that it would materially and substantially disrupt the work and discipline of the school. (p. 39)

Can the institution be held legally responsible for inappropriate posts of LC members? The Communication Decency Act of 1996 section 230[19] protects organizations from liability for third-party defamatory statements (e.g., RSS feeds, blogs, comments left by others). It states, "No provider or user of an interactive computer service shall be treated as the publisher or speaker of any information provided by another information content provider." This act could provide limited protection for LC stakeholders if a member posts defamatory comments on an LC post as long as the post is not specifically selected and republished by the LC. However, the safer approach would be to have member comments and dialogue within the learning management system instead of public forums. This would also help to protect members from cyber attacks and other threats in open-source media.

Free speech and academic freedom involve an extensive body of law that is beyond the scope of this text. However, Table 6.2 outlines significant considerations in this area as they relate to LCs.

If the LC leader is a college faculty member, academic freedom based on the 1940 ACE-AAUP Statement on Academic Freedom and Tenure (2006) applies. The first paragraph of the AAUP's Statement on Ethics articulates professors' responsibility "to seek and state the truth as they see it" (2006, p. 133). The ACE-AAUP Statement on Academic Freedom is designed to protect freedom of inquiry in academic settings. It is not set by law but rather generally accepted in academia and outlined in institutional policies and procedures. Accordingly, lawsuits are sometimes filed against college professors for controversial comments they made or subject matter they introduced within a learning setting.

TABLE 6.2
Considerations for LC content.

Key Factors	Description	LC Considerations and Actions
Free speech	Based on First Amendment to US Constitution (and many state constitutions) Does not protect speech • designed to incite violence • involving defamatory comments • related to clear and present danger • that uses obscenity Applies in educational settings • if government restraint applies to private and public institutions • if internal institutional restraint applies only to public institutions Student speech not protected if • disruptive • lewd or interferes with school's basic educational mission. *Tinker v. Des Moines Independent Community School District* (reasonably cause "substantial disruption of school activities")	The LC should • Support free speech of instructors and students involved with LCs. • Address violent, defamatory, dangerous, or obscene statements in writing or in person.
Academic freedom	Freedom to • pursue scholarship, • communicate facts or ideas, • teach and/or learn within broad educational parameters and free from interference Can establish and enforce relevant, reasonable, and clear standards of behavioral conduct for students and faculty Should not place greater limits in electronic mediums than print See AAUP Statements[a] on • Rights and Freedoms of Students • Academic Freedom (1940) • Academic Freedom and Electronic Communications	The LC should • Communicate support for academic freedom and open discourse. • Clarify standards of behavior essential to the LC educational mission and community life. • Clearly define offenses and outline reasonable and relevant consequences for violations.

Speech codes and "Academic Bill of Rights"	There is debate about whether these documents promote or unduly chill and censor free speech.[b] Courts have found that while some university speech codes are well intentioned to promote diversity, tolerance, and respectful dialogue, they may include overbroad definitions that "could certainly be used to truncate debate and free expression by students." *Bair v. Shippensburg University*, 280 F. Supp. 2d 357, 373 (M. D. Pa. 2003). (In that case the court enjoined removal of anti–Osama bin Laden posters from dorm room doors for being "offensive" to the campus community because the speech code being enforced was overly broad in violation of students' First Amendment rights.)	LCs should be cautious not to draft ground rules and written expectations regarding diversity, mutual respect, communication, or harassment too broadly or they could be interpreted as an unconstitutional speech code. Reviewing the broad language in Shippensburg's code of conduct that was overturned could be instructive for LCs.[c]

[a] Available at www.aaup.org/aaup/pubsres/policydocs/.
[b] See AAUP Statement on Speech Codes available at www.aaup.org/aaup/pubsres/policydocs/.
[c] See thefire.org/article/6111.html.

The same could apply to LC instructors and/or coordinators. In addition to legal concerns, if the LC leader has not worked out mutually agreed-to boundaries, statements may very well be made that can have an undesirable chilling effect on freedom of expression and exploration within the group that can seriously undermine needed learning.

By contrast, if an employee makes public comments to other employees related to terms of employment those comments will likely be considered "concerted activity," protected under the National Labor Relations Act (NLRA). This speech is protected regardless of whether the institution is public or private or has a union or not. Thus, if an employee makes comments about employment to other employees in a PLC or an LO, those comments may be protected speech under the NLRA. This protection applies even if the comments might otherwise appear to be defamatory to the organization or administration. However, this NLRA protection may be outweighed if that speech includes violations of FERPA, HIPAA, or other privacy laws.

LC Content Integrity and Ownership Issues

Content and ownership issues are complex and raise many questions. For example, B. Anderson and Simpson (2007) ask:

Is it an instructor's responsibility to ensure that information provided within a teaching environment is protected? Do we need to provide students with skills, strategies and information specific to online environments? Should we help them in a planned and deliberate way to deal with the types of issues we have raised? The text-based nature of online learning environments raises other questions as well. How long are text-based records of course discussions kept? (p. 132)

Further, are universities legally and ethically responsible to police their networks? If so, does this violate academic freedom? To what extent should they interfere with peer-to-peer file sharing—particularly given the potential for cheating, Internet piracy, and copyright issues? All of these issues can arise for LCs, particularly as they relate to enforcement of institutional policies and procedures.

Given that the institution will most likely drive the responses to these questions, LC coordinators need to know the position that their organization takes on these issues and their responsibility to report and/or enforce them. Although they are beyond the scope of this text, they should be addressed in the LC development process. For example, SLC ground rules (and syllabi where applicable) should specifically address and/or cross-reference the institutional copyright, intellectual property, cheating, and plagiarism policies. Useful resources regarding plagiarism, citation, and writing might also be provided to members. Where applicable, LC coordinators should include the Technology, Education, and Copyright Harmonization (TEACH) Act and other relevant disclaimers reminding members that use of materials beyond the scope of the course is prohibited and grounds for discipline. This would include presentation slides and audio recorded from guest speakers. Where possible, the LC coordinator may want to have guest speakers sign a permission-to-record statement authorizing the LC to record and use the presentation. This will be particularly important if lecture from a face-to-face class is recorded for use with an online section of the class. Under the TEACH Act, instructors may use a wider range of works in distance learning and students have greater latitude for storing, copying, and digitizing materials (see www.copyright.gov/legislation/archive for the TEACH requirements).

Privacy Versus Confidentiality

Privacy and confidentiality are closely related but different legal concepts. On its website, the University of California, Irvine's Office of Research Administration explains this distinction in its simplest terms: "Privacy is about people. Confidentiality is about data."[20] Ethically, both deal with individuals' autonomy to control information about themselves and obligate those with fiduciary duties to honor those decisions absent countervailing legal requirements. Figure 6.1 illustrates how privacy and confidentiality differ. Note that unlike violation of confidentiality, there is government enforcement but no private cause of action if privacy is violated.

Privacy

Privacy supports the constitutional right of an individual to have "control over the extent, timing, and circumstances of sharing oneself (physically, behaviorally, or intellectually) with others" (US Department of Health and Human Services, n.d.). State and federal laws provide sanctions when these privacy rights are violated in particular areas of education and health. The primary federal privacy laws are FERPA and HIPAA.

FERPA is designed to safeguard personally identifiable data (e.g., name, address, social security number) included in a student's education records.[21] It applies to public and postsecondary institutions that receive federal funds. The term *education records* is broadly defined in the regulations to include records that are (a) directly related to a student, and (b) maintained by an educational agency or institution or by a party acting for the agency or

FIGURE 6.1
Privacy versus confidentiality.

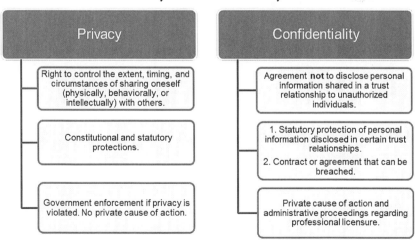

institution.[22] FERPA governs a student's right to control disclosure of personally identifiable information and request amendment to those records. The act also provides a list of limited circumstances in which information in a student's records can be released without the student's prior written permission. SLC coordinators will often have access to members' education records and are obligated to follow the privacy protections required under FERPA.

The Administrative Simplification provisions of HIPAA include a federal privacy rule that requires health care providers, health plans, and relevant clearinghouses ("covered entities") implement safeguards to protect patients' health records and other personally identifiable health information ("protected health information," or PHI).[23] The rule sets conditions on the uses and disclosures of PHI without patient authorization and clarifies the rights of patients to examine, request corrections of, and obtain a copy of their health records. HIPAA is relevant to LCs because there is sometimes an important interplay between FERPA and HIPAA.[24]

CONFIDENTIALITY

Confidentiality is both a legal and an ethical concept. Mary Ellen Lawless (2011), a research nurse in the School of Medicine at Case Western Reserve University, defines it as follows: "Confidentiality pertains to the expectation that information an individual has disclosed in a relationship of trust will not be shared to others in ways that are inconsistent with the understanding of the original disclosure without permission. Confidentiality is an agreement and can be breached."

Confidentiality is based on the fiduciary or contractual relationship that existed when the information was disclosed. While there are state laws that protect confidentiality in certain trust relationships (e.g., physician-patient privilege protects patients from having physicians testify about their medical information without authorization), to be legally enforceable it is a contractual right or agreement with the party to whom the information was disclosed (e.g., a credit card company violates contractual and/or privacy policy terms and conditions by releasing your information to an unauthorized person who steals your identity).

Expectation of Confidentiality in an LC

It is clear that the LC coordinator is obligated to follow privacy statutes, such as not releasing a student's private health information in the education record. Questions arise as to what level of confidentiality is expected among members and whether the LC coordinator is legally responsible for ensuring that information provided within an LC is protected from disclosure. The level of trust and closeness (in the psychological and social sense) that can develop in a powerful LC may lead to unguarded sharing about one's self and beliefs that contributes to learning. This is often done in more intimate detail than might be shared in broader educational or social settings.

Accordingly, it will be important that the coordinator effectively lead discussion and gain internalized agreement from every community member regarding appropriate/permissible disclosure, discussion, and social boundaries. This assurance will lead to heightened trust and minimize the number of unfortunate personal disclosures that may arise. Powerful LCs should establish written ground rules about the boundaries of discussion and expectations of confidentiality and privacy that members can expect. Nevertheless, members may still reveal personal problems or characteristics about themselves (e.g., bouts of depression, thoughts of suicide, or perceptions of being ugly) that they would not reveal in another setting.

Although the group should honor these expectations of confidentiality/ privacy, the assurances should not go so far as to "guarantee" that disclosures will remain confidential. This is particularly important given that the coordinator may be legally obligated to report a situation to government agencies (i.e., mandatory abuse reporting) or institutional officials (referral of a depressed, suicidal, or potentially dangerous student), as discussed next.

Mandatory Reporting

In certain cases, the LC coordinator is ethically and legally responsible for ensuring that information is reported. For example, the Clery Act requires institutional officials responsible for campus and student activities to report instances of campus crime to administration and/or supervisors. Resident assistants, coaches, and faculty who advise student organizations are specifically listed as mandatory reporters under the act. In that light, LC coordinators would likely be obligated to report under the act as well. The only exceptions are if the coordinator is a counselor, health provider, or member of the clergy or if the coordinator is also the victim.

The obligation to report begins as soon as the coordinator becomes aware of a reportable crime, regardless of whether the alleged victim wants it to be reported. For example, suppose that an LC member reports a sexual assault to her coordinator but asks the coordinator to keep it confidential. In that case the coordinator must tell the member that she is obligated to report it to the proper authorities of the institution, who may in turn involve law enforcement as dictated by the laws of that jurisdiction. The coordinator should then reassure the victim that confidentiality will be maintained as much as practicable and should take steps to do so. The Department of Education can impute substantial fines on the institution if the coordinator fails to report even a single crime.[25]

There may be peer-reporting obligations between members if there is a suspected violation of the institution's honor code or professional integrity code. Failure to report can lead to discipline for both LC members. Likewise, if two or more members of an LC—whether an SLC or a PLC—are professionals licensed by a state, they likely will have mandatory legal and ethical peer-reporting obligations. In the graduate health care LC setting, this could also involve reporting potential Medicare fraud and abuse, which can result in federal imprisonment, substantial fines, and other penalties for the reported members. Many institutions have other legal reporting requirements related to violence, sexual assault, harassment of any kind (sexual, verbal, and physical), and discrimination.[26]

The National Association of College and University Attorneys holds that for safety reasons there may be times when an LC coordinator should report otherwise confidential information to appropriate institutional officials or support personnel. As Tribbensee and McDonald (2007) state:

> A student's statements or behavior sometimes may raise concerns regarding the safety of the student or others. To prevent such harm from occurring, college and university administrators, faculty, and staff who become aware of such statements or behaviors may want to tell someone else—another campus employee, a parent, an outside health care professional, a law enforcement officer, or those with whom the student may interact—about what they know or believe. . . . They also may be concerned, however, that the Family Educational Rights and Privacy Act ("FERPA") . . . prevents them from doing so. Concerns about the ability to communicate critical information in an emergency are, in large part, the result of misunderstandings about FERPA. . . . FERPA is not a significant obstacle to appropriate (and desirable) communications intended to protect student, campus, or public safety. Depending on the relevant context and jurisdiction, however, additional restrictions may arise under other applicable state or federal laws.

Coordinators will need to follow institutional guidance and training about how to meet all reporting obligations related to the LC. There must be clear LC policies and procedures highlighting how to report. The Brazelton Center for Mental Health Law provides resources to help institutions of higher learning support students with mental health issues (see www.bazelon .org / Where - We - Stand / Community - Integration / Campus - Mental - Health .aspx).

References and Letters of Recommendation

LC coordinators in SLCs or PLCs may be in a special position to serve as a member's reference or to write a letter of recommendation for a job; rank, promotion, and tenure application; or other opportunity. Some institutions have policies that do not allow employees to serve as references or have strict guidelines; therefore, when a request is made coordinators must follow any institutional policies and procedures before agreeing to write a recommendation. Coordinators should be empowered to say no or to suggest another person who can provide the recommendation if they are not comfortable or do not have time. When coordinators do provide a recommendation, they should be honest but avoid making statements that could be perceived as defamatory. Coordinators also should not disclose any private or confidential information about LC members.

The coordinator may be aware of information about an LC member that is protected from disclosure under FERPA, HIPAA, or other privacy statutes. Accordingly, the coordinator is legally prohibited from divulging information about any physical or mental impairments that were disclosed during a request for accommodation under the ADA. Given the relaxed and trusting environment in a powerful LC, members may share or inadvertently disclose personal information about themselves that they wish to remain confidential. Ethically the coordinator should abide by LC ground rules not to divulge confidential information shared with LC members. If the coordinator believes that the disclosure would be in the member's best interest, he or she can seek permission from the member to share that information.

Liability

Liability is not just about lawsuits; it encompasses a number of legal and ethical obligations and concerns. These can involve statutory, contract, or tort claims against the individual person (e.g., the LC instructor, the coordinator, or a member) and/or the institution. Most LCs are not separate corporate legal entities so they themselves cannot be held liable. Accordingly, the sponsoring organization will often be held legally responsible for the actions of the LC, instructor, coordinator, and/or members under doctrines such as corporate negligence, ostensible authority, or vicarious liability.

Consider the situation in which an LC member is sexually assaulted by a person with a criminal history of assault who was hired as a guest speaker for the LC. In addition to the likely criminal and civil consequences for the alleged perpetrator, the coordinator and institution may both be civilly liable for negligent hiring, failing to screen and/or conduct a criminal background check and violating the institution's violence-free campus policies. Therefore, every violation, adverse outcome, or negative encountered can be a source of potential liability that will require documentation and appropriate response. The coordinator is the first line of defense in preventing and responding to potential liability situations that may arise in an LC. From that perspective, institutions should invest in training and resources to support LC coordinators' compliance with the law.

There is potential liability in all of the areas discussed in this chapter—discrimination, access, relationship issues, academic dishonesty, plagiarism, breaches of privacy/confidentiality, and mandatory reporting. Liability related to LCs tends to mirror that typically encountered by sponsoring organizations. Accordingly, the following discussion is intended to highlight the most notable areas of liability encountered by higher education generally: defamation and specific types of negligence.

Defamation

Defamation is a state law criminal or civil charge involving "any intentional false communication, either written [libel] or spoken [slander], that harms a person's reputation; decreases the respect, regard, or confidence in which a person is held; or induces disparaging, hostile, or disagreeable opinions or feelings against a person." It is not necessary to use a person's name to state a defamation claim. The person only needs to be reasonably ascertainable.[27] It also is not just use of a particular phrase that is probative; rather, it is the context in which it was used.

The court analyzes whether a reasonable person would confuse the opinion given as a statement of fact. Statements such as calling a specific business-person a fraud, an attorney a crook, or a woman a prostitute would likely be actionable whereas calling someone a jerk, clueless, or even a dumb-ass would be considered opinion in most situations. The court in *Vogel v. Felice* (2005) explained this distinction: "Plaintiffs were justifiably insulted by this epithet, but they failed entirely to show how it could be found to convey a provable factual proposition. . . . If the meaning conveyed cannot by its nature be proved false, it cannot support a libel claim" (p. 1020).

To illustrate this point, consider the situation of members of a PLC having a heated discussion about quality standards for student research and one member saying to another, "You shouldn't even be involved in this discussion because everyone knows you routinely plagiarize and take credit for your students' work!" This statement appears to be a provably false factual assertion,[28] it was made in front of third parties (the PLC members), it does not involve a public figure, and it reasonably could be considered damageable to the person's personal and professional reputation.[29] Based on these factors, it appears that the remarks were defamatory (slanderous) and could subject the person to civil or even criminal charges. The same analysis could apply to similar written statements provided to third parties, including online and/or social networking sites.

Negligence

The FindLaw (n.d.) dictionary defines *negligence* as follows:

> Conduct that falls below the standards of behavior established by law for the protection of others against unreasonable risk of harm. A person has acted negligently if he or she has departed from the conduct expected of a reasonably prudent person [or LC] acting under similar circumstances.

A straightforward case of negligence would be one in which an SLC member is injured while walking into a classroom because he trips on a broken rubber stopper sticking out of the carpet that the university was aware of but did not replace. In that case (a) there was a duty to the member (and other invitees to the campus) to have a safe learning environment and it was foreseeable that a person could trip on the broken stopper and be injured, (b) the stopper was not fixed in a timely manner and a warning sign about the potential risk of tripping on the broken stopper was not placed at the site, (c) the member tripped on the stopper and was injured, and (d) the injury was caused by the trip on the broken stopper.

Negligence covers a huge body of complex tort law, which is beyond the scope of this chapter. Table 6.3 briefly outlines common areas of negligence experienced in higher education. Here we discuss specific areas of particular note for LCs.

LCs have a duty to take adequate measures to protect members, guests, the organization, and/or the public from harm related to the activities of the

TABLE 6.3
Key considerations for LC negligence.

Types of Negligent Liability	General Description	LC Considerations and Actions
Premises liability	Institutional duty to maintain reasonably safe buildings, grounds, and equipment (landowner or lessee) Liability for injuries to students or others invited for failure to maintain reasonably safe campus: • Did the institution know or should it have? • Was the injury foreseeable? • Was the injury caused by reasonable use or foreseeable misuse of the property? • Did the institution take reasonable steps to warn about hazards? (not necessary if obvious hazard)	Coordinators should scan the physical LC environment in advance of activities (if possible): 1. Is the site accessible for all members and guests? 2. Are there any safety hazards? If so: • Correct or report immediately (follow up). • Change LC locations. • Post signs or other warning regarding potential dangers.
On-campus instruction	Liability for injuries occurring during on-campus activities part of LC or SLC—especially if required: • Was reasonable informed consent given? • Did the LC fail to instruct? • Were clear written guidelines provided? • What is the level of experience of the member (novice more direction needed vs. experienced)	• Provide clear instructions and written directions—more if new members. • Warn if no obvious hazards. • If required LC activity, address in the syllabus. • If optional, be clear about all known risks/benefits.
Off-campus instruction (e.g., service-learning, field trip, internship, study abroad)	Liability for injuries even though no direct control over learning environment if: Required, scheduled LC activity or selected site means duty not to expose to unreasonable risk of harm. See *Delbridge v. Maricopa County Community College District*, 893 P.2d 55 (Ariz. App. 1994). Need to use contracts and other mechanisms to ensure other parties with control meet their obligations to keep students safe. Must use care when assigning students to sites, even if students ultimately select from a list of potential sites. See *Gross v. Family Services Agency and Nova Southwestern University, Inc.*, 716 So.2d 337 (Fla. App. 1998).[a]	LCs responsible for protecting members from undue harm if require, schedule, or select site. Environmental assessment of potential risks and addressing in contracts with site are important. • Orient members in advance. • Provide clear instructions and written directions—more detail needed if new members. • If required LC activity, address in the syllabus. • If optional but select or schedule site, vet all sites and be clear about all known risks/benefits of potential sites.

Cocurricular and social activities (e.g., party is hosted at the home of member; employees socialize outside of regular duties)	Generally no custodial duty for adult college student; see *Freeman v. Bush* case. Was event purely private affair or authorized, supervised, or controlled by the association? See *Stitt v. Raytown Sports Association*, Ct. of App., W. Dist., WD 53894 (Feb. 2, 1998). Is there a nexus between activity and LC? If sponsored or related there is a clear duty May allege "Special Relationship"; see *Denver v. Whitlock*, 744 P.2d 54 (Colo. 1987). If prohibit or take control may assume undertaking duty to protect; see *Furek v. University of Delaware*, 594 A.2d 506 (Del. 1991).	• LC generally no duty for non-LC events even if LC members are involved. • Sometimes gray area between private member and LC official activities and events. Should spell out in ground rules. • If aware of private party or event reinforce that it is not LC event. • Do not offer or allow use of LC property, personnel, or other things that evidence authority, supervision, or control. • Do not be so explicit in prohibitions or control that LC takes on duty to protect.
LC outreach (community programs, summer camps, or nonstudent groups)	Institution's responsibility to supervise student employees or invitees to campus and to report inappropriate conduct; see article by Brad Wolverton (July 12, 2012), "Penn State's Culture of Reverence Led to 'Total Disregard' for Children's Safety," *The Chronicle of Higher Education* (online edition). May be held vicariously liable for actions of employees, students, or contracted individuals if exposure to invitees is in the scope of performance; see *Grambling State University, Dismuke v. Quaynor*, 637 So.2d 555 (La. App. 1994).	Ensure there are appropriate supervision and rules in place to prevent harm to invitees from members, employees, or others affiliated with the LC.
Educational malpractice	Common law detrimental reliance claim Not cause of action recognized by most jurisdictions but: • *Blank v. Board of Higher Education of the City of New York*, 273 NYS.2d 796 (NY Sup. Ct. 1966) (detrimental reliance on advisor's advice was sufficient to hold advisor and institution responsible) and • *Johnson v. Schmitz*, 119 F. Supp. 2d 90 (D. Conn. 2000) (academic misconduct on the part of doctoral advisor supported finding of liability).	*Caution:* LC coordinator is analogous to (and may function as) advisor function so may be liable for advice and/or misinformation provided. May be liable to member if LC coordinator engages in academic misconduct.

Note. Adapted from W. A. Kaplan and Lee (2007), pp. 87–104.
[a] Gross and Delbridge cases.

LC. The organization may be held liable for the harm created by the LC. Instructors and coordinators may also be personally held liable if they fail to meet their duties. Fortunately, in most of these situations there is sufficient institutional significance that overarching policies, procedures, risk management practices, and liability insurance are already in place to protect stakeholders throughout the organization—including the LC coordinators and members. Some particularly risk-averse individuals might even take the extra step of purchasing personal liability policies that would cover losses attributed to them in their role as an LC coordinator—but that generally would not be necessary.

In most cases the standard institutional incident-reporting process and casualty insurance/workers' compensation system would be implicated. Depending on the circumstance, institutional legal counsel may determine that there is governmental immunity for the institution and/or the LC coordinator or that the member somehow contributed to the injury herself. Most allegations of negligence by a sponsoring institution arise when the LC member is operating in an environment for which the institution and/or LC has little or no direct control, such as field-based service-learning experiences, internship or practicum sites, field trips, or en route to such places. For example, a student at a health care site might be exposed to a communicable disease. For virtual LCs, cyberspace might even count as such a space. Thus, negligence could relate to interactions between students and/or institutional personnel (including students) and/or noninstitutional personnel.

Off-campus sites may create institutional liability for student actions while students are engaged in LC activities. It may relate to having college-age students having contact with minors, dependent adults, or other vulnerable populations. Or it could include a breach of contract with the host organization, such as failure to follow up on promises to conduct a background check. There can also be a risk of damage to individuals, property, or technology at the host site.

The key consideration in such cases is that the LC does not have control and cannot assure conditions to its members or to others at the host site. The LC should enlist the cooperation of all students in following procedures as well as monitor compliance with and the effectiveness of those procedures. In addition, the LC should look at any risks inherent to the location and the activities in which students will be participating, and think through and answer the following key risk management questions:

- What can go wrong? (Risk identification)
- What can we do so that nothing goes wrong? (Risk control/plan)

- If something does go wrong, how do we respond, remediate, and/or pay for it? (Risk financing)

It may be impossible to supervise every "event" associated with an LC (although maintaining a certain degree of formality may lessen the risk of injuries and other forms of liability). However, at the very least, sponsoring organizations need to verify that they have sufficient insurance for any acts of LC employees, students, and volunteers that are found to be within their supervision or control. They may also wish to ensure that coordinators and others interacting with the LC (e.g., field experience sites) have adequate insurance of their own. Likewise, the hosting organization does not have control over students and others from the LC and must rely on the assurances of the LC representatives. Both the LC and the other party may seek to insulate themselves from liability by negotiating contract clauses requiring specific performance and/or indemnifying the other party if found liable for negligence that the other party caused. Several respondents to the 100-Institution Survey alluded to the importance of involving attorneys in negotiating language designed to limit liability.

Legal documents such as waivers, consent forms, and permission slips can provide some limited liability protection for the LC and institution. Generally, these documents do not transfer liability or restrain members from filing suit, but they document that members knew or should have known about the risks disclosed when deciding whether to participate.

Use and Misuse of Background Checks

Much like the college and university campuses with which they are affiliated, LCs may weigh the benefits and drawbacks of asking students to self-disclose criminal history and/or conducting background checks. These checks may relate to participation in the LC itself. They may also be linked to a particular activity in which LC members will participate, such as a service-learning project or an internship at a hospital that requires a criminal and/or abuse registry background check to protect patients who might interact with LC members. In such cases, failure to conduct an adequate check may result in not only breach of the contract, but the requirement to indemnify the site for any liability that resulted from breaching that duty.

LC members work closely with one another, sometimes living in the same residence. Thus, they are not immune from conflict that can escalate to potential violence. Tragedies such as the murders at the University of North Carolina and University of Virginia, where the students involved had criminal and/or mental health histories, raise the question: Could violence have been prevented if there had been background checks? At this time, colleges and universities are increasingly being held legally responsible for failing to protect individuals if there are outbreaks of violence involving students or faculty.

However, there are a number of concerns regarding background checks, including that most programs that conduct background checks often do not have training for staff to interpret the information appropriately. Nor do they have policies on whether/when criminal checks should be required and how information gathered should be used. Furthermore, institutional leaders, faculty, and staff are generally not aware of what biases to watch out for in background checking or how background checks can be applied in an unevenhanded, discriminatory manner.

Blumstein and Nakamura (2009) in particular discuss concerns about discriminatory use of background and credit checks, which can weigh against confidentiality and protection of particular group members. In her response to the 100-Institution Survey, Tae Nosaka at Colorado State University indicated that the university's SLCs are very active and include field trips, which can potentially lead to other liability issues. Given the potential liability, she expressed concerns as to whether all students should be required to participate in a particular activity in order to obtain academic credit. For example, a service-learning setting such as a homeless shelter might involve dangerous situations for participants. Nosaka feels it is important legally to give students options as to how much they wish to participate or not.

Unfortunately, despite rigorous planning, mistakes can be made and/or a lawsuit filed. Coordinators must be sufficiently familiar with the litigation process and institutional attorneys so that they will know whom to work with and how to respond if they receive a subpoena or discovery request or are personally served a complaint to initiate a lawsuit. Failure to respond in a timely, competent, and professional manner will only serve to make a bad situation worse.

The Rest of the Story

Mary, the coordinator for the SLC, made several errors that have negative consequences for LC stakeholders. Overall, she did not consider and plan for the substantive risks associated with the field learning experience, and she did not coordinate expectations or policies and procedures with FRCF. For example, it was not clear who, if anyone, was responsible for doing a background check. As LC coordinator, she may be liable for negligence in several incidents:

- **Incident 1: Resident falls and breaks her pelvis.** Clearly Matt's actions in mopping the floor without an appropriate warning sign have opened FRCF, PNC, and Matt himself to a negligence suit from the injured resident. The facts suggest that a jury could assign blame to FRCF because its staff did not provide the sign and instructed Matt to go ahead with the cleanup or to PNC and Matt because he is the one who mopped the floor knowing he did not have the appropriate sign. It is unclear from the facts given whether issues pertaining to work conditions, liability, indemnity, or other standards were spelled out in a written contract between the college and the service-learning site. For example, was PNC or FRCF responsible for orienting Matt about safety standards and precautions? Finally, this scenario demonstrates the complexities associated with background checks that LCs should be aware of and incorporate into their written agreements.
- **Incident 2: Student gets stuck by a needle.** The FRCF nurse's failure to follow federal blood-borne pathogen standards and institutional policies may have exposed Avery to serious infectious diseases, requiring her to undergo extensive and costly testing and treatment. She may sue the nurse for gross negligence in leaving the dirty needle on the cart; FRCF for corporate negligence in not having enough sharps containers and for hiring the nurse; Coordinator Mary for selecting FRCF as the site, negligence in setting up the field experience, and promising but failing to provide "a safe, fun, and rewarding experience"; and PNC, which has vicarious liability for the negligence and assurances made by its agent (Mary) and corporate liability for approving the service-learning experience.
- **Incident 3: Resident privacy is breached.** Posting a photo of a resident on a public site without proper permission is a violation of the federal HIPAA Privacy Rule because the photo is personally identifiable and is PHI because the post says she is a resident at FRCF. This can expose Susan and FRCF to substantial legal penalties. Depending on FRCF's agreement with PNC, the college may be obligated to indemnify FRCF for any penalties incurred. Unless there are provisions in a contract regarding unauthorized blogs or other public communications, the post by the second student about the "dirty parts" of nursing is not illegal because it does not include PHI. It is general in nature and is not likely to damage FRCF's reputation. It could even be seen as protected free speech in some contexts. However, the coordinator should visit with the student about ethical considerations related to the post and how it does not reflect well on her, PNC, or FRCF. The third student used highly derogatory terms to describe PHI about a resident that could be considered defamatory in addition to violating HIPAA. Although she does not mention the resident's name, she provides enough information that he could be identified. The student, PCN, and FRCF are facing not only government penalties for HIPAA violations but potential lawsuits from the resident involved.

- **Incident 4: Intoxicated bus driver crashes van and causes injury to student.** LC member Susan is injured and taken to a hospital by ambulance because the bus driver had been drinking and crashes the van. It is likely that the driver and transport company will be sued by Susan and any other student members who allege they were injured by the crash. Although it is probable that the driver and transport company will bear primary liability, it appears that Mary and/or PNC failed to adequately screen the transport company and could also be found negligent. The importance of risk management, background checks, and other prudent measures for off-site LC activities is demonstrated. When Mary shares confidential information about Susan's medical condition with the other LC members, she may have acted unethically. Although Susan or her family may have authorized her to share this information, it is possible that Susan did not want anyone to know about the extent of her injuries—especially if there is a mental impairment. Although we do not have enough information to say affirmatively that Mary violated the FERPA and HIPAA federal privacy laws, the facts suggest that she may have done so when she shared Susan's PHI. Again, the guarantee of a "safe, fun, and rewarding experience" was not met and could be another basis for liability.

Conclusion

Organizations that sponsor LCs must maintain awareness of legal and ethical concerns. Particular areas of concern include membership and access; relationships; and integrity, privacy, and liability. LC coordinators must address discrimination and access issues related to membership; ensure proper relationships by building and maintaining crucial "instructor presence" and defining boundaries and guidelines for promoting positive, healthy relationships within the community, including monitoring appropriateness of content; and promote quality content, protect confidentiality and privacy, and prepare for potential liability.

For Reflection

As you create your own meaning from ideas in this chapter, begin to think about a specific LC at your institution (or at an institution you know about if you are in a governmental or other noninstitutional role) and how it can inform your work or interests. Use that LC to answer the following questions and help you reflect on practical implications of the material in this chapter:

- In what ways might you fail to practice completely fair and equal selection and treatment within the LC? What are the most effective ways to prevent that from happening?
- What is the possibility of discrimination occurring that is based on gender, age, socioeconomic level, genetic information, or other characteristics protected by law? How can you best prevent such discrimination from occurring?
- What are your affirmative action obligations pertaining to this LC? How can you legally promote diversity within the LC?
- How would access issues such as disabilities and/or LEP contribute to such diversity? What accommodations would be necessary so that these individuals could be full LC participants?
- What discrimination would be illegal? What discrimination would be legal but unethical?
- What specific legal liabilities does the LC need to address to be protected? Has the LC coordinator received proper orientation and training on steps that must be taken to ensure such protection?
- How prepared is the LC to meet any liability situation that unexpectedly occurs? What contingency plans are in place to respond appropriately to such situations that might occur?
- How positive and healthy are the member-member and member-coordinator relationships within this LC? Do the LC relationships and interactions meet the specific moral and ethical standards discussed in this chapter? What are concrete ways that "instructor presence" and the relationships in your LC can be improved so as to maximize individual and group learning?
- Have your LC members received written ground rules up front, along with verbal reinforcement, that strongly emphasize expectations regarding boundaries, discrimination, and acceptable types of interaction?
- Do you have LC planning to head off ethical dilemmas and limit legal liability if sued?

Now that you have read and reflected on this chapter, you should be able to complete the following items on the Powerful LC Planning Form in Appendix C:

- Section II: #2. "How will you select members for your LC?"
- Section III: #5. "Is the LC prepared to deal with significant legal and ethical issues?"

Notes

1. Among the authors is an experienced attorney and mediator who teaches graduate courses on legal and ethical issues in face-to-face, online, and hybrid formats. Another author has extensive experience dealing with legal and ethical issues as an academic dean/vice president and authored the well-received course "Personal and Organizational Ethics" that has been taught in both face-to-face and online settings in locations across the country.

2. This chapter is intended to be a general overview of some legal and ethical issues pertaining to LCs, not legal advice. Note that legal and ethical issues are addressed as practical suggestions for sponsoring organizations to consider and adapt to their unique institutional circumstances rather than as a formal legal or ethical treatise on LCs. Readers with legal questions are encouraged to seek the advice of their legal counsel.

3. If the sponsoring institution is public, LC coordinators should recognize that 42 U.S.C. Section 1983 provides a federal remedy, in the form of an injunction, monetary damages, and recovery of attorneys' fees, for the violation of constitutional rights by the government, government officials, administrators, and employees. The sponsoring institution can also be found liable under this statute for failure to anticipate and train LC coordinators and members on how to avoid discrimination and other constitutional issues. A good analogy is found in the law enforcement context. See *City of Canton v. Harris,* 489 U.S. 378, at 387–88 (1989). See also footnote 10 on page 390 of the case.

4. Some protected classes do not have this high of a level of judicial scrutiny, such as age and disability.

5. See *Flanagan v. President and Directors of Georgetown,* 417 F. Supp. 377 (D.D.C. 1976); and *Regents of the University of California v. Bakke,* 438 U.S. 265 (1978).

6. At the time of this publishing the US Supreme Court has granted a writ of certiorari to reconsider the *Fisher v. University of Texas* case that may impact the court's holding on the permissible use of diversity as a factor in admissions decisions. Available at www.supremecourt.gov/Search.aspx?FileName = /docketfiles/11-345.htm.

7. See Department of Education Civil Rights Division, "Guidance on the Voluntary Use of Race to Achieve Diversity in Postsecondary Education," at www2 .ed.gov/about/offices/list/ocr/docs/guidance-pse-201111.pdf.

8. See *A Guide to Disability Rights Laws* at www.ada.gov/cguide.htm# anchor62335.

9. At present this requirement does not apply to all institutions in higher education. However, prudent organizations are planning to comply in anticipation that it will be the standard for all soon.

10. See www.washington.edu/doit/CUDE/app_postsec.html.

11. Exec. Order No. 13166, 28 C.F.R. 401–415. Exec. Order 13166, reprinted at 65 C.F.R. 50121 (August 16, 2000).

12. See Federal Register, January 12, 2004, Vol. 69, No. 7, pp. 1763–1768 (available at www.archives.gov/eeo/laws/title-vi.html).

13. See Federal Register, Vol. 75, No. 209, p. 66899.

14. See Higher Learning Commission (May 20, 2011), "Information for Institutions on the Higher Learning Commission's Credit Hour Policies," p. 1 (available at www.ncahlc.org/Information-for-Institutions/federal-compliance-program.html).

15. See Karen Osterholm, Deborah Horn, and William Kritsonis, "College Professors as Potential Victims of Stalking: Awareness and Prevention: National Implications," *Focus on Colleges, Universities, and Schools* 1, no. 1 (2007): 1–7.

16. For more information on promoting cultural competence, see www.racon line.org/topics/culture/culturalcompetencyfaq.php#fedactivities.

17. Two user-friendly resources summarizing practical strategies to address hyperbonding and groupthink are University of Wyoming, "The Impact of Hyperbonding: Exploring Student Relationships Within Courses," *LeaRN: Brown Bag Lunch* (available at www.uwyo.edu/learn/_files/docs/brownbag_docs/hyperbonding .pdf); and Ben Dattner, "Preventing 'Groupthink': Take Your Team Off Autopilot," *Psychology Today* (April 20, 2011) (available at www.psychologytoday.com/blog/ credit-and-blame-work/201104/preventing-groupthink).

18. By documenting separately, it falls into the sole source data exception to FERPA and does not require disclosure.

19. Most of the act was found to be unconstitutional limitation of First Amendment individual rights. However, Section 230 withstood judicial scrutiny and remains in effect.

20. See http://research.uci.edu/ora/hrpp/privacyAndConfidentiality.htm.

21. See 20 U.S.C. §1232g; 34 CFR Part 99. FERPA regulations and information can be found at www.ed.gov/policy/gen/guid/fpco/index.html.

22. See 34 CFR § 99.3.

23. See 45 CFR Parts 160, 162, and 164. Information on the HIPAA Privacy Rule is available at www.hhs.gov/ocr/hipaa.

24. See Departments of Health and Human Services and Education (November 2008). *Joint Guidance on the Application of the Family Educational Rights and Privacy Act (FERPA) and the Health Insurance Portability and Accountability Act of 1996 (HIPAA) to Student Health Records* (available at www.hhs.gov/ocr/privacy/hipaa/ understanding/coveredentities/hipaaferpajointguide.pdf).

25. See US Department of Education's The Handbook for Campus Safety and Security Reporting (February 2011) at www2.ed.gov/admins/lead/safety/handbook. pdf and National Association of College and University Business Officers' Campus Crime Reporting: A Guide to Clery Act Compliance (July 2002) at www.nacua.org/ documents/ACE_NACUBO_CleryAct.pdf.

26. See www.dol.gov/dol/topic/discrimination/ethnicdisc.htm and www2.ed.gov /about/offices/list/ocr/docs/sexharoo.html.

27. *West's Encyclopedia of American Law*, 2nd ed. Copyright 2008 The Gale Group, Inc. Available at http://legal-dictionary.thefreedictionary.com/defamation.

28. If the statement is true, the defendant (person who made the statement) could use this as a defense in a defamation suit. There are other defenses that could be used in a suit of this nature.

29. In most jurisdictions, damage may be established through evidence of mental anguish or "per se" defamation where damage is presumed—in this case because the statements involved attacks on the person's professional character/standing and allegations of "crimes" involving moral turpitude.

7

ASSESSMENT GUIDELINES FOR DIFFERENT TYPES OF LCs

What's the Story?

Maria Rey and Lamont Briggs work at Local Community College (LCC). Nearly a year ago, they developed a learning community (LC) proposal for their institution. The proposal noted the historical benefits of LCs, including increased retention, increased social and academic involvement, and enhanced academic success. The administration approved the proposal because it is concerned about retention and academic success. The administration also shares an interest in offering more high-impact experiences to students. Budget monies were allocated to create a number of new LCs on campus.

Because of budget cuts at the state level, however, LCC administrators now have to make some difficult choices. Across the institution, each department and program has been asked to provide a justification report to receive financial resources in the upcoming year. Reports must include a summary of activities, alignment of activities with the current strategic plan, resources required to maintain progress, and evidence of program impact.

Maria and Lamont have administered the new LCs all year, although these responsibilities were an add-on to their previous roles at the institution. They did not do any assessment prior to start-up. They focused most of their time on recruiting faculty and students, providing professional development, working with the registrar, and troubleshooting problems along the way. Little time was devoted to the assessment of the program. Lamont now desperately scans through a list of standardized assessment tools to find a quick one that they can administer to the students in the LCs. He finds a five-minute test that was used successfully by an art conservatory on the East Coast. Meanwhile, Maria drafts up a student satisfaction survey. Although there are many anecdotes that support the positive impact of the program, they are just not sure what else they can use at this point.

What assessment advice would you give to Maria and Lamont?

> My point is that excellent teaching . . . entails an ethical and
> moral commitment—what I might call the "pedagogical impera-
> tive." Teachers with this kind of integrity . . . inquire into the
> consequences of their work with students.
>
> —Shulman (2003, p. 1)

We start this chapter with a series of three anecdotes that touch on the importance of understanding how people learn and its implications for assessment. First, a September 2011 article in *Time* magazine told the story of computer gamers who solved a puzzle that may help offer new treatments for AIDS. For years, scientists worked on modeling the structure of a specific protein. Using a visual game, individuals were able to offer a solution for the structure of this critical protein in a matter of weeks. Current methods of modeling require significant time and money, even when using computers. The visual game, however, takes advantage of humans' puzzle-solving intuitions and ability to think three-dimensionally.

Second, in a study titled "Your Brain on Google" several researchers compared the brain activity of an Internet-savvy group with that of an Internet-naïve group when conducting an Internet search. The study found that Internet searching

> may engage a greater extent of neural circuitry not activated while reading
> text pages, but only in people with prior computer and Internet search
> experience. These observations suggest that . . . prior experience with
> Internet searching may alter the brain's responsiveness in neural circuits
> controlling decision making and complex reasoning. (Small, Moody, Sid-
> darth, & Bookheimer, 2009, p. 116).

Third, the National Institute for Learning Outcomes Assessment recently released an article detailing the assessment of learning in online courses. The authors describe the increased ability to collect information about students as they engage in the learning process. Information about students' behavior (e.g., how often they access specific resources, how often they respond to peers' comments) and their understanding of essential information within a module is available to faculty and course designers. These "learning analytics" can enable "rapid changes in instructional practices and curriculum, and . . . empower students to make informed decisions about their learning behaviors" (Prineas & Cini, 2011, p. 6).

These three anecdotes may seem to be a strange collection at the start of an assessment chapter. However, they go right to the heart of certain assumptions about what assessment means. Although one may be tempted to say that a common theme across these stories is the use of technology, there is a different essential component that warrants attention for the purposes of this book. Each of these stories provides an appreciation for assessing how the individuals engage in the learning process. Whether through measuring the time it takes to solve a "puzzle" rather than a "problem," monitoring changes in brain activity for different media, or actively tracking student behaviors, each of the stories demonstrates assessment of the learning process.

Assessment is not just about verifying that learning has occurred; it offers important insights into ways to enhance the learning process itself. Assessment is less about getting the "data" and "analytics" and more about understanding ways to promote powerful learning. It is a way of inquiring into the consequences of the effort to meet the "pedagogical imperative" that Shulman (2003) mentions in the introductory quote to this chapter. Presented in this way, the rationale for doing assessment work is not rooted in pressures for external accountability but instead focuses on the challenging problems that educators face today, the changing context of how human beings access information, and the evolving tools for understanding learning.

The purpose of this chapter is to discuss how assessment and evaluation can help move LCs into the next stage of educational transformation. The first part of this chapter provides a foundation for the purpose of assessment and provides a connection between assessment work and the improvement of learning in an LC. Then the next section introduces the assessment cycle that will help both learning organizations (LOs) and individual LCs develop assessment plans. Finally, the chapter examines strategies for applying the assessment cycle to LCs.

Connections to Research

Often, practitioners find themselves in the position of needing to design and conduct an assessment. Frequently these efforts fail to acknowledge the main purpose of assessment. Here, we make the case that assessment can serve as an important foundation for LC development and improvement.

Connecting Assessment and Learning

Two significant pieces of research provide clarity regarding the purpose of assessment as it relates to the work in LCs. The first comes from Huba and

Freed (2000), who offer a framework for learner-centered assessment. This learner-centered paradigm is different from a traditional teaching paradigm in several ways, as seen in Table 7.1.

Learning is the focus and the purpose of every LC, whether it is a student LC (SLC), a professional LC (PLC), or an LO. Huba and Freed (2000) explain that assessment helps to shift attention to a learning-centered paradigm. When focusing on learning, teachers/facilitators ask, "What have LC members learned, what contributed to their learning, and how well have they learned?"

The second piece of significant research comes from Blaich and Wise (2011), who provide advice on how to move beyond gathering data to actually using it: "Assessment data has legs only if the evidence collected rises out of extended conversations across constituencies about (a) what people hunger to know about their teaching and learning environments and (b) how the assessment evidence speaks to those questions" (p. 12). They explain that the process of collecting evidence alone will *not* have an impact on LCs that exist within the reality of busy institutions. They also explain that the time and effort it often takes to develop, implement, and support ongoing programs (such as LCs) interferes with the ability to actually use assessment information to prompt discussion and review of their effectiveness.

Taken together, these two perspectives shift attention to a learning-centered approach that is rooted in the critical questions of practice. Huba and Freed (2000) define *assessment* as follows:

> The process of gathering and discussing information from multiple and diverse sources in order to develop a deep understanding of what students

TABLE 7.1
Teacher-centered paradigm versus learner-centered paradigm.

Teacher-Centered Paradigm	*Learner-Centered Paradigm*
Knowledge is transmitted to learners.	Learners construct knowledge.
Learners passively receive information.	Learners actively absorb, assimilate, and apply information.
Assessment helps to monitor learning.	Assessment helps to promote and diagnose learning.
Learning is individualistic.	Learning is cooperative and collaborative.
Students are learners.	People learn together in community.

Note. Adapted from Huba and Freed (2000).

know, understand, and can do with their knowledge as a result of their educational experiences: the process culminates when assessment results are used to improve subsequent learning. (p. 8)

Note here that we do not use the terms *assessment* and *evaluation* interchangeably (Lenning & Ebbers, 1999; Upcraft & Schuh, 1996), like many educators do. We describe assessment as the process used to gather, analyze, and interpret information about learning (ultimately for the purpose of improving subsequent learning). By contrast, evaluation refers to the process of judging the merit or worth of a program or activity and/or (usually more important) judging how to improve it. Furthermore, in planning or in implementing assessment activities, we subscribe to the proposition originally formulated by Lenning (1981) that one should focus on the measurement phase (measures and/or indicators and processes used for gathering data), assessment phase (analysis and interpretation), and evaluative phase (judgment) separately but at the same time consider/be cognizant of what is specifically occurring in the other two phases.

B. L. Smith, MacGregor, Matthews, and Gabelnick (2004) identify six major strands of inquiry that shape assessment work.

1. *Program evaluation, helps promote organizational improvement through information that explores program progress, problems, and impact.*
2. *Educational assessment work,* explores the student learning process.
3. *Student development,* examines the social, intellectual, and ethical development of students in college.
4. *Student learning outcomes*—focusing on the need to identify intended learning outcomes, design tasks aligned with those outcomes, and provide students with feedback on the outcomes.
5. *Feedback to teachers* through classroom assessment techniques.
6. *Systematic inquiry* into practices that influence learning.

The work of this chapter touches on all of these strands but most closely aligns with a focus on exploring the student learning process and the assessment of learning outcomes.

Three Essential Findings About Learning

In their book *How People Learn: Brain, Mind, Experience, and School,* Bransford, Brown, and Cocking (1999a) outline three essential findings about learning that have important implications for both the development of learning experiences and efforts to assess the impact of these experiences.

1. *People bring preconceptions about the way the world works to their learning experiences.* This means that new concepts and information need to connect with individuals' initial understandings in order to engage learners. As its members work together to create new knowledge and understanding, a successful LC needs to build on the existing knowledge and understanding of its members.

An example of this principle comes from the work of the Collegiate Learning Assessment, which offers faculty a professional workshop to design performance tasks that will challenge students to demonstrate critical thinking and writing skills (see Performance Task Academy at http://collegiate learningassessment.org/pta.html). Participants are asked to answer the following question: "Where does the mass of a tree come from?" The participants then can form groups based on people who come up with similar answers to the question. The groups then engage in a discussion about their individual reasons for the common answer and about the type of questions they would like to pose to members in other groups to better understand their thinking. As the entire group begins to process the responses and listen to the questions raised by the small groups, there is usually a powerful moment when some people begin to move to other groups. This creates a visible moment of how the members in this LC have a profound influence on the understanding of others.

The implications of this principle for assessment work are twofold. First, the design of assessment tools and strategies should incorporate an understanding of learning that is situated in individuals' previous knowledge. Educators need to find ways to understand and explore this dynamic nature of learning and how knowledge changes over time. Second, learning becomes an integrative process that can be significantly influenced by the other members of the community.

2. *To develop competence in inquiry, individuals must have deep foundational knowledge, be able to apply a conceptual framework to that knowledge, and organize knowledge in ways that facilitate retrieval and application.* Research indicates that expert problem solvers' ability to apply concepts allows them to transfer knowledge to new problems. For an example of this principle, consider students in a course on statistics. Throughout the semester the students practice various types of problems (e.g., graphing data, calculating means, conducting various statistical tests). At the end of the semester,

students are presented with an open-ended problem that requires them to take data from a research study, analyze the results, and present their findings. To be successful in this task, students must have the opportunity to develop a deep understanding of the foundational principles and practices behind the various problems that they practiced.

Without a conceptual framework that integrates the individual problems, a student would likely struggle with a new problem that offers few cues for the specific statistical technique needed to solve the problem. The implication for assessment work is that the focus of inquiry must move beyond cataloging knowledge of facts, and expand attention to include an understanding of how individuals and communities apply conceptual frameworks and organize knowledge. In short, assessment efforts need to move beyond the multiple-choice or short-answer strategies to more complex ways of exploring thinking.

3. *A metacognitive approach to learning can help individuals take control of their own learning as they define learning goals and monitor their own progress.* The implication here is that assessment can provide both individuals and organizations with an opportunity to reflect on their learning. Efforts to include individuals in self-assessment will offer them an opportunity to reflect on their learning and also contribute to the learning process while educators gather additional information about the potential impact of experiences on participants' learning. In other words, metacognitive skills should be incorporated into the assessment process as another opportunity to support learning. An example of this principle would be a service-learning experience that includes a structured reflection exercise in which the participants consider their assumptions from before the experience, the areas of learning (interpersonal, cultural, ethical) that happened during the experience, and the ways that they might apply the learning to future experiences. The designers of the LC can then review this information as indicators of student learning.

A Critique of Current Efforts

Bransford, Brown, and Cocking (1999b) critiqued current efforts in teaching and learning (including LCs), noting that educators do not always apply the three principles just discussed, particularly when working with adult learners or providing professional development. For example, instead of grounding professional development in an understanding of learner-centered approaches, administrators expect individuals to attend particular workshops rather than ask their faculty or staff what they need. In addition, new teaching and learning techniques or concepts are presented without the opportunity for individuals to understand why, when, where, and how the information or technique might be integrated into current practices.

Professional development opportunities are not always assessment centered. Once the workshop or conference is over, individual faculty or staff members must often work out how to integrate the material into their jobs or classes on their own. If a given technique fails to work, there is often no professional feedback as to how to adapt and improve it. For LC members to change practices or develop new understandings, they need to provide opportunities for individuals to try things out and to receive feedback along the way. LC designers and administrators do not always make space for individuals to assess the impact of a new technique or strategy but, rather, make implementation the end goal. Furthermore, Bransford et al. (1999a) note that many professional development activities are not community centered and that they occur in isolation. Proper assessment efforts should consider the ways that assessment can support a learner-centered, assessment-centered, and community-centered LC effort.

The Assessment Cycle

This section offers a conceptual tool to assist in meeting the challenge of assessing the impact of LCs. The tool is an overview of the assessment cycle, but it is presented in a way that considers its role in overall program planning and implementation. Figure 7.1 presents the assessment cycle based on assessment and curriculum design models (Huba & Freed, 2000; Wiggins & McTighe, 2005). Clearly, application of the assessment cycle is foundational to effective assessment of LCs and deserves extensive discussion. Strategies for each phase of the cycle are described in more detail in the following section. However, a few important aspects of the assessment cycle are worth special note here.

What many people associate most strongly with assessment—collecting and interpreting evidence or data—is only one of the five phases in the cycle. It is neither the first phase nor the last. Without the important foundation provided by the assessment cycle, institutions may start at the bottom of the cycle as they design programs and then apply various assessment tools to determine whether the programs worked. We contend that assessment must be a focus early in the planning process. To begin exploring the impact of

FIGURE 7.1
Assessment cycle for improved learning.

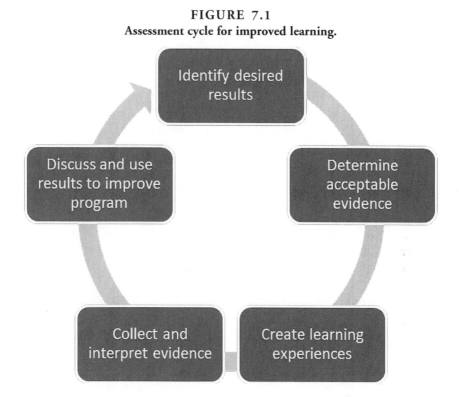

LCs, it is important to begin at the top of the cycle and first identify desired results (e.g., learning outcomes, broad programmatic goals such as retention) that serve as a guidepost for programs and activities. Wiggins and McTighe (2005) describe this as a backward design process, in which one begins with the intended end results. It is analogous in many respects to the concept of strategic planning. In strategic planning, one develops a vivid vision of what the institution should initially look like and accomplish in the next three to five years, and then one goes through an extensive process of analyzing what the institution can and should do now to make that vision become reality.

It is also important to note that the cycle relies on the discussion and use of results to improve the program. This phase restarts the cycle at a new level. Assessment findings emerge from discussion of the data, not directly from the data themselves. In other words, this is an ongoing process that requires institutions and individuals to discuss and use information in order to revise efforts consistently. The cycle explains that this is a systematic and ongoing effort, rather than an exercise in collecting data and then stopping. We encourage the use of this model as planners develop and implement an assessment plan.

We recommend that a steering committee or work group, with pertinent representation from the primary stakeholders as discussed in "Building Partnerships to Support Powerful LC Development" in chapter 2, work with the LC assessment coordinator in planning all phases of the assessment/evaluation. Full participation in this group by one or two students is desirable. The group should be large enough for legitimate representation but small enough for fruitful discussion, perhaps no fewer than 5 members and no more than 12–15. Note that once the work group identifies the assessment plan and proposes a cycle of implementation (e.g., focusing on one or two specific goals at a time), subsequent assessment work will be less difficult as the process matures and develops useful tools. A useful planning guide for this process is Walvoord's (2004) *Assessment Clear and Simple*, which provides a short and direct overview of how to design and implement an assessment plan.

B. L. Smith et al. (2004) offer several reasons why this cycle often is *not* used in practice. First, institutions and LCs are not as systematic as implied in the cycle. This is particularly true for assessment efforts, which sometimes appear to be an afterthought in response to a question or charge. Second, different individuals work on the various components or parts of the cycle, so it can be difficult to integrate information about goal setting and design, communicate results, and/or use analysis to inform practice. Third, programs such as LCs often operate with limited time and resources that may be focused on logistics and operations to support the program. This leaves little time and money for assessment. Fourth, individuals used to the framework of assessment being primarily at the end of a program may put off assessment until the program is more fully developed and then rush through the cycle.

As the start of this chapter made clear, we feel strongly that for LC assessment there must be a close connection between learning and assessment. While the cycle presented offers a structured approach, we note that this is a fluid process and that it is iterative. The following discussion offers additional insights into how LC planners can use the cycle to inform assessment. Although there are clear benefits to the backward design process, we recognize that the phases will often need to be considered at various points in time, rather than flowing in the more sequential fashion shown in Figure 7.1. The discussion does not occur only at the end but often carries through each of the different phases in the cycle.

Strategies for Assessment to Create Powerful LCs

LC planners can create powerful LCs by applying the strategies of the assessment cycle. Each of those strategies will now be presented.

Identify Desired Results

Assessment first needs to provide useful information that addresses the key questions, purpose, and/or goals associated with the LC. The end goal here is to design assessment processes in a way that supports the utility of the effort, including who needs the assessment results and what basic questions each group needs answered, rather than to construct perfect instruments. For example, assessment data directed to learners themselves may answer the question: Am I learning efficiently? Assessment directed to teachers and facilitators may use data to gauge what material needs to be reviewed or clarified. Or to the director of a program, assessment data may answer questions necessary to justify the need for additional resources.

Suskie (2004) recommends starting with clear statements about the intended goals/objectives of the program. These statements should include specific details about both the broad program-level goals and the goals for individual participants within the program. The key in both cases is that the goals/objectives be stated in tangible, concrete, action-oriented terms that are unambiguous and clear-cut (e.g., analyze and solve problems, advocate personal views, and refute opposing views; make appropriate inferences from information and explain how inferences apply to practice).

There should be intentional alignment between the program activities and the intended outcomes. The effort to match goals, activities, and assessment measures not only is important for the development of effective assessment, but also promotes intentional design of LC activities and programs. Efforts to explicitly state intended learning outcomes and to intentionally align learning experiences with the intended outcomes will support the ability to gather accurate information within the financial, social, legal, and other limitations.

The overall format used in Table 7.2 was developed at Iowa State University (ISU) to help develop intended learning outcomes for individual SLCs and can also be used with PLCs. This outcome writing model follows the acronym ABCD (**A**udience, **B**ehavior, **C**ondition, and **D**egree) in order to outline the various components that need consideration when developing an intended outcome and provides key questions for each component (Heinrich, Molenda, Russell, & Smaldino, 1996). It is helpful for individuals who

TABLE 7.2
Developing intended learning outcomes.

Item	Key Questions for Consideration
Audience	Who does the outcome pertain to—students, peer mentors, faculty, staff?
Behavior	What do you want them to be able to know, think, or be able to do? Check program statements or syllabus for ideas.
Condition	What circumstances or context will support the intended learning behaviors? What activities will help to ensure that the intended learning happens?
Degree	To what degree will the learning occur? How will you know if the learning occurred?

are new to writing outcomes and allows a clear focus on the questions of who, what, how, and how much. In other words, LC planners can develop clear statements about learning or performance in terms that are clear and consistent. Table 7.3 presents an example for the development of a global awareness learning outcome. Using such a table, LC developers can formulate a specific outcome through thoughtful consideration of the answers to key questions and discussion of the intended learning.

The importance of starting with the intended learning outcomes cannot be understated. Take, for example, the case of SLC development at Skagit Valley College. Faculty at Skagit Valley began SLCs in the 1980s as part of an effort to begin integrating the disciplines. In 1993, the faculty established several learning goals in a revision of the general education requirements, including helping students understand connections among disciplines. Skagit then determined that SLCs could be an effective structure to support achievement of the outcomes and made them an integral part of its general education program and degree requirements from that date forward. Currently Skagit schedules more than 50 SLCs each year. About half of Skagit's SLCs are team taught with the course work fully integrated and the faculty from each course in the classroom at all times, for instance, "Feast or Famine" (Nutrition and Sociology) and "Sex.comm" (Human Sexuality and Mass Communication).

A second SLC structure links pairs of courses with one or more overlapping assignments. These include most composition-based and all developmental SLCs, for example, "Stating the Matter" (Chemistry and English Composition) and "Reading Between the Numbers" (developmental Math and Reading). While the level of integration varies, the expectation is that

TABLE 7.3
Example of learning outcome development for global awareness.

Broad goal: Connect global and multicultural awareness to students' understanding of self and their future roles in the discipline.

Item	Responses to Key Questions for Consideration
Audience	• First-year students in an LC.
Behavior	• Better understand self as part of a global society. • Enhance understanding of own culture (self-identity) and awareness of other cultures. • Analyze how global issues apply to the discipline. • Develop awareness of global/multicultural perspectives and how to explore their impact.
Condition	• Explore self-identity through group activities. • Write guided reflective papers and do critical exploration. • Work in teams (teamwork) to identify and explore a global or multicultural issue that impacts the discipline. • Present in teams (written, oral communication) one disciplinary process or method that is influenced by culture or global context. • Identify similarities and differences based on local/global contexts in presentation.
Degree	• Students will identify specific issues, disciplinary processes, or knowledge that is influenced by cultural or global contexts. • Students will explain how their cultural identity influences their understanding of self and their disciplinary field of interest. • Students will articulate similarities and differences of disciplinary processes or knowledge that result from different cultural/global contexts. • Students will develop an awareness of and a curiosity of the impact of global/cultural issues (both personally and professionally). • Students will develop their ability to assess the influence of cultural/global issues on their professional field and formulate strategies for personal development.

Resulting Outcome: Students in the ACME first-year SLC will explore cultural self-identity and articulate similarities and differences of disciplinary processes in different cultural and global contexts through guided self-reflection activities, identification of cultural/global issues that influence the discipline, group presentation of similarities and differences in disciplinary practices in various global contexts, reflection of personal application to demonstrate understanding of self-identity, and application of cultural/global contexts and understanding to disciplinary practices or issues.

all SLCs emphasize collaborative, interdisciplinary learning and that students work together in small and large groups to prepare projects, panels, or papers that show their understanding of the connections between the two fields of study. The point here is that the structure of learning experiences follows the development of intended learning outcomes, which are the foundation of powerful learning.

Determine Acceptable Evidence

Once programs determine intended learning outcomes, they should direct attention to ways of measuring those outcomes; in addition to measures, there may be supplemental indicators (indirect evidence of the outcome) that can contribute to evidence that the intended outcome did/did not occur. This section provides an overview of various tools available to LCs. Before providing examples of specific tools, we provide a brief overview of different forms and purposes of assessment tools (formative vs. summative, direct vs. indirect, quantitative vs. qualitative).

Assessment tools can be characterized as either formative or summative. Formative assessment is used as a midpoint check to help improve the program and support its development; participants provide information about their experiences in a way that allows program developers to adjust activities. For example, a faculty LC may offer its participants formative assessment when reviewing a sample assignment design. Other faculty members might provide feedback to the faculty member and offer strategies for additional changes to the assignment. Another example of formative assessment is ISU's use of a satisfaction survey to explore students' perceptions of a common reading program used within several SLCs. Results from the survey help to determine ways to improve the program in the future, such as ensuring that there was a direct connection to the course and an effort to integrate the discussion with current content.

Summative assessment typically happens at the end of a program and provides information about the overall impact or success of the program. For example, at the end of a semester-long learning circle program, a faculty LC may provide individual members with summative assessment by critiquing the teaching philosophies they each developed throughout the course. Another example of summative evaluation is an evaluation of the program-level goal of improving student retention. Whalen and Shelley (2010) tracked SLC participant and nonparticipant retention rates at ISU from 1998 to 2008. The longitudinal impact of improved student retention brought about by the university's SLCs demonstrates the financial value of the program, which pays for itself through additional tuition revenue from students who would otherwise not have remained at the institution (see www.lc.iastate .edu/reports_overview.html).

Assessment tools can also be characterized as either direct or indirect. Direct measures are tangible sources of information that come from participants' work. Examples of direct evidence include scores of student papers using a rubric or reviews of self-reflection essays, capstone experiences, work samples, portfolios, poster presentations at the end of a development program, or peer review of syllabi. Indirect measures are often self-reported measures of individuals' perceptions or levels of satisfaction. These might include satisfaction surveys, ratings of knowledge and skills, student placement rates, or other secondary data from institutional records.

When comparing these two forms of assessment, indirect assessment data may provide an indirect measure of the outcome or goal but should be viewed as an indicator. Indirect measures may not relate a complete story and are often less clear or less convincing (Suskie, 2004), but their presence can add important support to the evidence provided by direct measures.

The last set of categories for assessment tools divides them into quantitative and qualitative. Quantitative assessments use numbers to categorize individuals' responses (e.g., test scores, ratings using a scale, or rubric scores). Qualitative assessments use flexible and natural processes (e.g., interviews, focus groups, or self-report questionnaires). Our purpose in this chapter is to highlight specific strategies and tools for assessment, rather than discuss methodology for specific types of assessment activities (e.g., quantitative survey design, focus group protocols). For a useful overview of assessment methods, interested readers can consult *Assessment Methods for Student Affairs* by Schuh and associates (2009).

The choice of assessment tools should flow from the questions posed about the LC. Tables 7.4 through 7.7 (placed toward the end of this chapter) offer example tools that institutions use to assess SLCs. However, the goal is not simply to select a tool, but to ensure that the information from that tool will align with the intended learning outcomes for the LC. We subscribe to the notion that the tool should not drive the data collection effort; if a commercially available tool or one used by others does not exactly measure your intended outcomes, it may be preferable to develop your own customized tool. As Maslow (1966) noted, if all you have is a hammer, everything you see starts to look like a nail.

Here is where individuals engage in an important phase of the backward design described by Wiggins and McTighe (2005). Recall that following the assessment cycle, individuals developing the LC (or reviewing its current efforts) have identified the intended results. Now the emerging design considers these types of assessment questions as adapted from Wiggins and McTighe:

- What evidence would show that participants achieved the desired results?
- What types of tasks, products, or other evidence will support achievement of these results and guide the design of learning experiences in the community?
- What should we look for to determine the extent of learning in the LC?

Often people do not naturally ask these types of questions when planning an LC. Instead, it is easier to jump to the design of activities, assignments, and program logistics without asking about the alignment of these efforts with the intended outcomes. There is a distinct approach to this backward design process that involves thinking like an assessor. Instead of asking, "What activities would be interesting for the LC?" ask, "What would be sufficient and revealing evidence of learning that resulted from our activities?" The distinction here is important and moves beyond semantics. Once LC designers establish a clear sense of the intended learning outcomes or results of the program, individuals should consider the questions presented here as a way to think about how to assess those outcomes.

In the structure of this chapter, a summary of some useful tools that can assess LC efforts has been intentionally put toward the end of the chapter, in the subsection entitled "Review Desired Results, Evidence Needed, and Other Steps of the Assessment Cycle." This summary is included in the hope that readers will continue to think about the entire assessment cycle and fully consider the benefits of how a holistic review can inform the development and implementation of assessment that will promote learning in the LC. In other words, we hope to avoid some of the pitfalls mentioned earlier that interfere with the use of the assessment cycle by reducing the temptation to find a simple solution in an existing assessment instrument.

Instead, LC organizers might consider the benefits of this grounded approach. In its response to our survey, Cabrini College noted that one of the most important aspects of its LCs is that "quantitative data pertaining to student outcomes [indicate that LCs] are 'value added' and demonstrate direct impact." Here, Cabrini College recognizes the benefit of collecting evidence regarding students' achievement of the intended results. We are confident that programs that attend to the backward design can also explore the question: "How does our LC have impact?"

Collect Needed Evidence

Earlier chapters in this book address the third component of the assessment cycle, "create learning experiences," so we shift attention now to the process of collecting evidence. This phase moves beyond the backward design process but provides the return on investment for earlier work in thinking about how to assess the intended results. The process for collection (and later the analysis and interpretation) of evidence will largely depend on the first parts of the assessment cycle. For example, a group trying to assess the needs and interests of a developing PLC in order to develop an ongoing program will collect different information than a group trying to determine the ways that an online LC promotes engagement with course material and class discussions. Therefore, we provide less structure here about the steps of this process but instead offer some suggested practices.

First, the group that is developing an assessment plan should consider what information might already be available (e.g., previous assessment, embedded program information, institutional research, campuswide surveys) that could offer evidence that aligns with the intended program results. Note here that the criteria for selecting these data begin with a clear focus on the intended results.

While it is common for higher education programs to ignore or simply be unaware of existing assessment information (Blaich & Wise, 2011), it is also common to experience a data dump, in which individuals struggle to sift through an excessive amount of information to find out what is truly relevant or useful for the program. We encourage developers to think about what data could help to inform the program and to develop partnerships with other parts of the institution that could help to identify information needs or assist with future LC development efforts.

Second, the group should consider what are the most cost- and time-effective strategies for gathering evidence (B. L. Smith et al., 2004). As already implied, assessment activities should make use of multiple measures and indicators to improve assessment reliability and validity, but even more important, those activities must be manageable. Institutions should focus their efforts on a few instruments and data collection activities that target the key program outcomes and result in the most impact. They should also limit the number of data collection activities so that the collected information is used to address the key outcomes for the LC (Suskie, 2004). Furthermore, the data collected and the methods used to collect it are of no avail if one does not collect it with care.

The first step, which considers existing evidence, is also a great start for this strategy because it avoids wasting resources on replication of existing data. Another cost- and time-effective strategy is for LC organizers to identify the most pressing questions about the LC and focus attention on a select number of outcomes or goals. This effort will allow the group to narrow the scope of assessment and determine how best to answer those questions. The assessment cycle is an ongoing process, so it is perfectly reasonable for LCs to invest in and consider different areas of focus at different points in time.

Another effective strategy for reducing cost and time is to take full advantage of the backward design process through embedded assessments. Here the term *embedded* refers to tasks that result in products that align with both intended learning outcomes and the evidence needed to demonstrate achievement of the outcomes. Embedded assessments can thus do two jobs for the price of one: enhancing learning and assessing it.

An example of this comes from LC developers at Portland State University, who describe their SLC courses as "assessment-driven." Portland State worked with the Carnegie Foundation for the Advancement of Teaching on a three-year project devoted to integrative learning that began in January 2004. The purpose of the project was to provide students with purposeful, progressively more challenging, integrated educational experiences. Portland State's LCs were developed so that students would experience peer-to-peer connections, obtain deeper thinking, and have a place where they can have a sense of connection. They use embedded assessment (exercises, quizzes, dilemmas, etc. used periodically throughout the semester that contribute to student learning at the same time it charts progress being made) to gather evidence about student outcomes. The university describes its SLC assessment process as "incredible!"

Several institutions have an SLC program that involves many individual LCs (e.g., different majors). This shapes how developers think about and frame the assessment process in a way that allows assessment at multiple levels (individual LC and collective program as a whole). One way to support both of these efforts and to track the collection and interpretation of evidence is to incorporate assessment into the planning templates or program proposals.

Consider the example from ISU that is presented in Table 7.4. Note that this format helps to align individual and program-level outcomes and supports the alignment of outcomes with both learning experiences and evidence. In short, this simple format not only helps to promote the ability to consider ways of aligning assessment efforts, but it also encourages individuals to follow the backward design process.

To reiterate what was discussed earlier, assessment activities should make use of multiple measures and indicators to improve assessment reliability and validity, but even more important, those activities must be manageable. Institutions should focus their efforts on a few instruments and data collection activities that target the key program outcomes and result in the most impact. They should also limit the number of data collection activities so that the collected information is used to address the key outcomes for the LC (Suskie, 2004). Furthermore, the data collected and the methods used to collect it are of no avail if one does not collect it with care.

Analyze and Interpret the Evidence

When planning and conducting the data collection, carefully consider how to go about viewing, analyzing, and interpreting the evidence once the data are compiled. This is true even though the assessment phase should be a completely neutral and separate activity that is not biased by expectations engendered during that earlier process. When analyzing and interpreting the data, one must completely understand and be cognizant of everything occurring during the earlier phases while not letting that knowledge bias assessment results.

Knowledge about what was discussed in the previous two subsections must be brought to bear when trying to understand the data and what the data mean. For instance, identify which data are direct measures and which are indirect measures (and possible sources of error). In fact, during the planning phase or prior to looking at any of the actual data, it is recommended that one develop "dummy data tables" and enter expected results, write summary statements about those expected results, and ask whether the questions driving the assessment will be answered by those data. Conducting such a preactivity will help one interpret the actual data within a proper context. One useful activity is to pilot instruments or to conduct an initial review of existing data to begin the process of making meaning from the data. We find that it is important to return to the initial goals outlined for

TABLE 7.4
Sample assessment template.

Intended Learning Outcome	Corresponding Program Outcome	Specific LC Experiences That Promote This Outcome	Assessment Plan: Evidence or Artifacts to Determine Whether Outcome Has Been Achieved
Example: Students will develop competency in communication and technical skills to make effective presentations.	Be able to present an effective oral report.	• Students training in basic PowerPoint skills • Individual and group presentations in class • Guest speakers and attendance at one or more events in the lecture series • Follow-up discussion after lecture series events	• Instructor and peer evaluation and critique • Final presentation showcasing skills learned • Self-review and critique of videotaped student presentations
Example: Students will use critical thinking and problem-solving skills in applied situations.	Be able to apply knowledge to solving real-life problems.	• Linked course assignments • Analysis of case studies • Field trips to observe actual work situations • Service-learning projects • Study groups and team problem-solving exercises	• Instructor evaluations of projects and assignments • Student journals and self-evaluations • Observations of students • Follow-up discussions on case studies, field trips, and service-learning experience

the LC as a way of ensuring that the data and interpretation align with the important assessment questions. Thus, if discrepancies between the expected and actual outcomes occur, one will generally know where to look for explanations.

Unlike empirical research studies, assessment/evaluation generally uses only simple descriptive statistics such as means, medians, modes, standard deviations, cross-tabulations, frequencies, and percentages. Much useful information can be obtained if (a) such statistics are profiled graphically for the group and subgroups therein, and (b) similarities and differences in the patterns are examined. It is important to remember that "means" can be misleading if the frequency distribution is not examined at the same time, that the possibility of response bias should be analyzed in questionnaire and interview data, and that group differences on other characteristics (e.g., input variables) should be taken into consideration during the analysis of specific learning outcomes.

Statistical tests such as *t*-tests, chi squares, analysis of variance, and correlational analysis will often be needed to supplement useful "eyeballing" across groups and profile analysis. However, one should steer clear of using pre- and postchange scores, and instead examine final status on the variable of concern for individuals with similar initial levels on the variable; those who have more sophisticated statistical backgrounds or who have assistance available from statisticians might prefer to apply analysis of covariance using a standard statistical package such as SAS or SPSS.

The LC assessment coordinator should develop one or more written reports that show analysis and interpretation of the data through tables, profiles, and interpretive narrative. It is recommended that different tailored reports be prepared as appropriate for different user groups. And one should not forget that discussion of the data—not the data themselves—leads to the pertinent answers, decisions, and actions. Too often such reports end up in a filing cabinet or on a shelf, and they never get discussed or contribute to the formulation and carrying out of decisions and actions. In many ways, the phase that follows is the most important phase of all.

Discuss and Use Results

Blaich and Wise (2011) noted that the initial plan for the Wabash National Study of Liberal Arts Education was to develop a series of useful assessment instruments that would allow institutions to gain insight into important factors that influence student learning. The study designers initially thought that the problem facing institutions was the lack of information, but they quickly realized that the challenge was not the difficulty in collecting information, but instead the inability to make meaning from the information they collect and then turn that meaning into actionable strategies.

This brings us to the critical aspect of the assessment cycle that stipulates programs need to (a) determine the effectiveness of the program activities in relation to the intended outcomes, (b) determine the ongoing progress of the program, and (c) discuss how to improve the program. This book subscribes to what, in the authors' personal experience, has commonly been called a "judgments team" approach, which involves a diverse group of individuals meeting periodically to discuss in depth all of the relevant data that have been made available to and studied by them ahead of time and arrive at actionable conclusions.

It is valuable to involve a number of participants with different perspectives in the work of making meaning from assessment information. The judgments team could be the same group as the steering committee/work group discussed earlier for the planning phases of the assessment cycle. Perhaps more desirable, however, is a judgments team with representation from all important stakeholder groups that is selected and recruited solely for the evaluative (judgments) phase. This strategy will introduce a fresh, more neutral perspective and get additional stakeholders involved, which could become important later.

The judgments team should definitely not limit its observations and discussion to the intended outcomes. Sometimes unintended and serendipitous outcomes—whether negative or positive—end up being the most important outcomes of all for the program director, stakeholders, and institution to acknowledge, grapple with, and act on. For example, the team may note that students participating in the LC are more likely to develop group study sessions that continue throughout students' careers. Even if this was not an explicit outcome for the program, designers should note this impact and its potential benefits.

The judgments team should be provided with the analysis and assessment phase report or reports (tables, profiles, and interpretive narrative) well ahead of the initial meeting of the team. The team should then study it ahead of the meeting and be prepared to discuss and make judgments about what has been reported.

It is very effective for the judgment sessions to be held during a couple-day retreat following the academic year. Or sessions could be conducted periodically over several weeks during the academic year at dates and times convenient for all members. Normally the judgments team sessions will be chaired by the area or program director, although another respected member of the group who has experience in facilitating group discussion could be selected for the task.

Essentially, this group judgment process is a logical exercise. It is similar in many respects to a detective solving a crime based on gathered and organized clues, or to a weatherman predicting the weather based on information about various conditions, or to a medical doctor making a diagnosis after studying the charts, or to a mechanic troubleshooting to discover what is wrong with an automobile. These analogies may in fact be usefully presented to members new to the judgments team process.

It is crucial that members maintain a complete record of the judgments team sessions Follow-up findings and related recommendations for improvement emerging from the discussions should also be communicated to constituents in an effective/motivating manner. In addition, it is desirable to send brief tailored memos to pertinent decision makers. In the memos the needs and recommendations (why and how) for specific actions in a particular area and how those actions will contribute to program improvements and sustenance should be detailed.

Review Desired Results, Evidence Needed, and Other Steps of the Assessment Cycle

Recall that in Figure 7.1 an arrow from the final step in the circle returns one to the desired results step. Now that you have reviewed the data-reporting and use step, for example, you may be able to state the results desired in a way that will be more concrete and useful to the pertinent decision makers. Similarly, at the next circular step you may realize that other evidence than what you had proposed and how to best gather it may be more readily accepted and illuminating to those decision makers.

Since by this time in the cycle, the second time around, you have presumably considered the entire picture and noted all of the cautions to consider, now may be a critical time to take a careful look at, and be stimulated by, the three tables of data-gathering examples, Tables 7.5, 7.6, and 7.7. As noted previously, carefully examining this summary earlier in the process may have caused you to be less circumspect and open to other data gathering methods, instruments, and processes that could in fact be more useful for your institution and culture. Conversely, after having gone through the entire cycle in a preliminary manner, you should now have a better total picture of your assessment needs to guide you in making your assessment choices.

TABLE 7.5
Participants' ratings of experiences/learning.

Instrument	Overview
Washington Center LC student survey	Information on dimensions of student experience that are associated with LCs, such as integration of concepts from different disciplines. See www.evergreen.edu/washcenter/project.asp?pid = 108.
ISU LC survey	Student perceptions of the LC experience combined with modules that explore how experience contributed to specific learning outcomes (e.g., communication, teamwork, understanding of self). See www.lc.iastate.edu/assesstools.html.
Classroom assessment techniques	Taken from the work of Angelo and Cross, these represent formative assessment tools to gain a quick insight into participants' learning. • Focused listing: Give to students a word or phrase connected with an important concept. Students write list of words and phrases related to the topic. • Misconception check: Create a simple question to elicit information about students' ideas and beliefs related to a common misconception. Explain the reason for using the technique and ensure anonymity. • Minute paper: What was the most important thing you learned during this class? What important questions remain unanswered?
Focus group protocol	Readers will want to create their own protocol to solicit participant feedback in targeted ways. A simple format comes from the Group Instructional Feedback Technique in Angelo and Cross (1993), which asks: (a) Give an example of something that helped you learn, (b) Give an example of something that interfered with your learning, (c) What are you (as an individual) doing that contributes to your learning? and (d) What are you doing that detracts from your learning? Readers can also consult Schuh and associates (2009) for more information.
MAP-Works	MAP is the acronym for "making achievement possible," and this comprehensive assessment and early warning system (also an insight-stimulating teaching tool about self) was developed over a number of years by Ball State University in partnership with Educational Benchmarking (EBI). This online system provides immediate feedback to the students and also transmits relevant student information to her or his advisor for review and contact with the student as needed. See www.webebi.com/retention.

TABLE 7.6
Assessment of student work.

Instrument	Overview
VALUE Rubrics (Association of American Colleges and Universities)	The VALUE rubrics reflect faculty expectations for essential learning in the Essential Learning Outcomes identified by AAC&U (e.g., critical thinking, written communication, problem solving, civic knowledge, and engagement). See www.aacu.org/value/rubrics.
National Project on Assessing Student Learning in Learning Communities Assessment Protocol	Qualitative collaborative assessment protocol used to review samples of student work. See www.evergreen.edu/washingtoncenter/docs/intlearning/protocol.pdf.

TABLE 7.7
General assessment resources.

National Institute for Learning Outcomes Assessment (NILOA)	Provides information on tools that universities and colleges commonly use for assessment. See www.learningoutcomesassessment.org/ToolKit.html for a tool kit that includes instruments that measure learning, such as tests, surveys, portfolios, and curriculum mapping.
Assessing Online Learning	"Assessing Learning in Online Education: The Role of Technology in Improving Student Outcomes," found at www.learningoutcomesassessment.org/documents/OnlineEd.pdf, considers how emerging techniques, such as data mining and learning analytics, allow the use of performance and behavioral data to improve student learning.

The Rest of the Story

Look back at the scenario at the beginning of the chapter. Maria and Lamont did not consider the assessment cycle before they began their LC program. Now they face the task of demonstrating the impact of the LC without a baseline measure. Even though they may not have explicitly considered the assessment cycle, Maria and Lamont can still use the assessment cycle. They should identify the intended outcomes or results of the program that they expressed in their initial proposal. They should think about evidence that might align with the stated out-comes, conduct an audit of existing data that might serve as evidence, and examine any additional sources of information that could be useful.

Rather than randomly search for a "quick and easy" assessment—from an institution that is quite different from theirs—or creating a "satisfaction" survey that does not relate to their proposal, they should specifically look for a tool that measures their intended outcomes. They could review some of the instruments identified in Tables 7.5–7.7 to see if there are aspects that would help inform their assessment of the program or they could conduct a series of focus groups with current participants. They could also use a team approach in which multiple individuals would assist in the process of making meaning from the information.

Conclusion

Effective assessment offers important insights into ways to promote powerful learning. Assessment and evaluation that focuses on LC improvement and is well designed must be integrated early in the LC development planning process. The design must be learner centered and focus on helping the LC optimize learning. It is also crucial that faculty and other key stakeholders see the process as assisting and supporting them in improving the program toward an optimum level of performance.

A variety of data collection approaches, including qualitative and quantitative methodologies as well as direct and indirect measures and indicators, is desirable. Differentiating among the data-gathering process, the assessment process (analyzing and interpreting data used to describe effectiveness), and the evaluation process (using assessment evidence to make judgments about worth and how to improve effectiveness) is important. It is crucial to realize that it is group discussion of the data (e.g., by a judgments team) and effective dissemination of findings emerging from that discussion that lead to action solutions, not the data themselves.

For Reflection

As you create your own meaning from ideas in this chapter, begin to think about a specific LC at your institution (or at an institution you know about if you are in a governmental or other noninstitutional role) and how it can inform your work or interests. Use that LC to answer the following questions and help you reflect on practical implications of the material in this chapter:

- How has assessment/evaluation been a part of the earliest planning for the program? Has it been discussed seriously by an effective program planning steering committee/work group with representation from all important stakeholder groups?
- How has LC assessment at your institution provided individuals and the total institution with an opportunity to reflect about optimum student learning?
- To what degree has the backward design process of the assessment cycle for improved learning been applied to LC assessment/evaluation at your institution? How could this be improved?
- How does the assessment/evaluation process at your institution view the purpose of data?
- Do data at your institution serve to provide action solutions or provide fodder for discussion that leads to action solutions? If so, how? If not, why?
- What should an appropriate judgments team for assessment/evaluation of the LC program at your institution do and how should (does) it operate?
- What is the best strategy for LC assessment at your institution?
- What foundational questions do you need to ask when starting an assessment effort?
- Which of the keys to good assessment practice in this chapter are true of assessment for your LC program and which are not?
- Which of the tools commonly used by colleges and universities to assess learning (see Tables 7.5–7.7) should your LC consider adding to its assessment toolbox?

Now that you have read and reflected on this chapter, you should be able to complete the following items on the Powerful LC Planning Form in Appendix C:

- Section III: #3. "What norms do you want members to follow and how will you ensure accountability?"
- Section III: #4. "What resources are needed for your LC to be successful?"
- Section IV: #1. "Brainstorming Your Learning Plan."
- Section IV: #2. "Developing Your Assessment Plan."
- Section IV: #3. "Closing the Loop."

8

PREVENTING AND
ADDRESSING POTENTIAL
PROBLEMS

8

What's the Story?

Dr. Graves, president of Private College (PC), is committed to learning communities (LCs) and would like to make the institution a premier learning organization to rival nearby Liberal Arts College (LAC). Despite a lack of enthusiasm from the faculty and staff, Dr. Graves pushes forward with a plan modeled after LAC.

LAC gained national recognition for the way that its LCs aligned with the college's mission to "promote social justice and educate students to be globally aware." Thus, its linked courses tie core requirement classes in social justice with composition classes. Although PC does not require social justice courses, Dr. Graves assigns the sociology chair, Lynn Glum, to design and oversee the linked courses.

The development office is able to raise some funds for the linked course initiative. Unfortunately, processing the linked courses overloads the computer registration system. Repairing the system was expensive and time-consuming. In addition, several staff members had to manually redo numerous student schedules. Because of the extra expense, no funds remain to train instructors or to offer stipends and workload reductions as originally promised. By the end of the term, most of the sociology faculty feel burned out.

The next semester Dr. Glum cannot get enough sociology faculty members to volunteer to teach a linked course, so she feels pressured to teach one herself. Her course is linked with a course taught by new faculty member, Dr. Rios. Dr. Rios asks to set up a few meetings to discuss how they will integrate their courses, but Dr. Glum says she does not have time to meet; she just sends him a copy of her syllabus and assignments. Dr. Rios is annoyed but does not say anything.

Dr. Rios spends a lot of time promoting social interaction in his class. Although he does not lay down any ground rules, the students bond very closely

8

with one another. Cliques form in the group and students develop immature rivalries. At times, students get completely off task, but Dr. Rios chalks that up to the costs of having lively discussion. One student bursts into tears after the rest of the group called her a "wimp" for not aligning with the prevailing opinion of the group. When the group goes to Dr. Glum's class, the students often behave in the same way. They tell her that Dr. Rios is "much cooler" and that Dr. Rios told them they did not have to do one of Dr. Glum's assignments. Dr. Glum is furious.

What problems and pitfalls does this LC face?

Our students invite change even as they demand new ways to earn their degrees, and our society seeks leaders who will ask the difficult questions and have the courage to identify good solutions to big problems. In learning communities, open inquiry and a desire for connection are nourished and taught. The future of learning communities is ours to construct.

—B. L. Smith, MacGregor, Matthews,
and Gabelnick (2004, p. 345)

This quote is a reminder that LCs provide a "good solution to big problems" only if we are willing to ask the difficult questions regarding what students need for optimum learning to occur and also have the courage to press ahead with complex rather than less effective simple solutions. The previous chapters have described in some depth the process and techniques that lead to constructing and sustaining powerful student LCs (SLCs) that yield optimum student learning. Constructing and sustaining powerful nonstudent LCs (professional LCs and learning organizations) that play an important role in creating such long-lasting SLCs and that are similar in concept and operation have also been discussed in detail.

Here we provide a revealing overview of the book by returning to key topics and discussing potential problems and pitfalls and proposing their solutions.

Overcoming Potential Problems for LC Success

The research literature discussed previously demonstrates conclusively that well-designed/implemented SLCs significantly and positively affect both students and faculty in important ways. However, for such SLCs to flourish and thrive, their supporters may have to prevent or overcome various potential problems. Lenning and Ebbers (1999, pp. 70–72, 75–85) identify and discuss many potential problems and pitfalls that can threaten "the fruition and longevity" of LCs if they are not dealt with in an effective manner.

Based on their experience in developing and implementing SLCs, respondents to the 100-Institution Survey identified additional potential problems that LC designers and coordinators must be cognizant of and prepared to overcome. We have organized these potential barriers into 10 broad thematic categories, which are listed in Table 8.1 along with sample concerns that typify each category as well as the number of responses that related to each thematic concern.

Some responses addressed multiple concerns, and some fit into more than one category. Figure 8.1 highlights the percentage of respondents who reported at least one item that fit into a given potential problems category. Thus, the categories with a high percentage of responses can be seen as areas of greater concern for LC attention. For example, nearly half of the respondents identified administrative concerns, while only 19% identified recruitment concerns and only 11% identified assessment. Although recruitment is an important potential problem, administrative concerns rank higher. Ideally of course, one must be aware of all potential problems and make efforts to avoid or transform them. Specifics pertaining to each category and suggestions for overcoming the problems identified are summarized in the following subsections.

Administrative

Possible Concerns. A total of 47% of the respondents mentioned administrative concerns. Administrative buy-in is an area of particular concern. There can be either too little or too much buy-in by the administration. Too much buy-in often results in a top-down mandate that causes faculty and support staff to feel left out of the process. In such cases, faculty/staff often have a lack of real commitment, excitement, and effectiveness about implementing and maintaining powerful SLCs. One survey respondent reporting such a problem indicated that the administrative problem had been resolved over time, but that vestiges remained in the minds of some faculty and these traces may never completely go away.

Too little administrative buy-in results in a general lack of interest and limits appropriate incentives (financial or otherwise) and infrastructure support for SLCs. The lack of buy-in affects LCs at all types of institutions, as shown in the following three examples. One state university survey respondent stated, "The administration can be a problem through saying or implying that LCs are not cost-effective or are too expensive, providing

TABLE 8.1
Categories of potential problems for LC success as reported in the 100-Institution Survey.

Thematic Categories of Potential Problems	Sample Concerns Identified	Number of Respondents Reporting Concerns
Administrative	Administrative buy-in, top-down decision making without getting adequate lower-level input, planning, coordination, oversight, funding, infrastructure, top-level support	38
Assessment	How complicated it is to assess effectiveness of LCs, need for assessment that demonstrates financial value of LCs, lack of knowledge locally pertaining to effective LC assessment	15
Curricular	Curricular planning, integration, interdisciplinary concerns, designing across disciplines, course linking, consistency	21
Faculty/staff participation	Lack of faculty/staff interest, commitment, buy-in, enthusiasm, participation, involvement, and shared vision; also loss of interest and burn-out	18
Faculty/staff interaction	Team interaction, relationships, workload, team communication, staffing, training	28
Collaboration	Collaboration, flexibility, community development	29
Recruitment	Student recruitment, targeting, marketing, topics attraction, student demand and expectations	15
Logistical	Student registration, selection, placement, scheduling, logistics, technology problems	27
Student conduct	Lack of discipline/responsibility, groupthink, hyper-bonding, immaturity, misconduct, cliquishness, oversharing, poor participation, poor attitudes, social focus rather than academic	22
Other potential problems	Lack of role models, inadequate advising, need for ground rules, confusing of quantity with quality	7

inconsistent support or conversely micro-managing." A respondent from a private college commented, "LCs sometimes begin with external funds and then later face difficulty institutionalizing the initiative when the funding runs out." A community college respondent reported, "It can be difficult to obtain administrative buy-in to team-teaching and large-credit courses."

FIGURE 8.1

Percentage of institutions reporting for each category of potential problems pertaining to LCs.

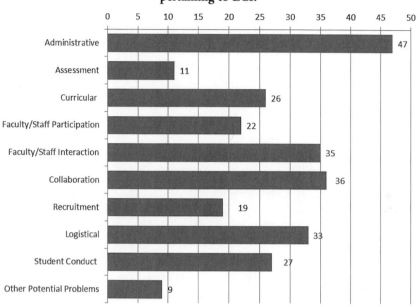

Moreover, even at institutions where there is initial buy-in, other concerns may distract the administration from focusing on LCs. Included among these distractions are economic recession and budget problems, to which a number of respondents referred; the unbridled growth of the institution, to which one state university respondent referred; and various other campus incidents that may occur, such as alumni complaints or student demonstrations.

It should also be realized that strong administrative buy-in and effectiveness in gaining total campus support for LCs do not ensure that there will be administrative effectiveness in organizing, coordinating, and providing oversight for LCs. As one state university respondent stated, "There is good support from the top administration on down (think LCs are very important) and they have good connections with the department chairs, but it is a challenge to convince others on campus about the value of LCs." Another state university respondent stated, "Deciding how to address such issues is a complicated problem." Still another state university respondent stated, "I think the greatest challenge in sustaining them [LCs] is finding the structures that will provide what students and faculty/staff need to keep going." A respondent from a private university reported, "I think the greatest challenge in sustaining LCs is finding the structures that will provide what students and faculty/staff need to keep going."

Survey responses that illustrate other common administrative problems—such as coordination, planning, funding, and infrastructure—include the following:

- "Balancing faculty, staff and student interests can be difficult."
- "The LCs need to perform in the ways that we tell students and parents that they will."
- "Figuring out who is doing what can be a problem."
- "The maximum numbers of students per section needs to be lowered, but we could not close off sections."
- "When the grant dollars ran out in 2005, money for LCs became scarce and the program leader was reassigned; SLCs . . . thus lacked leadership."
- "In some institutions, divides exist between academic affairs and student affairs that would make collaboration difficult or impossible to achieve; effective collaboration is necessary for an LC to work."
- "We build as we go, but it would be better to perceive well ahead of time what might help."
- "This program is very resource intensive for the academic departments, which in turn places a strain on the college's resources."

A respondent from a private university emphasized the danger that "the maintenance and sustenance of LCs can become stale and neglected." This danger is illustrated by a public university that in the first half of the previous decade had an array of well-developed arts and sciences college SLCs that, according to a former LC coordinator of the program, "faded away" because:

1. "Firm institutional commitment and funding from the top" within the College of Arts and Sciences eroded after the admission standards changed, the associate dean went back to the classroom, the college was reorganized, and several LC coordinators were transferred to different areas or left the university. "Perhaps the LCs would have survived if they had reported to the provost with campuswide academic commitment and funding."

2. "Faculty enthusiasm and intellectual leadership" waned because the "LC coordinators' leadership and recognition from the dean's office" disappeared. Gradually the full-time faculty tired "of the extra work involved in planning integrated, theme- or major-based linkages" and "academic departments did not always support their best faculty members' expending extra time and effort on LC work." As a result, increasingly "part-time faculty or TAs who lacked time for or consistent interest in LC involvement" were assigned the "general education classes needed for the LCs."

3. The formerly "capable and committed administrative assistants willing to do the intensive, summer-long enrollment management necessary to offer the LCs at summer orientations" began to lose their commitment to it being "a student-centered effort" and to view this task primarily as a "job." The new First-Year Experience (FYE) course does not provide "an academic or pre-professional focus for . . . LCs, . . . just an advising or student orientation focus" and "is taught by staff or TAs, not faculty from a general education discipline. FYE is not linked to any content class(es), major, or theme. . . . Thus, while personal support and learning and adjustment strategies are offered, this class is no longer part of a larger LC."

Possible Solutions. Called for is an enlightened and sensitive but forthright and active administration fully knowledgeable about and committed to the importance of effective SLCs and providing appropriate incentives for and to them. One respondent stated, "Having support from administration, getting faculty support, managing the logistics (housing assignments, pre-enrollments in courses, etc.), and developing assessment are all key activities." Another stressed, "The programs need to be endorsed and supported—ongoing—from the top, support that solicits active participation from the institution's departments, and values faculty participation."

Such an administration works together harmoniously and in full partnership long term with all relevant groups throughout the institution on exploring, adopting, and supporting financially and otherwise the development and maintenance of optimal SLCs. An extremely important part of this process, as made clear by one community college respondent, is to provide "vital and motivating professional development in the efficacy of LCs so that administrators, faculty, and students 'buy in' to the concept." Through such means, the administration is in effect promoting and helping to create a powerful learning organization culture, as discussed in chapter 5.

A state university respondent made a related and equally important suggestion:

> I think the common often-mentioned problem is gaining respect and acknowledgment from department chairs. I've found, though, that two components may change this. First—the curricular theme. We were always a social-justice-oriented program, but once we officially established a Peace Studies focus, then faculty began contacting us. Another element is the establishment of the LCs office—with a director whose charge it is to communicate with departments.

Similarly, another state university respondent reported, "There must be a strong and intricate collaborative partnership between academic affairs and student affairs for such LCs to succeed; in my experience, failure is assured [sic] if such a close and harmonious relationship is missing." A respondent from a small private college concurred and went beyond this statement, saying, "Working together and coordinating effectively with academic affairs, student services, admissions, registrar, and librarians as well as advising is critical."

The administration must also accomplish other important goals pertaining to LCs as summarized by the following respondent statements:

- "Start small and keep things as simple as possible—then grow the program as you have success and gain experience."
- "Don't forget to plan for and consider all the administrative functions that must happen behind the scenes if one is to have a successful LC program."
- "Sometimes hyper-bonding occurs; when it does occur we recognize that it is a management problem and not the LC that is at issue."
- "Develop and implement positive assessment."
- "Insure [sic] that the various LCs and faculty therein are monitored on an ongoing basis to be certain they are doing what they should be doing."
- "I think the leadership needs to be very clear about the LEARNING outcomes of the communities so that deeper learning remains the top priority (in addition to social and retention benefits)."
- "At times we may need to reeducate our campus community, including faculty. As new people join the faculty and staff it is important to orient them in a way that gets them excited about the program and

helps them internalize the original vision at the same time as they bring fresh ideas and insights that are helpful."

In our view, three respondent statements well summarize all of these:

1. "If the best faculty members are involved with students who are committed to the process, and the university provides the appropriate infrastructure and funding, then everything will go smoothly."
2. "Having a complete understanding of the academic landscape of your institution is crucial for implementing LCs. Don't follow a set model but adjust the model to fit your institution."
3. "You need to do assessment that will demonstrate the financial value of the program—ours more than pays for itself—it's an excellent investment, especially in tough budget times."

Where there is a will there is usually a creative way to overcome the LC problems faced, as illustrated by Lenning and Ebbers (1999):

> Those involved in initiating LCs at Iowa State University for the fall semester of 1995–96 reported they did not have time to focus on the long-term development and implementation of a well-designed and comprehensive assessment and evaluation plan for the project. They also felt that they lacked knowledge and expertise in both LCs and their assessment and evaluation. In response, the director of ISU's Center for Teaching Excellence asked the chair of ISU's Professional Studies in Education Department for help, and the authors were assigned to develop a plan for implementation and assessment. (p. 71)

Over the last 15 years, the SLCs at Iowa State have gained national prominence. Moreover, an article by Anne Krapfl (2011) titled "ISU Learning Communities: A 71 Percent Capture Rate and Growing" on the university's website in 2011 reported impressive student outcomes:

> Students don't pay any additional fees to belong to one, but history shows a LC goes a long way in their academic success at Iowa State. In a recent 15-year recap, the average one-year retention rate for Iowa State freshmen in LCs is 8 percentage points higher (89 percent vs. 81 percent) than those not in a LC. The average six-year graduation rate is 12 percentage points higher (74 percent vs. 62 percent). . . .
>   Last fall, nearly three out of every four freshmen (71 percent) participated in one of Iowa State's 84 LCs. The rates vary among Iowa State's

undergraduate colleges, from 98 percent in Design, to about 44 percent in Liberal Arts and Sciences. (Recall that undeclared students enroll in that college; those without a major are less likely to identify a LC.) In between were Business (54 percent), Human Sciences (74 percent), and Engineering and Agriculture and Life Sciences (about 86 percent each). (para. 1–2)

A full listing of ISU LC highlights from 1995 to 2010 is posted at www .lc.iastate.edu/LC_15yr_success.html. To see copies of the many formal reports of LC assessment studies conducted at ISU, visit www.lc.iastate.edu/ reports.html.

Assessment

Possible Concerns. Several areas represent potential problems as organizations look to integrate assessment into their LC efforts. One primary problem is a lack of organizational support for assessment. Some institutions or organizations fail to understand the assessment cycle and how it relates to program improvement in a systematic way. When assessment is viewed as an add-on activity designed to meet accountability pressures, it can limit the overall buy-in for the process. An additional problem is lack of clarity regarding the purpose of assessment as it relates to LCs. Often, assessment of programs or activities becomes focused on doing the assessment rather than having a grounded understanding of/focus on the end goal (e.g., improve learning in LCs).

A common problem that many assessment efforts face is not implementing a systematic process that attends to the full assessment cycle. This can create multiple challenges in different ways. For example, programs that do not identify the intended learning outcomes will eventually find it difficult to use any assessment measures in a meaningful way to support program improvement. Another pitfall is failing to review assessment efforts as part of the assessment cycle. A final problem to consider is the failure to develop an implementation plan for assessment plans.

Unfortunately, assessment is not a priority concern at many institutions. Assessment problems such as the aforementioned were only implied by the 15 respondents referring to assessment as a potential problem or pitfall to consider in implementing SLCs. For example, one respondent stated, "Deciding how to address problems is a complicated problem."

Possible Solutions. In conducting assessment, it is important to get all members throughout the campus involved in appropriate and effective ways. As emphasized in chapter 7, assessment must have a positive and clear-cut purpose that is understood and endorsed by all throughout the institution. One must speak to concerns, keep conversation positive, and focus on purpose and how that purpose can best be achieved.

One respondent remarked, "Develop and implement positive assessment." This means that the discussion and focus should be on affirming what we are doing right and how to improve, rather than on accountability; too often faculty in particular see the danger that assessment will be used to justify cutbacks and accountability rather than for formative purposes such as improving LC effectiveness and demonstrating that LCs are a good investment (see the quote about this in the previous subsection).

As also emphasized in chapter 7, there must be a systematic assessment plan that aligns with the stated purpose. Assessment should never be seen by anyone throughout the institution as an add-on and must be considered seriously at an early point in any program development activity. Questions to ask prior to creating an assessment plan include: Does the program have clear purposes that guide assessment? Why is the assessment being done? Who will use the findings? How will the information be used to improve learning? Simply put, the reasons for assessing the LC need to include more than "we need to do assessment."

When starting an assessment effort, planners should consider the following questions: Will assessment lead to improvement? Is assessment part of a larger set of conditions that will promote change? Is assessment focused on questions that people care about? Does assessment have institution-wide support and involvement? Without the necessary support for assessment, it can be difficult to sustain an effort to apply the full assessment cycle adequately.

Program planners should also consider the following questions: What are the most cost-effective and time-effective strategies for gathering evidence? What is a realistic timeline? Who will be responsible for gathering, interpreting, and reporting evidence? Do we have the right team to carry out activity? How will we communicate and use results? How and when should individuals share and reflect on results? What other stakeholders should receive information? One resource for developing implementation plans is the use of a logic model (see the *W.K. Kellogg Foundation Logic Model Development Guide* [W. K. Kellogg Foundation, 1998] for an example).

Programs that fail to study their assessment process (conduct an assessment audit) to ensure that it is complete and effective may neglect to integrate existing information into their assessment efforts. Assessment efforts that fail to examine information from different program activities or learning experiences separately and then compare and contrast the results across those entities (disaggregate) will struggle with cause-and-effect questions pertaining to identifying whether and how specific program activities are having a desired impact. Assessment efforts that end with a written report that summarizes data but fails to prompt shared conversations that lead to program improvement represent labor-intensive efforts that never close the loop. Incorporate the full assessment cycle into your efforts.

Curricular

Possible Concerns. Problems identified by the retired coordinator of a once strong SLC program that had "faded away" over a five-year period focused on a curricular problem: FYE is not linked to any "content class(es), major, or theme as was [the previous FYE course]. Thus, while personal support and learning and adjustment strategies are offered, this class is no longer part of a larger learning community." Statements such as this were common in the survey results; 26% of respondents reported that integration across courses and working across the disciplines too often does not get addressed adequately.

Particular respondents stated the problem as follows:

- "Not all faculty at the university are supportive of integration across the curriculum."
- "Traditional disciplinary structures tend not to fit and be supportive of interdisciplinary ventures."
- "An appreciation for integration across the curriculum is not being institutionalized."
- "Are courses really integrated or simply being taught 'parallel' (i.e., a common theme but two clearly separate courses)? If material is not truly integrated students may feel like they are wasting their time."
- "Sometimes too much priority is put on course scheduling; that is not the key to whether they are linked or not."
- "The large numbers of faculty required can get in the way of a focus on the interdisciplinary."
- "Creating the right kind of course for a broad audience can be difficult."
- "Sometimes the collaboration and coordination between linked courses breaks down."
- "There is danger that the courses could become stand-alone."
- "We have an open curriculum where students choose, so we have competing student interests."

- "Forty basic skills are dealt with, which is complex."
- "It may be difficult to deliver different curricula using the same model; e.g., it may not be possible to deliver Business in the same manner as Design."
- "The transfer student market needs such LCs also, but is often ignored."
- "The common goals may not be on some participants' own agendas."

Possible Solutions. In response to these problems, the following are specific solutions that particular institutions surveyed are using that could profitably be employed by others:

- "We are requiring faculty to produce a single syllabus for all LCs—thus encouraging them to address the issue of integrating material prior to getting into the classroom."
- "The design element receives input from experience outside the discipline."
- "Define exactly what you're trying to accomplish."
- "Although one leads to the other, student learning needs to be emphasized to faculty and students more than student bonding."
- "You must make sure that the curriculum is useful. The majority of LC classes fulfill general education credits. Students are becoming much more practical and they want to know they will gain the leadership skills they need—and the credits they need. We just happen to teach those credits with a greater emphasis on integration of disciplines, as well as on speaking, writing, and research."
- "From an institutional perspective, it may be tempting (and easier) to create LCs for special groups of students, but then the initiative may remain as an add-on to the rest of the curriculum."
- "It is important to avoid 'boutique' LCs—ones that appeal to the faculty, but do not necessarily help students meet their educational goals."
- "Check with the advising staff before finalizing the LC course offerings!"

Other responses were more philosophical but also suggestive:

- "Keep students' needs at the center of the program, which requires careful planning and implementation (what courses do students need/ want to take? What times work best for them? etc.)."

- "No problems if you talk to and obtain agreement from *all* relevant constituencies and stakeholders."
- "It can also help if *all* faculty members agree to read, during the summer, several of the same books on innovative teaching and learning."
- "A third consideration is course selection—departments and/or faculty may want to cluster courses that don't make sense for the target population of students, or that have a time conflict, or prerequisites."

Faculty/Staff Participation

Possible Concerns. For SLCs to become powerful, full-time faculty throughout the institution (including senior faculty) must be interested in and enthusiastic about SLCs, committed to leading and participating in them, and have a strong personal vision of what SLCs can accomplish for students if done well. However, as reported by 22% of the survey respondents, obtaining acceptance and/buy-in from the faculty is a serious problem at some institutions. For example, a community college respondent reported, "Getting faculty buy-in, especially from full-time faculty, can be difficult." Other respondents reported similar observations:

- "Faculty member interest in doing LCs is spotty."
- "Finding enough willing faculty to lead these various efforts can be a serious problem."
- "Our faculty members in LCs are now beginning to move on to other things."
- "Getting new faculty involved in LCs can be a problem."

A number of survey respondents reported more-specific problems in this area pertaining to faculty members:

- "Others may not see this as exciting and invigorating as you do."
- "A common faculty vision and plan and faculty interest may be lacking; if the faculty members are not excited about the LCs it is not good for the students."
- "There is difficulty of getting full-time faculty involved in the integrated LC courses when no release time is provided to faculty; they have had to get lots of adjunct faculty involved, and it is not the same."

Possible Solutions. Again, respondents reported activities that helped them overcome such problems: A state university respondent stressed, "Develop a vision statement and publish your intended outcomes." Another stated, "LCs are not likely to work if they are directed from 'the top down'; their success depends on faculty creating collaborations and driving the development of courses."

You must not only get faculty/staff interest but maintain it. "Develop a plan to replace people so that when one 'champion' leaves a program does not disappear." "Develop a reward and recognition program to publicly show people are valued." Other solutions are implied in the way the following two respondents expressed their concern regarding faculty interest. "Faculty participation in LCs does not feed naturally into the promotion and tenure system." "There is difficulty of getting full-time faculty involved in the integrated LC courses when no release time is provided to faculty; they have had to get lots of adjunct faculty involved, and it is not the same." Faculty are busy people, dealing with many time-consuming responsibilities and expectations. Providing incentives such as tenure credit and release time can help gain and maintain faculty interest. Ultimately, LCs being faculty inspired and initiated is a key.

While there are clear benefits to LCs, not all faculty are aware of how LCs can help them and their students. As one respondent noted, "Faculty need to be educated about LC benefits and processes." Appendix H: "Call for and Evidence of Educational Change" reviews the research results documenting the many important benefits to faculty from participation in SLCs, and we contend that realization of those faculty outcomes provides the best way to prevent or overcome the problems for faculty just identified. As one institution reported:

> LCs have been much more effective than we had imagined in fostering collaboration and cooperation among faculty from different disciplines. We had envisioned that the recruitment of faculty to participate in the program would be problematic and we were pleasantly mistaken. Faculty report that their teaching and enthusiasm in the classroom have been reinvigorated. The somewhat experimental nature of our LC program has provided faculty the opportunity to be more creative and innovative in the classroom.

Faculty/Staff Interaction

Possible Concerns. A total of 35% of the respondents referred to faculty/staff interaction as a problem area. A respondent from a private university summarized the problem as follows: "It is difficult to develop and cultivate the close peer and faculty relationships that are needed; and too often we get needed timely information out too late. We are searching for more-effective training and organization that will achieve the kind of interaction desired, and a better method of sharing with shareholders." A community college respondent saw this as the primary problem area for the college and summarized the concern in just a few words: "Getting the faculty to work together, scheduling and staffing." A respondent from a small private college raised the faculty load issue: "Because of the time and energy required to have such close linkage across courses, it places a heavy workload on the faculty members."

Other respondents provided additional specifics that can help one better understand the concern:

- "Team teaching and integration *requires* especially close and collaborative instructor relationships."
- "Some teachers want to do traditional teaching in the LCs and not collaborate with faculty colleagues in that activity."
- "Building trust; faculty members have fears of other faculty looking into what they are doing or not doing and making judgments."
- "Keeping everyone working together is a constant battle requiring much energy."
- "Just as good matches between instructors carries over to the students, so do poor matches when they occur."
- "There is extra workload for the faculty members early in the process."
- "Faculty participation in LCs does not feed naturally into the promotion and tenure system."
- "There is always a danger that some faculty members will revert back to stand-alone teaching techniques."
- "Faculty members must be careful not to let the LC sessions exceed the given time limit; if the discussion is hot and heavy, let them continue it outside of class."
- "Sudden shifts in faculty staffing can lead to problems."
- "Many faculty members want to teach, not facilitate and flexibly challenge."
- "Our LCs do not need great additional cost or overhead [so] faculty/staff sometimes dedicate limited time to them and feel some courses do not need the linkage specified."

Possible Solutions. A primary recommendation for solving problems and issues in this area is to have the institutional reward structure provide meaningful credit toward rank and tenure for LC collaborative activities with faculty colleagues. A state university respondent to our survey stated, "The faculty reward structure (for promotion and tenure) rewards loyalty to the disciplinary research agenda, which can interfere with faculty loyalty to the interdisciplinary goals of the LC program and cooperation with colleagues in such collaborative activities." Equally important, one respondent suggested, "The institution needs to provide more financial reward for investing time in this endeavor, which will encourage related faculty collaboration."

Ongoing professional development and training was another primary recommendation provided by a number of respondents:

- "The importance of ongoing professional development for faculty in designing, teaching, creating assessments, and assessing integrative experiences cannot be overemphasized."
- "At times we may need to reeducate our campus community, including faculty. As new people join the faculty and staff it is important to orient them in a way that gets them excited about the program and helps them internalize the original vision at the same time as they bring fresh ideas and insights that are helpful."
- "Have frequent professional development opportunities to keep people involved and connected to others who are doing similar things."
- "Visit other schools to see what they're doing and send a group of people to a conference."

Still another primary recommendation was provided by a respondent from a private college:

From the perspective of each LC, it is important for faculty to be in communication with each other and prepared to respond to student dynamics. Faculty members who have not communicated with each other about expectations may find students playing one faculty member off against the other (as in "We weren't told that in Prof. Smith's course" or "Prof. Smith didn't say we had to cite our sources").

Collaboration

Possible Concerns. By definition, LCs are designed for extensive discussion and other collaboration among and between all LC members. When such collaboration is missing or ineffective, the LC is not effective. A total of 36% of the survey respondents perceived this as a potential problem. They described the problem and its components as follows:

- "Not all collaboration is effective."
- "LC members need to be flexible and collaborative, and sometimes that does not happen."
- "Students need to be more flexible."
- "There needs to be effective social collaboration and flexibility among faculty, among students, and between students and faculty in order for LCs to work, and sometimes that can be difficult to stimulate into happening."
- "Collaboration involves effort, challenges, and bridging that many are not willing to attempt."
- "Sometime[s] we try to force community, and that is not productive."
- "In some institutions, divides exist between academic affairs and student affairs that would make collaboration difficult or impossible to achieve. Effective collaboration is necessary for a LC to work."
- "Engaging in LC can be a very natural thing, but sometimes (especially early in the process) it is not. Sometimes things get so busy and hectic within a LC that it is difficult to schedule needed appointments with important stakeholders."
- "In the nursing learning LC there is too much competition among the students, which gets in the way of collaboration and cooperation."
- "Too often there is a culture or atmosphere of not participating."
- "What should the professor do if students do not seem amenable to discuss and work together?"

The opposite collaboration problem can also develop, which one respondent referred to as "groupthink."

As indicated by the following respondent comments, faculty members' ineffectiveness in collaborating with students can also become a problem:

- "Faculty members can become defensive and not transparent at times."
- "Faculty and students *must* work more closely together."
- "Faculty should include students in the planning whenever possible."

- "The biggest challenge is topics that are continually changing through rotation and replacement, and all first-year seminar faculty members rotate through a cycle."
- "Sometimes focusing on the theme gets left out."

Possible Solutions. The following specific solutions to these problems that are being used by particular surveyed institutions could profitably be employed by others:

- "Communicate extensively with everyone so that they all know what is going on. During LC orientation and training, whether intended for LC leaders or for participants, encourage them to collaborate by trying to give more than they take and give credit to the other person."
- "There needs to be more celebrating in a LC, e.g., celebrating the end of the academic year by visiting a museum in the city."

A respondent from a private residential university had this to say about collaboration:

For the first 10 years, all aspects were basically "owned and operated" by the faculty and existed separate and apart from the Student Life division. . . . [The LC] was directed by an associate dean who reported to the dean of academic affairs. . . . Under a relatively new president and a new dean of students, the program was restructured such that the residential aspects of the program were now under the purview of the Student Life division. The program is still ultimately administered by the associate dean . . . (who) works closely with the Director of Residence Life . . . to coordinate the residential component of the program with all other aspects of the program. This structure is much more effective at taking advantage of the relative expertise of the two divisions, creating a stronger program overall. However, this structure is impossible without effective communication and a collaborative approach to making decisions about the program.

Two ways we increase that collaboration is by having a joint retreat each year among the student life staff who work with first-year students, the academic staff who work with the program, and all of the faculty teaching within the program. In addition, we have a policy-making body . . . council . . . chaired by the associate dean . . . and [it] includes four elected faculty and one appointed staff member from Student Life. Hence, Student Life is always "at the table" when important decisions are being made about the program.

Recruitment

Possible Concerns. A total of 19% of the survey respondents refer to effectiveness of marketing LCs to students and recruitment of LC members as a serious problem for many SLCs, although one respondent reported that it was a problem only in the beginning and now the demand for LCs exceeds the availability. Several of the respondents indicated that they see this problem area as the most serious one that they face with respect to SLCs.

The reasons that student recruitment into SLCs is a problem area are illustrated by a number of respondents' comments:

- "Figuring out how to best market LCs is complicated."
- "Getting the word out to such a large and diverse student population is *not* easy."
- "Sometimes the formation of new communities has not been student interest/need driven."
- "Some topics—e.g., the sustainable environment themes—attract students better than other topics."
- "The faculty members have to recruit the students."
- "The LCs have not been keeping their visibility up."
- "Not all of our advisors believe that LCs work; they advise their students against taking LCs, which makes it difficult to populate them."
- "We have limited counseling and advisement for new students, so it is difficult to communicate with students about why they might be interested in taking LC courses."
- "Not meeting the demands of students is potentially the big problem."

Ineffective recruitment of SLC students may lead to SLCs that are too small to be effective, desirable, and cost-effective; this can lead to the cancellation of needed SLCs. It can also lead to student dissatisfaction with the experience or have other unintended consequences such as students (and/or their parents) perceiving they were misled. One respondent stated, "If the message is not clear, sometimes it is not clear in students' minds as to what LCs are all about so they get into the wrong LC and lack commitment to it."

Possible Solutions. It is important that students receive, are stimulated by, and pay attention to promotional messages about LCs, and that they truly come to understand what LCs are all about and get into the right LC for their needs. Therefore, the messages conveyed to students must be eye-catching, accurate, concise, timely, and "hip" and be seen by them as plausible and true. Multiple messages that mutually reinforce one another and that are sent through different channels and modes of communication are essential. Attractive, high-quality brochures that will reach the students are needed, as well as brief and well-designed reinforcing messages through a well-designed and attractive institutional web page, press releases, institutional publication articles, direct faculty contact, phone messages, e-mails, texting, Facebook, Twitter, and so forth. Encourage current LC members to tell prospective students and current student nonparticipants about the LC and their positive experiences therein.

Several survey respondents offered additional suggestions:

- "The LCs need to perform in the ways that we tell students and parents that they will."
- "Students are becoming much more practical and they want to know they will gain the leadership skills they need—and the credits they need. We just happen to teach those credits with a greater emphasis on integration of disciplines, as well as on speaking, writing, and research."
- "When implementing student LCs, it is imperative to have student feedback and buy-in for the community to be successful. Faculty and staff can identify a great 'idea' but if students are not interested, the community will not flourish and be successful."

Logistical

Possible Concerns. A third of the survey respondents referred to logistical concerns as potential problems. More often than not, their comments referred to problems with computerized registration and scheduling systems. The following comments are from respondents at a community college, a private college, and a state university, respectively:

- "We have the Banner administrative software system for course registration, and it does not lend itself to registration for groups of courses; it has to be done manually, which makes student registration for LCs difficult."

- "Scheduling blocks of time for specific student cohorts and for team teaching is a complex and time-consuming matter because the computerized administrative software system is not designed for such matters."
- "The registration system does not allow block registration, so the scheduling for LCs must be done manually."

One institution indicated that because of the time and energy required to register and schedule students manually, it had gone from scheduling four courses per LC cohort to two courses.

Sometimes registration and scheduling problems do not pertain to technology, as indicated by the following comments:

- "It is difficult to have a LC targeted at certain student majors, such as education, because they have too many courses to get in during the first year of college."
- "It becomes confusing to students if you give them too many options."
- "Scheduling and logistics are the most serious potential problem. So many of our students work and have families."
- "Sometimes too much priority is put on course scheduling; that is not the key to whether the courses are linked or not."
- "Another problem is that registration is all online."
- "Keeping everyone on the same page and making the logistics work."
- "The mechanism for dropping and adding is inadequate."
- "Self-enrollment of students becomes a LC logistical problem."

Possible Solutions. If the registration system is not compatible for logistics and scheduling, it is important to work with the software provider and/or your technical staff to get the problem corrected. Attaining and maintaining powerful LCs is too important for manual registration and scheduling of LCs to become a long-term solution. Several survey respondents made helpful suggestions that pertain to LC registration, scheduling, and placement, such as the following:

- "Simplify the registration process."
- "Having support from administration and getting faculty support for the proper management and assessment of LC logistics (housing assignments, pre-enrollments in courses, etc.) is important."

- "Simplify the registration process."
- "Students in learning communities have priority registration in key courses in the community."
- "If you select only one of the classes in the learning community when you register, the registration system will ensure you are registered for the other class(es)."
- "What makes our learning community program unique is special registration where the LC team registers students for their fall classes."

Student Conduct

Possible Concerns. A total of 27% of the survey respondents referred to student LC misconduct problems. The majority of these misconduct issues are related to groupthink and what some have called "hyper-bonding." The following respondent statements describe these concerns and their causes:

- " 'Groupthink' can become a problem."
- "Hyper-bonding, where students feel so comfortable that they talk in class, interrupt, and engage in other inappropriate behavior."
- "Because of the open and free environment within the LCs, sometimes community members lose self-discipline and exhibit undesirable hyper behavior."
- "The free-flowing interaction that is encouraged could in some cases lead to hyper-bonding that can result in immature behaviors, talking in class, or even joining together to go against a disliked professor."
- "Cohort mentality sometimes leads to students knowing each other too well, which can result in noise in the classroom, them doing what they want to do rather than what we want them to do, sharing of sensitive matters such as roommate problems, etc. Things are messier in a LC."
- "Hyper-bonding—students become too comfortable and speak while the instructor is speaking—is sometimes a problem."

Other disruptive attitudes and inappropriate behavior by individuals or the group can also lead to problems, as illustrated by the following survey responses:

- "Absences and late papers can be a problem."
- "Some of the students are savvy enough to operate outside the set boundaries."

- "Everything is so familiar to the students that it becomes difficult to maintain a structured environment."
- "Students who know one another before entering the LC [can engage in behavior that] can result in classroom disruptions."
- "Sometimes traditional-age students naturally revert to high school behavior, e.g., boyfriend–girlfriend issues."
- "Some students fall behind in one or more classes and are invited to withdraw."
- "Interest in the LC varies for different students—some students do not feel the connection—and students' interests change over time."
- "The common goals may not be on some participants' own agendas."
- "Some participants do not see LCs as exciting and invigorating."

Possible Solutions. Hyper-bonding interferes with LC relationships and both individual and group learning, so it is essential to plan ways to deal with it. Some of the survey respondents spoke to this:

- "Cliquishness can develop; we are alert to it, so insure [*sic*] there are some things that all students do together."
- "Hyper-bonding, where the students are more into the social than the academic and exhibit cliquish and other inappropriate behavior, is an early challenge that is new for full-time faculty getting involved for the first time in working with LCs. The faculty must be oriented and trained ahead of time in how to handle such student behavior when it arises."
- "When hyper-bonding occurs, we recognize that it is a management problem and not the LC that is at issue."

LC participants also need effective up-front orientation, guidance, and assistance for other reasons, such as managing personality conflicts and personal concerns or receiving accommodation for disabilities. Survey respondents made a number of suggestions to help accomplish this, including the following:

- "Define exactly what you're trying to accomplish."
- "We need to acknowledge that although engagement within an LC can be a very natural thing, sometimes (especially early in the process) it is not."

- "Although one leads to the other, student learning needs to be emphasized to faculty and students more than student bonding."
- "When grading together is used, make clear to the students who have the responsibility for assigning the grade."
- "Competition among the LC participants gets in the way of collaboration and cooperation, so discourage it."

Other Potential Problems

The survey respondents mentioned the following additional potential problems:

- "We are asking students to take a package [set program of tied components] where they might not live in a certain room."
- "Not all of our advisors believe that LCs work; they advise their students against taking LCs."
- "All freshmen co-gather so [they] have a freshman mentality; they need upper classmates as role models."
- "There may be too much competition among the students, which gets in the way of collaboration and cooperation."

Still other potential problems were worded as guidance rather than problem identification:

- "Some students are not prepared for participation in a social community, so up front the ground rules should be emphasized and made clear."
- "Trying to force people in a certain direction or to act in a certain way is generally counterproductive, so don't try it."
- "LCs are a great way to raise the bar and challenge students academically. But it is important to ensure that you are not confusing quality with quantity—giving students more work does not equate to students doing *better* work."
- "Make it fun and enjoyable."

Lenning and Ebbers (1999) identified other potential problems in a question-and-answer format. Some of those were alluded to but not identified by those responding to our survey.

The Rest of the Story

Look back at the scenario at the beginning of the chapter. The various episodes described illustrate problems and pitfalls in almost all of the thematic areas discussed in this chapter:

Administrative Concerns: There is too much administration buy-in by President Graves, so that LC work seems like a top-down mandate, while there is too little buy-in by the department chair. Oversight of allocated monies seems to be a problem.

Curricular Concerns: The linkage of courses is being applied based on what worked at another school, rather than integrating core courses from PC.

Faculty/Staff Participation Concerns: Because the LC project is top-down, many faculty are less than enthusiastic. Many feel burned out after one semester and refuse to participate more. Dr. Glum's participation is merely obligatory.

Faculty/Staff Interaction Concerns: Faculty do not receive promised workload reductions. Dr. Glum and Dr. Rios do not work well together. They feel angry and irritated with one another, but do not meet to resolve issues. This allows the students to pit the professors against one another.

Collaboration Concerns: Dr. Glum does not collaborate with Dr. Rios to integrate their courses.

Logistical Concerns: The registration system does not work, requiring costly repairs and manual registration.

Student Conduct Concerns: Dr. Rios allows the group to hyper-bond. The group grows cliquish, competitive, and disruptive. There are instances of groupthink, in which the majority of the group target a fellow student and Dr. Glum.

Conclusion

Many potential problems and pitfalls have been identified in this chapter. LC practitioners must be on the lookout for these issues and develop contingency plans to deal with them in an effective manner. Based on evidence provided by practicing LC coordinators, they may be avoided or dealt with swiftly and effectually.

For Reflection

As you create your own meaning from ideas in this chapter, begin to think about a specific LC at your institution (or at an institution you know about if you are in a governmental or other noninstitutional role) and how it can inform your work or interests. Use that LC to answer the following questions and help you reflect on practical implications of the material in this chapter:

- Which of the responses from the 100-Institution Survey resonate most for you or other members of this LC?
- Which of the categories of potential problems are most pressing for this LC? Why are these particular areas of concern?
- Which potential problems currently exist in this LC? How are members of the LC currently responding to these problems? Has this response been effective?
- What other practices or changes could be made to reduce or remove such problems?
- What contingency plans might be helpful for this LC to make in order to prevent or better prepare for potential problems that it has not yet experienced?
- How have the tools and resources included in the appendices— including the supplementary appendices G through M available in the e-edition of this book and at www.styluspub.com/resrcs/other/PLC .pdf—influenced the way that you now perceive this LC?

Now that you have read and reflected on this chapter, you should be able to complete the following item on the Powerful LC Planning Form in Appendix C:

- Section I: #7. "What are the potential problems for your powerful LC?" (Those problems, in turn, can relate directly or indirectly to any one of the other sections in the Powerful LC Planning Form.)

APPENDICES

A Note About the Appendices

For space reasons we have limited the number of appendices incorporated into the print edition of this book. The table of contents refers readers to seven additional appendices (G through M) that can be found online at www.styluspub.com/resrcs/other/PLC.pdf. They are also incorporated into the e-book edition of this volume.

APPENDIX A

Colleges and Universities Selected for the 100-Institution Survey

1. Abraham Baldwin Agricultural College
2. Appalachian State University
3. Arizona State University
4. Bowling Green State University
5. Brigham Young University
6. Brooklyn College
7. Bunker Hill Community College
8. Cabrillo College
9. Cabrini College
10. Cascadia Community College
11. Cerritos College
12. Chandler-Gilbert Community College
13. Citrus College
14. College of Charleston
15. Collin County Community College
16. Colorado State University
17. Crafton Hills College
18. Cuyahoga Community College
19. De Anza College
20. Delta College
21. Dickinson College
22. Dominican University
23. Duke University
24. Eastern New Mexico University
25. Elgin Community College
26. Flagler College
27. Florida Atlantic University
28. Fresno Pacific University
29. George Mason University
30. Grossmont Community College
31. Guilford Technical Community College
32. Hawaii Community College
33. Highline Community College
34. Hobart and William Smith Colleges
35. Holyoke Community College
36. Indiana University–Purdue University Fort Wayne
37. Inver Hills Community College
38. Iowa State University
39. J. Sargeant Reynolds Community College
40. Kennesaw State University
41. Kingsborough Community College
42. Kutztown University of Pennsylvania
43. LaGuardia Community College
44. Lane Community College
45. Lehigh Carbon Community College
46. Long Beach City College
47. Loyola University Chicago
48. MCC Blue River
49. Medaille College
50. Miami University
51. Middle Tennessee State University
52. Minnesota State University, Mankato
53. North Seattle Community College
54. Pace University
55. Passaic County Community College
56. Portland State University
57. Principia College
58. Richland College
59. Saint Louis University
60. San Diego City College
61. Seattle Central Community College
62. Skagit Valley College
63. St. Lawrence University
64. Stonehill College
65. SUNY Cortland
66. SUNY Potsdam
67. Syracuse University
68. Tacoma Community College
69. Texas A&M International University
70. The Catholic University of America
71. The Evergreen State College
72. The Pennsylvania State University
73. The University of Iowa
74. University of Alabama at Birmingham
75. University of Central Arkansas

76. University of Connecticut
77. University of Denver
78. University of Hawaii at Manoa
79. University of Illinois at
    Urbana–Champaign
80. University of Maryland, College Park
81. University of Michigan
82. University of Nebraska–Lincoln
83. University of New Mexico
84. University of North Carolina at
    Charlotte
85. University of North Carolina at
    Greensboro
86. University of North Dakota
87. University of Northern Colorado
88. University of Oregon
89. University of Rhode Island
90. University of Texas at Arlington
91. University of Washington
92. University of Wisconsin–Whitewater
93. Villanova University
94. Vista Community College
95. Wagner College
96. Washington State University
97. West Hills College Lemoore
98. Western Washington University
99. William Rainey Harper College
100. Yakima Valley Community College

APPENDIX B

Compendium of Key Factors Recommended in the Research to Build Powerful LCs

LC Design	Purpose and Goals	Collaborative Community	Culture for Learning	Group Norms and Accountability
Boyer Commission on Educating Undergraduates in the Research University (1998) 6 Guiding principles to understanding community	• Are purposeful	• Are caring • Are open • Are just • Are celebrative		• Practice discipline
Chickering & Gamson (1987) Principles of good practice to support learning in SLCs	• Have well-defined goals and objectives • Demonstrate shared purpose (participants, faculty, administration) • Have adequate funding	• Have common goals • Respect diverse talents/ learning styles • Encourage member and leader contact • Provide prompt feedback • Have reciprocity and cooperation among members	• Allow needed time for investigation • Encourage active learning	• Outline roles and responsibilities • Emphasize time on task • Communicate expectations

(continues)

Compendium of Key Factors Recommended in the Research to Build Powerful LCs (continued)

LC Design	Purpose and Goals	Collaborative Community	Culture for Learning	Group Norms and Accountability
Gardner (1990) 7 Elements of good academic communities		• Incorporate and value diversity • Practice shared learning • Have internal communication • Demonstrate caring, trust, and teamwork	• Foster development • Link to outside world	• Have group processes and governance strategies that encourage participation and shared leadership
Bielaczyc & Collins (1999) 11 Principles for LC design	• Show community growth • Show emergent growth • Articulate goals	• Have structural dependence • Show respect for others • Have diverse expertise • Share knowledge • Negotiate	• Practice metacognition • Go beyond the bounds • Are fail-safe • Privilege depth over breadth • Allow multiple ways to participate	• Have standards and expectations for quality of product
Wenger (1998) 4 Communities of practice		• Have a sense of identity	• Are meaningful • Demonstrate practice • Have sense of community	
Peck (1987) Introduction's definition of *community*		• Communicate honestly • Are inclusive • Have deeper relationships • Acknowledge differences and use consensus approach	• Are open to risk	• Practice conflict resolution

Lenning & Ebbers (1999) Definition of powerful LC	• Have common learning goals	• Demonstrate interaction/ interplay • Are celebratory • Maintain mutual trust and loyalty • Facilitate team building	• Focus on active learning • Are intentional	• Are accountable • Practice self-discipline
Moseley et al. (2005); Mentkowski and Associates (2000); B. L. Smith (2001)	Follow Association of American Colleges and Universities' educational outcome to help students successfully function in a "complex and volatile world"		• Develop strategic, reflective, and self-aware learners • Integrate thinking and promote deep learning	
Costa & Kallick (2000)		• Think and communicate with purpose and intention • Practice remaining open • Practice listening with understanding and empathy • Practice responding with wonder and awe	• Gather data through all senses • Create, imagine, and innovate • Think about thinking (metacognition) • Take responsible risks • Question and pose problems • Apply past knowledge to new situations • Think flexibly • Find humor • Engage in continuous learning	• Manage impulsivity • Strive for accuracy • Think independently

(continues)

Compendium of Key Factors Recommended in the Research to Build Powerful LCs (continued)

LC Design	Purpose and Goals	Collaborative Community	Culture for Learning	Group Norms and Accountability
Summary of evidence-based design factors	Are purposeful Have common, well-defined, and communicated: • LC purpose • LC objectives • Learning goals	Facilitate: • Relationships • Open and honest communication • Mutual trust, reliance, and loyalty • Shared learning • Team building	Intentionally plan to create: • A safe environment for risk taking and making mistakes • Multiple ways to participate • Opportunities for self/team reflection, awareness, and development Have activities to promote learning that is: • Active • Cooperative • Creative • Strategic • In-depth (time)	Clearly communicate: • LC group processes and governance strategies • Shared leadership roles • Member responsibilities • Expectations/standards • Timelines

APPENDIX C

Powerful LC Planning Form

This planning form correlates with the information from throughout the book. Use a separate form for each type of LC.

I. SETTING THE STAGE (see chapter 2)

A. Developing a Clear Purpose for Your LC

1. How did this idea for an LC come about? What was the trigger event? (see chapter 2)

_____

_____

2. Why are you doing this? (see chapters 2 and 5)

Check all that apply.

_____ New program
_____ Curriculum
_____ Student support (social)
_____ Student support (academic)
_____ Freshman experience
_____ Other _____

3. What are your overarching goals? (see chapters 2 and 5)

Prioritize the desired experiences (meaning) of the LC below.
a. Sharing of knowledge ____
b. Building of a solid foundation ____
c. Creation of depth and breadth of knowledge ____
d. Creation of quality ideas ____
e. Promotion of a variety of perspectives of content ____
f. Maintenance of process of governance structures ____
g. Shared leadership ____
h. Promotion of caring and trusting relationships ____
i. Shared experiences ____
j. Celebratory climate ____

4. Purpose Statement (see chapters 2 and 5)

Use your responses to the previous questions to create your LC's purpose statement.

_____

_____

_____

B. Conducting an Environmental Scan

5. Who are the stakeholders? (see chapters 2 and 5)

List the stakeholders, check whether they are a primary or secondary stakeholder, and explain why you feel they are a stakeholder.

Stakeholders	Primary	Secondary	Partnership

6. What resources (or sources of resources) are available to support the LC? (see chapters 2 and 5)

List resources already available to the LC and potential sources of resources.

Resources Available	Potential Sources

7. What are the potential problems for your powerful LC? (see chapters 2 and 8)

List problems you are concerned may impact your LC and provide possible solutions you could use to address or overcome them.

Problems	Possible Solutions

II. DESIGNING POWERFUL LCs (BLUEPRINT)

1. What will the LC look like? (see chapters 1–3 and 5)
a. Type of LC (check one):
_____ LO _____ PLC _____ SLC
b. Delivery format (check one):
_____ Face-to-face _____ Virtual/online _____ Hybrid
c. Duration of LC (check one):
_____ Brief _____ Short term _____ Long term/ongoing

2. How will you select members for your LC? (see chapters 2, 5, and 6)

a. List the criteria you will use to select your members, how you will define those criteria, and how you will address any relevant access and/or diversity issues you anticipate.

Criteria	Definition of Criteria	Access Issues	Diversity Issues

b. On a separate sheet, describe the selection and notification processes for including members by answering the following questions.

Key Elements of the Selection Process
How will you identify potential members? What will be your cutoff number of participants?
Will participation be mandatory?
If voluntary, how will you recruit?
Will there be an application process? If so, describe.
How will you contact selected members? Who will be assigned to do it?
How will you contact individuals who were not eligible or applicants who were not selected? Who will do it?
Will feedback be provided?
Will there be an appeal or reconsideration process? If so, describe.

3. What are the overarching goals of the LC? (see chapters 2 and 5)

In the following chart, list the top four overarching goals you identified for question 3 of "Setting the Stage." Create at least one objective, measurement, and time frame for each goal listed.

Overarching Goal	Objective	Measurement	Time Frame

III. BUILDING POWERFUL LCs (FOUNDATION)

Each of the following charts is designed around questions that you must address to build a powerful LC. The charts incorporate key practice components and considerations derived from the evidence-based research and principles presented throughout the book. For each component you should brainstorm implementation strategies and activities for your LC. Where possible, the LC members should work through this process together. However, in some situations it may be necessary to go through this exercise in advance and allow members to recommend changes.

1. How will you build community? (see chapters 2–5)

Building Community Component	Considerations	Implementation Strategies and Activities
Team Building	Buy-in Respectfulness Shared responsibility Mutual reliance/support Celebratory climate Trust/openness to risk	
Communication	Open and clear Persistent Honest Constructive feedback	
Diversity	Inclusive Individual identity Cultural awareness Social awareness Access	
Presence	Cognitive Social Teaching	

2. How will you develop a culture for learning? (see chapters 2–5)

Culture for Learning Component	Considerations	Implementation Strategies and Activities
Shared	Cooperativeness Learning Team decision making Discourse Problem solving Team reflection	

Culture for Learning Component	Considerations	Implementation Strategies and Activities
Metacognative	Self-reflection Justification of actions Refinement of action Creating meaning	
Experiential	Service-learning Internships	
Creative	Flexible thinking Innovating	

3. What norms do you want members to follow and how will you ensure accountability? (see chapters 2–5 and 7)

Group Norms and Accountability Component	Considerations	Implementation Strategies and Activities
Conduct	Integrity Confidentiality Loyalty Respectfulness	
Roles	Leader/shared leadership Static/rotating duties Governance	
Expectations	Meeting details Communication Conflict resolution Documentation of work Quality standards Timelines	

4. What resources are needed for your LC to be successful? (see chapters 2–5 and 7)

Describe needed resources, how they will support the LC, and how to get them.

Needed Resource	Use for LC	How to Get (or alternatives)

5. Is the LC prepared to deal with significant legal and ethical issues? (see chapter 6)

a. Fully address each of the following areas of concern in separate documents and check off once completed.

Issue	Policy/ Procedures in Place	Clear Expectations	Enforcement Strategies	Follow-up
Discrimination (selection/even-handed application)				
Access (ADA and LEP)				
Confidentiality/ privacy and reporting				
Instructor presence assurances				
Boundaries				
Response to harassment, violence, disruption				
Liability				
Negligence				

b. Check that each of these areas is:

___ Coordinated with institutional policy

___ Documented in writing

___ Supported by advice of legal counsel

___ Addressed in ground rules if
applicable

___ Coordinated with institutional policy

___ Part of coordinator and member
training

c. What other legal and ethical concerns might be particularly significant for this LC?

_____

_____

_____

IV. ASSESSING AND SUSTAINING POWERFUL LCs (see chapter 7)

1. Brainstorming Your Learning Plan

a. Identify the objective or goal your outcome is going to support.

b. Identify the audience.

c. What do you want them to be able to know, think, or do?

d. What circumstances or context will foster the learning?

e. To what degree will the learning occur? (Be specific!)

f. How will you measure the learning?

2. Developing Your Assessment Plan

Insert into a planning table your intended LC outcomes for the LC as a group and for its individual members, the specific LC experiences that should promote this outcome, and the evidence or artifacts to be gathered that will assist in determining whether the particular outcome has been achieved. Use the following table as a template.

Intended Learning Outcome	Specific LC Experiences That Promote This Outcome	Assessment Plan: Evidence or Artifacts to Determine Whether Outcome Has Been Achieved
Example: Students will develop competency in communication and technical skills to make effective presentations.	• Students training in basic PowerPoint skills • Individual and group presentations in class • Guest speakers and attendance at one or more events in the lecture series • Follow-up discussion after lecture series events	• Instructor and peer evaluation and critique • Final presentation showcasing skills learned • Self-review and critique of videotaped student presentations
Example: Students will use critical thinking and problem-solving skills in applied situations.	• Linked course assignments • Analysis of case studies • Field trips to observe actual work situations • Service-learning projects • Study groups and team problem-solving exercises	• Instructor evaluations of projects and assignments • Student journals and self-evaluations • Observations of students • Follow-up discussions on case studies, field trips, and service-learning experience
1.		
2.		

3. Closing the Loop

List each intended outcome in a table like the one here. Then for each intended outcome describe the reporting process and schedule (including date of most recent review) in the second column, and report how the information will be used and reported in the third column.

Intended Outcome	Reporting Process and Date of Most Recent Review	Use of Information (Documentation of Any Changes, Overall Results)

APPENDIX D

Experiential Evidence That Face-to-Face and Virtual LCs Depend on the Same Principles and Techniques

This appendix demonstrates from two personal experiences of the senior author that exactly the same principles and techniques are operating in powerful online learning communities (LCs) as in powerful face-to-face LCs. Moreover, it was that realization that initially led to the initiation of the idea for this book.

Throughout the 1980s, the senior author served as vice president for academic affairs and dean at Roberts Wesleyan College in Rochester, New York. During that time, he oversaw development of an evening bachelor's degree completion program for working adults called Organizational Management (OM).

OM is a good example of a "powerful LC." To enroll in OM, individuals had to be at least 25 years old and employed, had to have completed two years of lower-division work at a community college, and had to have had enough significant work experience and associated learning to earn an additional year of supporting course work credit through portfolio assessment. The program emphasized application of learning to a significant yearlong, on-the-job project.

Regardless of the time of year, once a group of 15–20 students had signed up for the OM program and been assessed and approved for enrollment, the students were introduced to their lead instructor, who taught some of the program modules and served as the group's mentor on an ongoing basis for the entire length of the program. Each lead instructor had the proper degree credentials and was specially oriented and trained to work with individuals as well as the total group, and to act as the students' advisor and a supportive friend. Each group of students took all of the OM modules together as one group, in a lockstep (specified order) manner.

Because the student groups completed the OM program at various times during the year—almost always many weeks or months before commencement—a special graduation dinner with a follow-up recognition ceremony and program was arranged for each class on completion of the program. Students' families, professors, and other available faculty and administrators from the college attended these events. As part of the program, the graduating students were always invited to share experiences and testimonials about the past year.

Invariably, they talked about the positive and rewarding experience of studying and socializing together inside and outside class, the helpful interaction with their lead instructor and other professors, and how the support from one another—and their instructors—had pulled them through and allowed them to succeed beyond their highest expectations. An extremely effective LC had developed for every class, and on the rare occasions when a student had to drop out it was because of serious illness or extreme circumstances. Each group of students and mentors/instructors developed a remarkable esprit de corps, and students' achievement and development of skills were superb. Employers noted how beneficial the program had proved to be for their employees.

In May 2011, the college held a special gala celebration to recognize the OM program's 25 years of success. Subsequent contact with the current program director (Penny Cannon) revealed that after 25 years the program is much larger but similar characteristics and outcomes persist (e.g., a student retention to graduation rate of well over 90%).

During the 1990s, with the assistance of an outside firm, Roberts Wesleyan's OM program was licensed and implemented with success by more than 70 colleges and universities across the country whose faculty tailored it to local needs. In addition, in 2001 a new start-up company, later renamed Bridgepoint Education, licensed the program. It then entered into a partnership with Charter Oak State College in Connecticut (an external degree institution regionally accredited by Middle States) to offer the program. Each student has both a Bridgepoint and a Charter Oak advisor, and after completion of the program students receive a bachelor's degree at Charter Oak.

The eight staff members comprising the core staff during the first several years of the company operated in a hybrid interaction mode. They were located in four states—Arizona (company headquarters and the CEO were in Phoenix), Florida, Iowa, and Washington (the company president was in Seattle)—and held a staff telephone conference call every Monday morning. Other staff communication was conducted by e-mail and telephone, with infrequent face-to-face staff meetings at the company headquarters. In spite of being spread out across the country, the staff members came to know one another well, and they became an effective/powerful professional LC that focused continually on achieving student learning success, as well as on strategic/tactical issues.

From the very beginning of the company, the senior author served as its director of assessment and program development, with responsibility for overseeing all curriculum and course development, including creation of guidelines and an organizational template to which all courses must conform. In addition to creating particular courses himself, he worked with many selected professors from across the country—using telephone and e-mail—to have them create course drafts, which he would then edit to ensure consistent quality and style. Within the template, instructors were given the freedom, and encouraged, to make significant changes prior to teaching it that would "make the course their own." Teaching was overseen by others within the organization and in consultation with the assessment/program development director.

After implementing a number of face-to-face classroom student cohorts in Phoenix, Arizona, and several other geographic areas across the country, development of comparable online programs utilizing the same courses, concepts, and a comparable template was begun. Soon online students began outnumbering the face-to-face students, and they were having equal success, which also demonstrates that similar concepts and principles apply to virtual and face-to-face LCs.

After four years, Bridgepoint's student numbers were projected to become larger than Charter Oak was then capable of registering and advising. Therefore, in March 2005, using funds that had been made available by a prominent venture capital firm (that firm became the majority owner of the company and installed a new CEO who moved the company headquarters to San Diego, California), Bridgepoint Education purchased a small (approximately 400 undergraduate and master's students) and financially failing Franciscan University of the Prairies in Clinton, Iowa, that had just begun an online program.

The university was renamed Ashford University, and with a full-time faculty to oversee curriculum development, the senior author's position was assumed by others. Over the next two years, however, he consulted on an ongoing basis with Ashford, served on its board of trustees (secretary of the board), and helped begin rapid online student growth and a move toward more than doubling its campus numbers.

Not only were the same principles and techniques operating online as had been so successful in the face-to-face setting, but they were leading to equally impressive outcomes. By the spring of 2011, Ashford's total student body had grown from fewer than 1,000 students five years earlier to 85,000 students (99% of them online), and a variety of data were being collected that suggested its students were attaining academic and personal success, satisfied with their education there, and willing to recommend Ashford to others (see https://assessment.ashford.edu).

To achieve such growth to a large-scale enterprise, with new curricular programs being added regularly, the student cohort concept (students in a particular program all taking the same courses in the same sequence and together as a cohort) was impossible. However, each student still has her or his own ongoing personal academic mentor to consult with and provide support throughout the entire process, and the courses utilize advanced technology to encourage and maximize ongoing student-student collaboration, and collaboration with the instructor, in the manner of a student LC.

As indicated in the beginning of this appendix, these two separate personal experiences of the senior author convinced him that similar concepts, strategies, procedures, and tools apply in both face-to-face and virtual LCs that are optimal in design. Further, powerful LCs are equally important for these two different educational delivery formats, as well as for the hybrid/blended LC format. And out of this realization sprang the realization that a book such as this is vitally needed throughout higher education.

APPENDIX E

100-Institution Survey Responses Regarding What Makes the Institutions' SLCs Unique or Innovative and Effective/Powerful

---

FIGURE E.1
How the institutions' SLCs are unique or innovative.

Each Factor Mentioned by Multiple Institutions (number out of 81 total respondents is in parentheses)

1. (23) Special emphasis on curricular integration (being fully integrated, unusually large number of linked courses, "course bundling," sophisticated course integration, having interdisciplinary courses, LC faculty work every week on course integration) as well as in some cases integrating in such things as the library and service-learning.

2. (19) Faculty-driven, use only full-time faculty; amount of faculty energy devoted to collaboration on topics, activities, and assignments; take special interest in students; make use of collaborative and blended instruction; yearlong seminar and faculty offices in and/or faculty members live in the residence halls.

3. (12) Assessment-driven; special focus on assessment that will make a difference, including MAP-Works or other data feeding into an early warning system; have a special method to collect "formidable information; unique approach to pilot testing"; developed a Request for Proposal process for obtaining needed institutional resources that required each LC to document their learning outcomes; outcomes achieved are noteworthy.

4. (10) Emphasizes service-learning or other focus on surrounding community (e.g., all first-year LCs are rooted in a community-based experience with service-learning projects and an end-of-year celebration), or even beyond.

5. (10) Special SLCs, e.g., focus on leadership, service, reflective writing, or social transitions; or designed solely for commuters, veterans, underprepared students, developmental education and adjusting to one's culture, or graduate students.

6. (9) Blends academic affairs and student affairs in a meaningful manner; emphasizes learning in the cocurriculum.

7. (9) Emphasizes active peer and faculty mentoring, e.g., "common peer mentor," "Master Learner Mentor," Peer Academic Leaders (PALs); every LC has a paid student.

8. (7) All first-year students are required to register for LCs in order to avoid a registration hold and/or LCs are required for graduation; one requires participation only for graduate students.

9. (5) Students (and participating faculty) involved beyond the freshman year.

10. (4) Counselor enhanced; 60% of all first-year students have LLC advising in the residence halls; amount of counselor involvement; and FYE counseling component.

11. (4) The variety of LC models and types of SLCs used, which varies depending on courses and targeted population (different models used for different student interests and needs).

12. (2) All must do science learning, or an emphasis on student research, creating knowledge, or creative investigation.

13. (2) Groups by majors or themes that are unique or grouped in a unique way.

14. (2) Special outreach focus to bring people in, or LC outreach to the high schools.

15. (2) Special training provided to LC coordinators and participating faculty, for example, through PLCs.

Each Factor Mentioned by a Single Institution

16. Students designing and leading their own community of interest.

17. Each thematic unit is an academic residential college with its own dean as coordinator.

18. The students' first semester is designed primarily around first-year LCs.

19. Provide "deep learning" experiences.

20. Emphasis within the LCs of students becoming work teams.

21. Emphasizes developing hands-on sophisticated projects and presentations of their choice.

22. Proxy LLC for commuter students.

23. "Steeped in the disciplines."

24. Unique program/LC structure.

25. Consciously changes assignments.

26. All academic learning communities are for credit and have a heavy writing component.

27. Unusually large number of options for topics.

28. The support provided for transfer students.

29. No adjunct faculty involved, only full-time faculty.

30. Space and time is provided to the LCs for reflection led by a counselor.

31. LC student composition ratio that is programmed (e.g., 50% commuter students and 50% students living on campus).

32. The special connection with fellow LC students and faculty.

33. Links basic courses (reading, writing, math, etc.) with career program courses.

34. Team-taught courses.

35. A special community hour ten times each semester when no other campus activities are scheduled, for LC students and their faculty mentor to join together in special activities planned by the mentor.

36. Group students at a similar place in the career-planning process who have similar bonding needs and interests.

37. "Embedded learning," where the LCs are subgroups of larger classes that they take together.

38. Mandatory tutoring for all LC members.
39. College-level courses and general education supporting one another.
40. Few prerequisites across LC courses.
41. Emphasize the spiritual side as well.
42. Sophomores in LCs have more mentoring and leadership opportunities.
43. Integrating writing into a continual reflection on their courses; varied experiences; and learning during their first year is at the heart [of] the LC program.
44. When completing their housing contract, students request which LLC they want to be a part of, not which hall they want to live in.
45. Student-oriented "try everything" faculty create and implement the LLCs, and the administrative support provided for the program is also unique and exemplary.
46. During the second year the students agree to a common read; all LC students, faculty, and staff are asked to read the book over the summer prior to the start of the fall semester.
47. Do not have a "one size fits all" LC model and the "sky is the limit" with regard to creating LCs; are creating new ones all the time.
48. ESL program has five tiers at four levels.
49. LCs are deeply imbedded in the culture of the university, last the entire first year of the students' career, and are mandatory for all students except honors students.
50. Resident assistants for LLCs receive 100 hours of special training.
51. The diversity of LCs available to students is great even though broader views and creativity are emphasized in all of them.
52. Has a 5-year LC strategic plan.
53. LCs are tied back to the university mission statement.
54. LCs are tied directly to the college's eleven Learning Values, the first [of] which is Application and Integration.
55. First-year SLCs are holistic in that they address all important aspects of the students' experience.
56. The SLCs are designed for sophomore students, not for freshmen.
57. The diversity of LC offerings is unusual.
58. Separate LC office that coordinates all SLCs, and two directors (one from Academic Affairs and one from Student Affairs, in a partnership), with the office budget coming from Academic Affairs.
59. The LC program has extremely strong collaborative relationships across the university, with an unusually large number of institutional "partners."
60. LC themes change each year.
61. Bringing their experiential learning experiences back into their seminar and English classes creates a powerful learning and growth experience for students.
62. The students pay a fee to participate in their LCs.
63. Report that the way they coordinate logistics is unique and LLC housing is generated as needed.
64. Use special student focus groups near the end of each semester as informal assessment to help identify improvements needed (not meant to be for a formal evaluation of any kind).

65. Have a residential college within the university that is a powerful SLC.

66. Uniquely unstable funding source and lack of faculty/top administration support led to the demise of the university's SLCs.

67. 80% of first-year students are in LLCs.

68. Unusually strong faculty commitment to the program but inconsistent administration interest.

"As far as we know, WWU's Teaching-Learning Academy is the only such university-wide learning community that includes faculty, staff, and STUDENTS, along with Bellingham community members and that is designed to study and enhance the learning culture campus-wide. We use a scholarship of teaching and learning model based on dialogue: Together we compose a big question of shared interest relating to teaching and learning that becomes the overarching research question for the academic year; we use it to gather data (from participants and others), analyze the findings, and then use our findings to advance individual and institutional change initiatives" (Dr. Carmen Werder, Director, Teaching-Learning Academy). More is reported about this development at Western Washington State University in the PLC section of chapter 5 in the book.

FIGURE E.2
What helps make the institutions' SLCs effective/powerful.

Each Factor Mentioned by Multiple Institutions (number out of 81 total respondents is in parentheses)

1. (34) Sense of true community; great sense of belonging, bonding, sharing, interaction, partnership, trust, caring, collaboration, learning from each other, and feeling of safety and security.

2. (32) Intentional aligned agendas, interdisciplinary, sense of integration, and emphasis on making connections.

3. (27) Strategic peer involvement; trained peer tutors and quality coordinator who are enthusiastic and motivated about their SLCs, collaborate effectively, and are fully invested in their students' needs.

4. (20) Intentional "value added" and impact data collection (including placement and early warning system tests) and collaboration in interpreting it.

5. (17) Institution-wide commitment to LCs, including strong faculty, staff, administration, counselor, and library support; both top-down and bottom-up support; it is critical that LCs be endorsed and supported by the institutional administration with financial needs being met, that there be buy-in by faculty department chairs, [and that] the program has a good connection to the total faculty and movers therein.

6. (7) Faculty participants believe in, know, and support the students in every possible way.

7. (7) Quality of the LC programming that emphasizes breadth of experiences and especially meaningful themes.

8. (5) Emphasis on deep learning and student engagement.

9. (5) Shared vision and goals, and high expectations for the LCs.

Each Factor Mentioned by a Single Institution

10. Quality, well-placed offices and a variety of LC choices available.

11. Think of LCs as labs to join students into community.

12. Cocurricular activities are coordinated with academic activities.

13. Emphasis on both the social and the academic.

14. Reporting to Academic Affairs is a key.

15. Residence experience is a key as is learning outside the classroom that complements classroom learning; our total campus is becoming a learning environment.

16. Ability to push both students and faculty beyond their comfort zones.

17. Encourage recognition that learning does not simply have to be a means to an end—it can be an enriching end in and of itself.

18. Participation in the various program activities is not optional for students selected into the LC.

19. The importance of developing self-confidence.

20. Study groups add stability.

21. Focused on the shared vision of the college.

22. Students must sign a commitment form.
23. Require attendance policy.
24. Match partners within the LC.
25. They are their own separate department and/or one needs to provide a social foundation for LCs.
26. The focus is on the major.
27. Provide stipends to faculty for LC involvement.
28. We provide faculty stipends for involvement in learning communities, there is a banked credit system in place that permits faculty to attain such things as release time for development of new student learning communities, and we have many faculty involved in faculty-led teaching circles that focus on improving teaching and learning.
29. The studying required outside of class.
30. All students except honors students are required.
31. Cooperative learning is emphasized.
32. Make extensive use of focus groups.
33. The study groups are crucial.
34. More than one LC is required for each student.
35. The opportunity for faculty to work intensely on these new students' critical thinking and communication skills without the concern for particular content requirements is the most effective aspect of the program.
36. Wide variety of offerings and student sense of variety, including student communities of practice.
37. They have a common experience free from isolation and there is continuity.
38. The broad emphasis on thinking, reasoning, communication, faith, and writing across all four years.
39. The housing assignments and matching up roommates carried out by student affairs is critical.
40. Faculty have a passion for student learning and sharing with their students.
41. The LC team (made up of faculty or staff directors, possibly other seminar instructors, student leaders, and partners) provides a rich resource and support structure.
42. Students gain a bigger understanding of the university, so they cope better and tend to graduate.
43. Students can co-enroll in LCs and the Freshman College.
44. All LCs are taught by full-time faculty.
45. Our emphasis on having LCs support social transition is important.
46. 60% of all first-year students have LLC advising in the residence halls.
47. Upper-division faculty working with first-year students is important.
48. Participating faculty members in LCs receive a $1,000 or more annual stipend for that involvement.
49. An inner core of faculty celebrate LCs at upscale country club at end of each year.
50. Incorporating an off-campus experiential component in the first-year and senior learning communities is an especially powerful way to bring theory to life for students.

51. Flattening the usual academic hierarchy and creating an environment where titles are irrelevant and all ideas are valued.

52. The opportunity to effect change—in terms of both individual and institutional teaching and learning practices.

APPENDIX F

Key Laws and Legal Resources Impacting LCs

TABLE F.1
Membership and access laws and legal resources related to LCs.

Legal Issues	Primary Relevant Laws and Legal Resources
Ensuring fair and equal treatment	• Higher Education Opportunity Act of 2008 (HEOA) Title IV (Reauthorization of the Higher Education Act of 1965 (HEA) • Higher Learning Commission: *Commission Statement on Diversity*
Discrimination	• Civil Rights Act of 1964 (CRA) (42 U.S.C. 2000d *et seq.*) • Equal Educational Opportunities Act of 1974 • Higher Education Act of 1965 (HEA), Part B, § 111(a) • Equal Employment Opportunity Act of 1972 (Public Law 92–261) • Education Amendments of 1972, Title IX (20 U.S.C. 1681 *et seq.*) • Age Discrimination Act of 1975 (42 U.S.C. 6101 *et seq.*) • Age Discrimination in Employment Act of 1967 (ADEA) • Genetic Information Nondiscrimination Act of 2008 (GINA) • Uniformed Services Employment and Reemployment Rights Act of 1994 (USERRA) • Pregnancy Discrimination Act • Relevant state and local laws
Diversity and affirmative action	• Institutional Affirmative Action provisions Title VII of the CRA • Equal Employment Opportunity Act of 1972 (EEOA) • The 14th Amendment of the US Constitution • Federal Regulations: 45 C.F.R. 80.3(b)—prohibits discrimination on the basis of race, color, or national origin in the awarding of federal financial aid • Relevant court decisions

TABLE F.1 (Continued)

Legal Issues	Primary Relevant Laws and Legal Resources
Disability: access and accommodation	• Americans with Disabilities Act of 1990 (ADA) 29 U.S.C. 2201 Title II—applies to all individuals with a covered disability • The Americans with Disabilities Act Amendments Act of 2010 (ADAAA) • Rehabilitation Act of 1973, § 508, 29 U.S.C. § 794d (as amended in 1998) • Rehabilitation Act of 1973, § 508 (as amended in 2008) • Assistive Technology Act • Carl D. Perkins Vocational and Technical Education Act Amendments of 1998, § 1 (b) (20 U.S.C. 2302) • Regulations on Financial Aid: 34 C.F.R. 1200.130(b)—Workforce Investment Act of 1998 (WIA) (29 U.S.C. §§ 188 and 701) • The Vietnam Era Veterans' Readjustment Assistance Act (VEVRAA): § 4212 • Telecommunications Act of 1996 (47 U.S.C. §§ 255 and 613) • Federal Government Procurement of Accessible Information Technology • Twenty-First Century Communications and Video Accessibility Act
Limited English proficiency: access and accommodation	• Civil Rights Act (CRA) of 1964 • Title VI: "Prohibition Against National Origin Discrimination Affecting Limited English Proficient Persons" • Presidential Executive Order 13166: "Improving Access to Services for Persons With Limited English Proficiency" • Office of Civil Rights Interpretive Guidelines • State "English Is the Official Language" laws

TABLE F.2
Relationship laws and legal resources related to LCs.

Legal Issues	Primary Relevant Laws and Legal Resources
Presence and contact	• State laws (e.g., Title V, § 55204 of the California Code) • Higher Education Opportunity Act of 2008 • Higher Learning Commission (HLC) Accreditation Standards • Department of Education, Program Integrity Issues, Final Rule 34 CFR 600.2 (Published October 29, 2010)
Diversity, inclusion, and cultural competence	• Higher Learning Commission (HLC) *Criteria for Accreditation*—Criterion One: "Mission and Integrity" ○ Core Component 1b ○ Core Component 4c *Commission Statement on Diversity*
Mandatory reporting requirements	• Jeanne Clery Disclosure of Campus Security Policy and Campus Crime Statistics Act (Clery Act), 20 USC § 1092(f) (2008) • Peer reporting under student honor code/professional integrity code • Professional licensing boards
Dealing with disruptive members and violent situations and individuals	• State violence-free and weapons-free workplace laws • The Campus Sexual Violence Elimination Act (SaVE Act) (S.834), Legislation • CAMPUS Safety Act of 2011 (S.1749), Legislation

TABLE F.3
Ownership, privacy, and liability laws and legal resources related to LCs.

Legal Issues	Primary Relevant Laws and Legal Resources
Copyright and intellectual property	• Acceptable use/terms of use policies • Copyright Act of 1976 • Fair Use Exception (17 U.S.C. 107) • Online Copyright Infringement Liability Limitation Act (OCILLA) • Digital Millennium Copyright Act (DMCA) • Public domain • Fair use doctrine • Technology, Education and Copyright Harmonization Act of 2002 (TEACH ACT) (17 U.S.C. § 110[2])
Privacy and confidentiality	• Family Educational Rights and Privacy Act of 1974 (FERPA) • Health Insurance Portability and Accountability Act of 1996 (HIPAA) • State professional licensing statutes and codes of ethics regarding confidentiality in special relationships
Negligence and liability	• Court cases • State statutes on negligence and negligent supervision • Respondent superior • Corporate liability • Ostensible or apparent authority • Risk management

REFERENCES

Ajjawi, R., & Higgs, J. (2008). Learning to reason: A journey of professional socialization. *Advances in Health Sciences Education, 13,* 133–150.

Akin, L., & Neal, D. (June 2007). CREST + model: Writing effective online discussion questions. *Journal of Online Learning and Teaching.* Available at http://jolt
.merlot.org/vol3no2/akin.htm

American Association of Colleges and Universities. (2007). *College learning for the new global century.* Report from the National Leadership Council for Liberal Education and America's Promise. Washington, DC: Author.

American Association of University Professors. (2006). *Policy documents and reports* (10th ed.). Baltimore, MD: Johns Hopkins University Press.

Anderson, B., & Simpson, M. (2007). Ethical issues in online education. *Open Learning, 22*(2), 129–138.

Anderson, J. (1995). *Courageous teaching: Creating a caring community in the classroom.* Thousand Oaks, CA: Corwin Press.

Anderson, L. W., & Krathwohl, D. R. (Eds.). (2001). *A taxonomy for learning, teaching and assessing: A revision of Bloom's taxonomy of educational objectives.* New York, NY: Longman.

Angelo, T. A. (1997, May). The campus as a learning community: Seven promising shifts and seven powerful levers. *AAHE Bulletin, 49*(9), 3–6.

Angelo, T. A., & Cross, K. P. (1993). *Classroom assessment techniques: A handbook for college teachers.* San Francisco, CA: Jossey-Bass.

Aronson, E. (2008). *The social animal* (10th ed.). New York, NY: Worth/Freeman.

Arum, R., & Roksa, J. (2011). *Academically adrift: Limited learning on college campuses.* Chicago, IL: University of Chicago Press.

The Association of Independent Liberal Arts Colleges for Teacher Education. (n.d.). *Moral and ethical dimensions of the learning community.* http://www.ailacte.org/images/uploads/general/Quality_I.docx

Astin, A. (1993). *What matters in college: Four critical years revisited.* San Francisco, CA: Jossey-Bass.

Ausubel, D. P., & Robinson, F. G. (1969). *School learning: An introduction to educational psychology.* New York, NY: Holt, Rinehart and Winston.

Barbour, M. (2011, December 5). Attendance and online learning. *Virtual School Meanderings* Blog. Available at http://virtualschooling.wordpress.com/2011/12/05/attendance-and-online-learning/

Barth, R. S. (2001). *Learning by heart.* San Francisco, CA: Jossey-Bass.

Baxter Magolda, M. (1999). *Creating contexts for learning and self-authorship: Constructive-developmental pedagogy.* Nashville, TN: Vanderbilt University Press.

Beck, J. C., & Wade, M. (2006). *The kids are alright: How the gamer generation is changing the workplace.* Boston, MA: Harvard Business School.

Beichner, R., Saul, J., Abbott, D., Morse, J., Deardorff, D., Allain, R., . . . Risley, J. (2007). Student-Centered Activities for Large Enrollment Undergraduate Programs (SCALE-UP) project. In E. F. Redish & P. J. Cooney (Eds.), *PER-based reform in university physics* (Vol. 1). College Park, MD: American Association of Physics Teachers.

Belenky, M. F., Clinchy, B. M., Goldberger, N. R., & Tarule, J. M. (1986). *Women's ways of knowing: The development of self, voice, and mind.* New York, NY: Basic Books.

Belsey, B. (2011). cyberbullying.org website. Retrieved from http://www.cyberbullying.org/

Bennis, W. G. (1993). *An invented life.* Reading, MA: Addison-Wesley.

Bielaczyc, K., & Collins, A. (1999). Learning communities in classrooms: A reconceptualization of educational practice. In C. M. Reigeluth (Ed.), *Instructional-design theories and models* (pp. 269–292). Mahwah, NJ: Lawrence Erlbaum. Retrieved from http://isites.harvard.edu/fs/docs/icb.topic541040.files/Bielaczyc%20and%20Collins-Learning%20Communities%20in%20Classrooms.pdf

Biggs, J. B., & Collis, K. F. (1982). *Evaluating the quality of learning—The SOLO taxonomy.* New York, NY: Academic Press.

Blaich, C. F., & Wise, K. S. (2011, January). *From gathering to using assessment results: Lessons from the Wabash National Study.* NILOA Occasional Paper no. 8. Urbana, IL: National Institute of Learning Outcomes Assessment, University of Illinois and Indiana University.

Blake, E. S. (1996, September–October). The yin and yang of student learning in college. *About Campus, 1*(4), 4–9.

Bloom, B. S. (Ed.). (1956). *Taxonomy of educational objectives: The classification of educational goals. Handbook 1: cognitive domain.* New York, NY: McKay.

Blumstein, A., & Nakamura, K. (2009, June). "Redemption" in an era of widespread criminal background checks. *National Institute of Justice Journal,* no. 263. Available at http://www.nij.gov/nij/journals/263/redemption.htm.

Bonwell, C. C., & Eison, J. A. (1991). *Active learning: Creating excitement in the classroom.* ASHE-ERIC Higher Education Report no. 1. Washington, DC: The George Washington University.

Borda, J., Kriz, G. S., Popejoy, K. L., Dickinson, A. K., & Olson, A. L. (2009). Taking ownership of learning in a large class: Group projects and a mini-conference. *Journal of College Science Teaching, 38*(6), 35–41.

Boston, W. E., Ice, P., & Gibson, A. M. (2010). Comprehensive assessment of student retention in online learning environments. In J. Sanchez & K. Zhang

(Eds.), *Proceedings of World Conference on E-Learning in Corporate, Government, Healthcare, and Higher Education* (pp. 1593–1599). Chesapeake, VA: Association for the Advancement of Computing in Education. Retrieved from www.westga .edu/~distance/ojdla/spring141/boston_ice_gibson141.html

Boyer Commission on Educating Undergraduates in the Research University. (1998). *Reinventing undergraduate education: A blueprint for America's research universities.* Stony Brook, NY: State University of New York at Stony Brook.

Bransford, J. D., Brown, A. L., & Cocking, R. R. (Eds.). (1999a). *How people learn: Brain, mind, experience, and school.* Washington, DC: National Academic Press.

Bransford, J. D., Brown, A. L., & Cocking, R. R. (1999b). Learning: From speculation to science. In J. Bransford, A. Brown, & R. Cocking (Eds.), *How people learn: Brain, mind, experience, and school* (pp. 39–66). Washington, DC: National Academic Press.

Brooke, C., & Gruenewald, D. (2003, June). *Building bridges between academic affairs and student affairs: Learning communities at Iowa State University.* Paper presented at the North Central Teaching Symposium, Minneapolis, MN.

Brown, A. L., Bransford, J. D., Ferrara, R. A., & Campione, J. C. (1983). Learning, remembering, and understanding. In J. H. Flavell & E. M. Markham (Eds.), *Handbook of child psychology: Vol. 3. Cognitive development* (4th ed., pp. 77–166). New York, NY: John Wiley.

Brown, A. L., & Campione, J. C. (1996). Psychological theory and design of innovative learning environments: On procedures, principles, and systems. In L. Schauble & R. Glaser (Eds.), *Innovations in learning: New environments for education* (pp. 289–325). Mahwah, NJ: Lawrence Erlbaum.

Brown, J. S. (1997, January–February). On becoming a learning organization. *About Campus, 1*(6), 5–10.

Browne, E. (2003, November). Conversations in cyberspace: A study of online learning. *Open Learning, 18*(3), 245–259.

Bruner, J. S. (1966). *Toward a theory of instruction.* Cambridge, MA: Harvard University Press.

Campbell, J. P., & Oblinger, D. G. (2007, October). *Academic analytics.* Retrieved from http://net.educause.edu/ir/library/pdf/PUB6101.pdf

Carlen, U., & Jobring, O. (2005). The rationale of online learning communities. *International Journal of Web Based Communities, 1*(3), 272–295.

Chickering, A. W., & Gamson, Z. F. (1987, March). Seven principles for practice in undergraduate education. *AAHE Bulletin, 39*(7), 3–7.

Christensen, C., Johnson, C. W., & Horn, M. B. (2008). *Disrupting class: How disruptive innovation will change the way the world learns.* New York, NY: McGraw Hill.

Church, E. B. (2008, September). Building community in the classroom. *Early Childhood Today.* Retrieved from http://www2.scholastic.com/browse/article .jsp?id=3749832

Costa, A., & Kallick, B. (2000). *Habits of mind: A developmental series.* Alexandria, VA: Association for Supervision and Curriculum Development.

Cox, M. D. (2004). Introduction to faculty learning communities: Using FLCs to solve problems and seize opportunities. In M. D. Cox & L. Richlin (Eds.), *Building faculty learning communities: New directions for teaching and learning,* no. 97 (pp. 5–23). San Francisco, CA: Jossey-Bass. Also available at http://www.vcu.edu/cte/programs/FLC/IntroductionToFLCs.pdf

Cox, M. D., & Richlin, L. (2004). *Building faculty learning communities: New directions for teaching and learning,* no. 97. San Francisco, CA: Jossey-Bass.

Dale, E. (1972). *Building a learning environment.* Monograph Series no. 3. Bloomington, IN: Phi Delta Kappa Educational Foundation.

Dattner, B. (2011, April). Credit and blame at work. *Psychology Today* blog. Retrieved from http://www.psychologytoday.com/blog/credit-and-blame-work/201104/preventing-groupthink

Dawson, S. (2010). "Seeing" the learning community: An exploration of the development of a resource for monitoring online student networking. *British Journal of Educational Technology, 41*(5), 736–752.

Delaney, A. M. (2009, October). Institutional researchers' expanding roles: Policy, planning, program evaluation, assessment, and new research methodologies. In C. Leimer (Ed.), *Imagining the future of institutional research: New directions for institutional research* (no. 143, pp. 29–41). San Francisco, CA: Jossey-Bass.

Deng, L., & Yuen, A. H. K. (2010). Designing blended learning communities. In F. L Wang, J. Fong, & R. Kwan (Eds.), *Handbook of research on hybrid learning models: Advanced tools, technologies, and applications* (pp. 228–243). Hershey, PA: IGI Global.

Domizi, D. P. (2008). Student perceptions about their informal learning experiences in a first-year residential learning community. *Journal of the First-Year Experience & Students in Transition, 20*(1), 97–110.

Doolittle, G., Sudeck, M., & Rattigan, P. (2008, October). Creating professional learning communities: The work of professional development schools. *Theory Into Practice, 47,* 303–310.

Drayton, B., & Falk, J. K. (2009). Introduction. In J. K. Falk & B. Drayton (Eds.), *Creating and sustaining online professional learning communities* (pp. 1–16). New York, NY: Teachers College Press.

Drayton, B., Obuchowski, J., & Falk, J. K. (2009). Epilogue. In J. K. Falk & B. Drayton (Eds.), *Creating and sustaining online professional learning communities* (pp. 203–218). New York, NY: Teachers College Press.

DuFour, R. (2004). What is a "professional learning community"? *Educational Leadership, 61*(8), 6–11.

DuFour, R., & Eaker, R. (1998). *Professional learning communities at work: Best practices for enhancing student achievement.* Alexandria, VA: Association for Supervision and Curriculum Development.

DuFour, R., Eaker, R., & DuFour, R. (2005). *On common ground: The power of professional learning communities.* Bloomington, IN: Solution Tree (formerly National Educational Service).

Duncan-Howell, J. (2010). Teachers making connections: Online communities as a source of professional learning. *British Journal of Educational Technology, 41*(2), 324–340.

Dunlap, L., & Pettitt, M. (2008, Spring). Assessing student outcomes in learning communities: Two decades of study at community colleges. *Journal of Applied Research in the Community College, 15*(2), 140–149.

Ellis, R. A., & Calvo, R. A. (2007). Minimum indicators to assure quality of LMS-supported blended learning. *Educational Technology & Society, 10*(2), 60–70.

Evans, N. J., Forney, D. S., & Guido-DiBritto, F. (1998). *Student development in college.* San Francisco, CA: Jossey-Bass.

Falk, J. K., & Drayton, B. (Eds.). 2009. *Creating and sustaining online professional learning communities.* New York, NY: Teachers College Press.

Feldmann, L. J. (2001). Classroom civility is another of our instructor responsibilities. *College Teaching, 49*(4), 137–140.

FindLaw. (n.d.). Available at http://dictionary.findlaw.com/definition/negligence.html

Fink, L. D. (2003). *Creating significant learning experiences: An integrated approach to designing college courses.* San Francisco, CA: Jossey-Bass.

Fullan, M. (2002). *The change leader. Educational Leadership, 59*(8), 16–20.

Gabelnick, F., MacGregor, J., Matthews, R. S., & Smith, R. S. 1990. *Learning communities: Creating connections among students, faculty and disciplines: New directions for teaching and learning,* no. 41. San Francisco, CA: Jossey-Bass.

Gagne, R. M. (1965). *Conditions of learning.* New York, NY: Holt, Rinehart and Winston.

Gannon-Leary, P., & Fontainha, E. (2007, September). Communities of practice and virtual learning communities: Benefits, barriers and success factors. eLearning Papers, no. 5. ISSN 1887-1542. Available at http://www.elearningeuropa.info/files/media/media13563.pdf

Gardner, H. (1999). *Intelligence reframed.* New York, NY: Basic Books.

Gardner, J. W. (1990). *On leadership.* New York, NY: Free Press.

Garrison, D. R., & Vaughan, N. D. (2008). *Blended learning in higher education: Framework, principles, and guidelines.* San Francisco, CA: Jossey-Bass.

Gednalske, J. (2010, March 29). *Human factors in online education.* TechEDge, California Community Colleges website. Retrieved from http://ccctechedge.org/news/miscellaneous/68-human-factors-in-online-education

Gibbs, J. (2006). *Reaching all by creating tribes learning communities.* Windsor, CA: CenterSource Systems.

Glenn, D. (2009, December 15). Matching teaching style to learning style may not help students. *The Chronicle of Higher Education.* Available at http://chronicle.com/article/Matching-Teaching-Style-to/49497/

Goodsell Love, A. (2004, June). A campus culture for sustaining learning communities. In J. Levine Laufgraben & N. Shapiro (Eds.), *Sustaining and improving learning communities* (pp. 14–30). San Francisco, CA: Jossey-Bass.

Gouge, K., & Yates, C. (2002). Creating a CA programme in the arts: The Wigan LEA Arts Project. In M. Shayer & P. Adey (Eds.), *Learning intelligence: Cognitive acceleration across the curriculum from 5 to 15 years* (pp. 85–102). Buckingham, UK: Open University Press.

Gregory, G. H., & Kuzmich, L. (2009). *Teacher teams that get results: 61 strategies for sustaining and renewing professional learning communities.* Thousand Oaks, CA: Corwin Press.

Gruenewald, D., & Brooke, C. (2007). Building collaborative student affairs-academic affairs connections through the development of learning communities at Iowa State University. In B. L. Smith & L. B. Williams (Eds.), *Learning communities and student affairs: Partnering for powerful learning* (pp. 35–46). Olympia, WA: National Association of Student Personnel Administrators and the Washington Center for Improving the Quality of Undergraduate Education.

Guell, R. C. (2003, April). *Isolating the impact of learning communities and first-year residence halls on first-year student retention and success.* Paper presented at the annual meeting of the Association of American Colleges and Universities, Phoenix, AZ. Available at http://irt2.indstate.edu/nca2010/assets/pdf/C3/Isolating%20the%20Impact%20of%20LCs%20and%20FYRHs.pdf

Guthrie, K. L., & McCracken, H. (2010, October). Teaching and learning social justice through online service-learning courses. *International Review of Research in Open and Distance Learning, 11*(3), 78–90.

Hannah, L. S., & Michaelis, J. U. (1977). *A comprehensive framework for instructional objectives: A guide to systematic planning and evaluation.* Reading, MA: Addison-Wesley.

Hanson, D. T. (1995). Teaching and the moral life of classrooms. *Journal for a Just and Caring Education, 2,* 59–74. Available at http://tigger.uic.edu/~lnucci/MoralEd/articles/hansen.html

Hardiman, J., Smith, B. L., Washington, K., & Brewster, E. (2007). Connecting with local communities. In B. L. Smith & L. B. Williams (Eds.), *Learning communities and student affairs: Partnering for powerful learning* (pp. 87–102). Olympia, WA: National Association of Student Personnel Administrators and the Washington Center for Improving the Quality of Undergraduate Education.

Harrell, I., II, & Hollins, T. (2009, Spring). Working with disruptive students. *Inquiry, 14*(1), 69–75.

Hauenstein, A. D. (1998). *A conceptual framework for educational objectives: A holistic approach to traditional taxonomies.* Lanham, MD: University Press of America.

Havel, V. (2000). Politics, morality, and civility. In D. E. Eberly (Ed.), *The essential civil society reader* (pp. 391–402). Lanham, MD: Rowman & Littlefield.

Heinrich, R., Molenda, M., Russell, J. D., & Smaldino, S. E. (1996). *Instructional media and technologies for learning.* Englewood Cliffs, NJ: Merrill.

Holyoke, L. B., Sturko, P. A., Wood, N. D., & Wu, L. J. (2012, April). Are academic departments perceived as learning organizations? *Educational Management, 40*(4), 436–448.

Hord, S. (1997). *Professional learning communities: Communities of continuous inquiry and improvement.* Austin, TX: Southwest Educational Development Laboratory. Retrieved from http://www.sedl.org/pubs/change34/

Huba, M. E., & Freed, J. E. (2000). *Learner-centered assessment on college campuses: Shifting the focus from teaching to learning.* Boston: Allyn & Bacon.

Hubbell, L., & Hubbell, K. (2010, June). When a college class becomes a mob: Coping with student cohorts. *College Student Journal, 44*(2), 340–353.

Huber, M. T., & Hutchings, P. (2005). *The advancement of learning: Building the teaching commons.* San Francisco, CA: Jossey-Bass.

Hurd, S. N. (2010). Introduction. In T. Peckskamp & C. McLaughlin (Eds.), *Building community: Stories and strategies for future learning community faculty and professionals* (pp. 4–5). Syracuse, NY: The Syracuse University Graduate School Press.

Illinois Online Network. (n.d.). *What makes a successful online student?* Available at http://www.cgspitt.org/medialibrary/File/Tips_For_Success/SuccessStudent713 06.pdf

Indiana University Center for Postsecondary Research. (2007). *Experiences that matter: Enhancing student learning and success.* National Survey of Student Engagement: Annual report 2007. Bloomington, IN: Author. Available at http://nsse.iub.edu/NSSE%5F2007%5FAnnual%5FReport/docs/withhold/ NSSE_2007_Annual_Report.pdf

Jacobs, J., & Yendol-Hoppey, D. (2010). Supervisor transformation within a professional learning community. *Teacher Education Quarterly, 37*(2), 97–114.

Jaffee, D. (2004, July 9). Learning communities can be cohesive and divisive. *The Chronicle of Higher Education,* B16.

Jaffee, D. (2007). Peer cohorts and the unintended consequences of freshman learning communities. *College Teaching, 55*(2), 65–71.

Jaffee, D., Carle, A. C., Phillips, R., & Paltoo, L. (2008). Intended and unintended consequences of first-year learning communities: An initial investigation. *Journal of the First-Year Experience and Students in Transition, 20*(1), 53–70.

Janis, I. L. (1972). *Victims of groupthink.* New York, NY: Houghton Mifflin.

Janis, I. L. (1982). *Groupthink: Psychological studies of policy decisions and fiascoes* (2nd ed.). Boston, MA: Houghton Mifflin.

Johnson, D. W., Johnson, R. T., & Smith, K. A. (1991). *Cooperative learning: Increasing college faculty instructional productivity.* ASHE-ERIC Higher Education Report no. 4. Washington, DC: The George Washington University Graduate School of Education and Human Development. (ED343465)

Jones, J. K., & Lawrie, J. D. (2010). Institutional pedagogies: Exploring two learning community programs. In T. Peckskamp & C. McLaughlin (Eds.), *Building community: Stories and strategies for future learning community faculty and professionals* (pp. 99–108). Syracuse, NY: The Graduate School Press, Syracuse University.

Joo, J. (n.d.). *Developing a model for blended professional learning communities: How to balance online and onsite teamwork for a global online professional development program for educators.* Available at http://projects.coe.uga.edu/edrconference/EDR%20Proceedings/papers/Joo%20Paper.pdf

Kagan, S. (1985). Co-op co-op: A flexible cooperative learning technique. In R. Slavin, S. Sharan, S. Kagan, R. H. Lazarowitz, C. Webb, & R. Schmuck (Eds.), *Learning to cooperate, cooperating to learn* (pp. 437–452). New York, NY: Plenum Press.

Kagan, S. (1989). *Cooperative learning resources for teachers.* San Juan Capistrano, CA: Resources for Teachers.

Kagan, S. (1992). *Cooperative learning* (2nd ed.). San Juan Capistrano, CA: Resources for Teachers.

Kaplan, S. (n.d.). *Building eLearning and blended learning communities.* Available at http://www.icohere.com/CollaborativeLearning.htm

Kaplan, W. A., & Lee, B. A. (2007). *The law of higher education* (4th ed.). San Francisco, CA: Jossey-Bass.

Kegan, R. (1994). *In over our heads: The mental of modern life.* Cambridge, MA: Harvard University Press.

King, P., & Kitchener, K. (1994a). *Developing reflective judgment: Understanding and promoting intellectual growth and critical thinking in adolescents and adults.* San Francisco, CA: Jossey-Bass.

King, P. M., & Kitchener, K. S. (1994b). Reflective judgment: Concepts of justifications and their relation to age and gender. *Journal of Applied Developmental Psychology, 2*(2), 89–116.

Kinzie, J., & Kuh, G. D. (2004, July–August). Going deep: Learning from campuses that share responsibility for student success. *About Campus, 9*(5), 2–8.

Kofman, F., & Senge, P. M. (1993). Communities of commitment: The heart of learning organizations. *Organizational Dynamics, 22*(2), 5–22.

Kolb, D. A. (1984). *Experiential learning: Experience as the source of learning and development.* Englewood Cliffs, NJ: Prentice Hall.

Kouzes, J. M., & Possner, B. Z. (1987). *The leadership challenges.* San Francisco, CA: Jossey-Bass.

Krapfl, A. (2011, May 19). ISU learning communities: A 71 percent capture rate and growing. *Inside Iowa State for Faculty and Staff* (online newsletter). Retrieved from www.inside.iastate.edu

Kuh, G., & Ikenberry, S. (2009). *More than you think, less than we need: Learning outcomes assessment in American higher education.* Urbana, IL: University of Illinois and Indiana University, National Institute for Learning Outcomes Assessment (NILOA).

Kuh, G. D., Kinzie, J., Schuh, J. H., & Whitt, E. J. (2010). *Creating conditions that matter.* San Francisco, CA: Jossey-Bass.

Lampert, M., Rittenhouse, P., & Crumbaugh, C. (1996). Agreeing to disagree: developing sociable mathematical discourse. In D. Olson & N. Torrance (Eds.),

Handbook of education and human development (pp. 731–764). Oxford, UK: Blackwell.

Lardner, E., & Malnarich, G. C. (2008, July–August). A new era in learning community work: Why pedagogy of intentional integration matters. *Change Magazine, 40*(4), 30–37. Retrieved from www.changemag.org

Lardner, E., & Malnarich, G. C. (Eds.). (2009). Washington Center's national project on assessing learning in learning communities [Special issue]. *Journal of Learning Communities Research, 3*(3).

Lave, J., & Wenger, E. (1991). *Situated learning: Legitimate peripheral participation.* Cambridge, UK: Cambridge University Press.

Lawless, M. E. (2011, December 14). Privacy and research studies: NetWellness. *The Plain Dealer.* Retrieved from http://www.cleveland.com/healthfit/index.ssf/2011/12/privacy_and_research_studies_n.html

Leavitt, L. H., & Oates, K. K. (2003). *Service learning and learning communities: Tools for integration and assessment.* Washington, DC: Association of American Colleges and Universities.

Leimer, C., & Terkla, D. G. (2009, October). Laying the foundation: IR office organization, staffing, and career development. In C. Leimer (Ed.), *Imagining the future of institutional research: New directions for institutional research* (no. 143, pp. 5–16). San Francisco, CA: Jossey-Bass.

Lenning, O. T. (1981). Assessment and evaluation. In A. Delworth & G. Hanson (Eds.), *Student services: A handbook for the profession* (pp. 232–266). San Francisco, CA: Jossey-Bass.

Lenning, O. T., & Ebbers, L. H. (1999). *The powerful potential of learning communities: Improving education for the future.* ASHE-ERIC Higher Education Report, vol. 26, no. 6. Washington, DC: The George Washington University Graduate School of Education and Human Development.

Lenning, O. T., Lee, Y. S., Micek, S. S., & Service, A. L. (1977). *A structure for the outcomes of postsecondary education.* Boulder, CO: National Center for Higher Education Management Systems.

Levine, T. H. (2010). Tools for the study and design of collaborative teacher learning: The affordances of different conceptions of teacher community and activity theory. *Teacher Education Quarterly, 37*(1), 109–130.

Levine Laufgraben, J., & Shapiro, N. S. (2004). *Sustaining and improving learning communities.* San Francisco, CA: Jossey-Bass.

Levine Laufgraben, J. L., O'Connor, M., & Williams, J. (2007, Fall). Supporting first-year transition: Learning communities and educational reform. In B. L. Smith & L. B. Williams (Eds.), *Learning communities and student affairs: Partnering for powerful learning* (pp. 47–55). Olympia, WA: National Association of Student Personnel Administrators and the Washington Center for Improving the Quality of Undergraduate Education.

Levine Laufgraben, J., & Tompkins, D. (2004). Pedagogy that builds community. In J. Levine Laufgraben & N. S. Shapiro (Eds.), *Sustaining and improving learning communities* (pp. 54–75). San Francisco, CA: Jossey-Bass.

Lewin, K. (1943). Defining the "field at a given time." *Psychological Review, 50,* 292–310.

Lichtenstein, M. (2005). The importance of classroom environments in the assessment of learning communities. *Journal of College Student Development, 46,* 341–356.

Light, R. J. (2001). *Making the most of college: Students speak their minds.* Cambridge, MA: Harvard University Press.

Lumina Foundation for Education. (2010, September). *A stronger nation through higher education: How and why Americans must achieve a Big Goal for college attainment.* Indianapolis, IN: Author. http://www.luminafoundation.org/publications/A_stronger_nation.pdf

Mandernach, B. J., Gonzales, R. M., & Garrett, A. L. (2005). An examination of online instructor presence via threaded discussion participation. *Journal of Online Learning and Teaching, 2*(4). Available at http://jolt.merlot.org/vol2no4/mandernach.htm

Marzano, R. J. (2001). *Designing a new taxonomy of educational objectives.* Thousand Oaks, CA: Corwin Press.

Maslow, A. (1966). *The psychology of science.* New York, NY: Harper & Row.

McEwan, A. E. (1993, April). *On becoming a sojourning community.* Paper presented at annual meeting of the American Educational Research Association, Atlanta, GA. (ED 359914)

McWilliam, E. (2008). *The creative workforce: How to launch young people into high flying futures.* Sydney, Australia: UNSW Press.

Means, B., Toyama, Y., Murphy, R., Bakia, M., & Jones, K. (2009). *Evaluation of evidence-based practices in online learning: A meta-analysis and review of online learning studies.* US Department of Education, Office of Planning, Evaluation, and Policy Development. Available at www.ed.gov/about/offices/list/opepd/ppss/reports.html

Meiklejohn, A. (1932). *The experimental college.* New York, NY: HarperCollins. Available at http://digital.library.wisc.edu/1711.dl/UW.MeikExpColl

Mentkowski, M., & Associates. (2000). *Learning that lasts: Integrating learning, development, and performance in college and beyond.* San Francisco, CA: Jossey-Bass.

Merrill, M. D., Jones, M. K., & Zhongmin, L. (1992). Instructional design theory: Classes of transactions. *Educational Technology, 32*(6), 12–26.

Meyers, C., & Jones, T. B. (1993). *Promoting active learning: Strategies for the college classroom.* San Francisco, CA: Jossey-Bass.

Mezirow, J. (1978). Perspective transformation. *Adult Education, 28,* 100–110.

Mezirow, J. (2003). Transformative learning as discourse. *Journal of Transformative Education, 1*(1), 58–63.

Michaelsen, L. K., Parmelee, D. X., McMahon, K. K., & Levine, R. E. (2007). *Team-based learning for health professions education: A guide to using small groups for improving learning.* Sterling, VA: Stylus.

Miller, A. S. (2009). *Collaborating in electronic learning communities.* (ERIC Document Reproduction Service No. ED505959). Retrieved July 2010 from www.eric.ed.gov.

Millis, B. (Ed.). (2010). *Cooperative learning in higher education: Across the disciplines, across the academy.* Sterling, VA: Stylus.

Morris, L. V., Finnegan, C., & Wu, S. (2005). Tracking student behavior, persistence, and achievement in online courses. *Internet and Higher Education, 8*(3), 221–231.

Morrison, J. Q., Sansosti, F. J., & Hadley, W. M. (2009). Parent perceptions of the anticipated needs and expectations for support for their college-bound students with Asperger's syndrome. *Journal of Postsecondary Education and Disability, 22*(2), 78–87.

Moseley, D., Baumfield, V., Elliott, J., Gregson, M., Higgins, S., Miller, J., & Newton, D. P. (2005). *Frameworks for thinking: A handbook for teaching and learning.* Cambridge, UK: Cambridge University Press.

Murphy, C. U., & Lick, D. W. (2005). *Whole faculty study groups: Creating professional learning communities that target student learning* (3rd ed.). Thousand Oaks, CA: Corwin Press.

National Center for Education Statistics. (2008, December). *Distance education at degree-granting postsecondary institutions: 2006–07.* Washington, DC: US Department of Education. Available at http://nces.ed.gov/pubs2009/2009044.pdf

National Center for Education Statistics. (2009, September). *Projections of education statistics to 2018.* Washington, DC: Author. Available at http://www.nces.ed.gov/programs/projections/projections2018/sec2c.asp

Northern Illinois University. (2010, September). *Vision 2020.* Dekalb, IL: Author.

Northern Illinois University. (2012, Winter). *President's report 2012.* Dekalb, IL: Author.

Ortquist-Ahrens, L., & Torosyan, R. (2009). The role of the facilitator in faculty learning communities: Paving the way for growth, productivity, and collegiality. *Learning Communities Journal, 1*(1), 29–62.

Palloff, R. M., & Pratt, K. (1999). *Building learning communities in cyberspace: Effective strategies for the online classroom.* San Francisco, CA: Jossey-Bass.

Palloff, R. M., & Pratt, K. (2007). *Building online learning communities: Effective strategies for the virtual classroom* (2nd ed.). San Francisco, CA: Jossey-Bass.

Panksepp, J. (1998). *Affective neuroscience: The foundations of human and animal emotions.* New York, NY: Oxford University Press.

Parry, M. (2009, May 29). Online professors pose as students to encourage real learning. *The Chronicle of Higher Education, 55*(38), A10.

Pascarella, E. T., & Terenzini, P. T. (2005). *How college affects students: A third decade of research* (2nd ed.). San Francisco, CA: Jossey-Bass.

Pashler, H., McDaniel, M., Rohrer, D., & Bjork, R. (2008). Learning styles: Concepts and evidence. *Psychological Science in the Public Interest, 9,* 106–119.

Paulson, D. R., & Faust, J. L. (2008). *Active learning for the college classroom.* Retrieved http://www.calstatela.edu/dept/chem/chem2/Active/main.htm

Peck, M. S. (1987). *The different drum: Community making and peace.* New York, NY: Simon & Schuster.

Peckskamp, T., & McLaughlin. C. (Eds.). (2010). *Building community: Stories and strategies for future learning community faculty and professionals.* Syracuse, NY: The Graduate School Press, Syracuse University.

Perlmutter, D. D. (2011, July 10). It's your fault. *The Chronicle of Higher Education.* Available at http://chronicle.com/article/Its-Your-Fault/128098/

Perry, W. G., Jr. (1970). *Forms of intellectual and ethical development in the college years: A scheme.* New York, NY: Holt, Rinehart, and Winston.

Peterson, M. W. (1999). The role of institutional research: From improvement to redesign. In J. F. Volkwein (Ed.), *What is institutional research all about? A critical and comprehensive assessment of the profession: New directions for institutional research* (no. 104, pp. 83–103). San Francisco, CA: Jossey-Bass.

Piaget, J. (1950). *The psychology of intelligence.* London, UK: Routledge and Kegan Paul.

Picciano, A. G., Seaman, J., & Allen, I. E. (2010, December). Educational transformation through online learning: To be or not to be. *The Journal of Asynchronous Learning Networks, 14*(4), 17–35. Available at http://sloanconsortium.org/jaln/v14n4/educational-transformation-through-online-learning-be-or-not-be

Pope, L. (2006). *Colleges that change lives: 40 schools you should know about even if you are not a straight-A student* (3rd ed.). New York, NY: Penguin Books.

Pratt, K. (1996). *The electronic personality* (Unpublished doctoral dissertation). Fielding Graduate University, Santa Barbara, CA.

Presseisen, B. Z. (1991). Thinking skills: Meanings and models revisited. In A. L. Costa (Ed.), *Developing minds: A resource book for teaching thinking* (pp. 47–53). Alexandria, VA: ASCD Publications.

Prineas, M., & Cini, M. (2011, October). *Assessing learning in online education: The role of technology in improving student outcomes* (NILOA Occasional Paper no. 12). Urbana, IL: University of Illinois and Indiana University, National Institute for Learning Outcomes Assessment.

Quellmalz, E. S. (1987). Developing reasoning skills. In J. R. Baron & R. J. Sternberg (Eds.), *Teaching thinking skills: Theory and practice* (pp. 86–105). New York, NY: W. H. Freeman.

Riel, M. (2009). *The learning circle model: Building knowledge through collaborative projects.* Retrieved fall 2010 from http://sites.google.com/site/onlinelearningcircles/Home/learning-circles-defined

Romiszowski, A. J. (1981). *Designing instructional systems: Decision making in course planning and curriculum design.* London, UK: Kogan Page.

Rovai, A. P., & Jordan, H. (2004, August). Blended learning and sense of community: A comparative analysis with traditional and fully online graduate courses. *The Internet and Higher Education, 5*(2), 1–17.

Rusnak, B. J., & Stout, D. M. (n.d.). Comparative book review: An exercise in collaboration on learning communities in higher education. *NOVAtions Journal.* Retrieved February 16, 2009, from http://novationsjournal.org/content/original_story.pl?story = 5

Ryan, S. (1994). The emergence of learning communities. In K. T. Wardman (Ed.), *Reflections on creating learning organizations* (pp. 95–105). Cambridge, MA: Pegasus Communications.

Rydell, R., & McConnell, A. R. (2006). Understanding implicit and explicit attitude change: A system of reasoning analysis. *Journal of Personality and Social Psychology, 91,* 995–1008.

Sanford, N. (1966). *Self and society: Social change and individual development.* New York, NY: Atherton Press.

Scardamalia, M., & Bereiter, C. (1994). Computer support for knowledge-building communities. *Journal of the Learning Sciences, 3*(3), 265–283.

Schein, H. K. (2005, October). The zen of unit one: Liberal education at residential learning communities can foster liberal learning at large universities. In N. S. Laff (Ed.), *Identity, learning, and the liberal arts: New directions for teaching and learning* (no. 103, pp. 73–88). San Francisco, CA: Jossey-Bass.

Schuh, J., & Associates. (2009). *Assessment methods for student affairs.* San Francisco, CA: Jossey-Bass.

Senge, P. M., Kleiner, A., Roberts, C., Ross, R., & Smith, B. (1994). *The fifth discipline field book: Strategies and tools for building a learning organization.* New York, NY: Doubleday.

Sergiovanni, T. (2000). *The lifeworld of leadership: Creating culture, community, and personal meaning in our schools.* San Francisco, CA: Jossey-Bass.

Servage, L. (2008, Winter). Critical and transformative practices in professional learning communities. *Teacher Education Quarterly, 35*(1), 63–77.

Shapiro, N. S., & Levine, J. H. (1999). *Creating learning communities: A practical guide to winning support, organizing for change, and implementing programs.* San Francisco, CA: Jossey-Bass.

Shelley, M., & Epperson, D. L. (2007). One-Year, Two-Year, Three-Year, and Four-Year University Retention Rates Associated with First-Year Participation in a Learning Community at Iowa State University by First-Time, Full-Time Students, Fall 1998 to Fall 2005 Cohorts. Retrieved from www.lc.iastate.edu/reports.html

Shulman, L. S. (2003). No drive-by teachers. *Carnegie Perspectives.* Retrieved from http://www.carnegiefoundation.org/perspectives/no-drive-teachers

Shumar, W. (2009). Interaction, imagination and community building at the math forum. In D. Akoumianakis (Ed.), *Virtual community practices and social interactive media: Technology lifecycle and workflow analysis* (pp. 269–282). Hershey, PA: IGI Global International.

Slavin, R. E. (1984). Team assisted individualization: Cooperative learning and individualized instruction in the mainstreamed classroom. *Remedial and Special Education, 5*(6), 33–42.

Slavin, R. E. (1995). *Cooperative learning: Theory, research and practice* (2nd ed). New York, NY: Allyn & Bacon.

Slavin, R. E., Madden, N. A., Dolan, L. J., & Wasik, B. A. (1996). *Every child, every school: Success for all.* Thousand Oaks, CA: Corwin.

Sloman, S. A. (1996). The empirical case for two systems of reasoning. *Psychological Bulletin, 119*(1), 3–22.

Small, G. W., Moody, T. D., Siddarth, P., & Bookheimer, S. Y. (2009). Your brain on Google: Patterns of cerebral activation during Internet searching. *American Journal of Geriatric Psychiatry, 17*(2), 116–126.

Smith, B. L. (2001, Fall). The challenge of learning communities as a growing national movement. *Peer Review, 4*(1). Retrieved from http://www.aacu.org/peer-review/pr-fa01/pr-fa01feature1.cfm

Smith, B. L., MacGregor, J., Matthews, R. S., & Gabelnick, F. (2004). *Learning communities: Reforming undergraduate education.* San Francisco, CA: Jossey-Bass.

Smith, B., & Smith, R. (2000). Bridging the gap: Constructing faculty-student relationships for mutual learning. In T. Peckskamp & C. McLaughlin (Eds.), *Building community: Stories and strategies for future learning community faculty and professionals* (pp. 70–74). Syracuse, NY: The Graduate School Press, Syracuse University.

Smith, B. L., & Williams, L. B. (Eds.). (2007). *Learning communities and student affairs: Partnering for powerful learning.* Olympia, WA: National Association of Student Personnel Administrators and the Washington Center for Improving the Quality of Undergraduate Education.

Smith, S. F., & Rodgers, R. F. (2005, September–October). Student learning community of practice: Making meaning of the student learning imperative and principles of good practice in student affairs. *Journal of College Development, 46*(5), 472–487.

Snart, J. A. (2010). *Hybrid learning: The perils and promise of blending online and face-to-face instruction in higher education.* Santa Barbara, CA: Praeger.

Sokolow, B. A., Lewis, W. S., Keller, J. A., & Daly, A. (2008, December 4). College and university liability for violent campus attacks. *Journal of College and University Law.* Available at http://ncherm.org/pdfs/Journal%20of%20College%20and%20University%20Law.pdf

Soven, M., Lehr, D., Naynaha, S., Olson, W. (Eds.). (2013). *Linked courses for general education and integrative learning: A guide for faculty and administrators.* Sterling, VA: Stylus.

Spady, W. G., & Schwahn, C. J. (2010). *Learning communities 2.0: Educating in the age of empowerment.* Lanham, MD: Rowman & Littlefield Education.

Stahl, R. J., & Murphy, G. T. (1981, April). *The domain of cognition: An alternative to Bloom's cognitive domain within the framework of an information processing model.* Paper presented at the Annual Meeting of the American Educational Research Association, Los Angeles, CA. (ERIC Document Reproduction Service No. ED208511)

Stein, J. (2008, April 9). *Defining "Creepy Treehouse"* [Blog post]. Retrieved from http://jaredstein.org/2008/04/09/defining-creepy-tree-house/

Sternberg, R. J. (2001). Giftedness as developing expertise: A theory of the interface between high abilities and achieved excellence. *High Ability Studies, 12*(2), 159–179.

Strack, F., & Deutsch, R. (2004). Reflective and impulsive determinants of social behavior. *Personality and Social Psychology Review, 8,* 220–247.

Strempel, E. (2010). The arts adventure LC: A classroom-to-community cultural connection. In T. Peckskamp & C. McLaughlin (Eds.), *Building community: Stories and strategies for future learning community faculty and professionals* (pp. 41–44). Syracuse, NY: The Graduate School Press, Syracuse University.

Strine Patterson, H. (2010). Learning communities: A structural overview. In T. Peckskamp & C. McLaughlin (Eds.), *Building community: Stories and strategies for future learning community faculty and professionals* (pp. 18–25). Syracuse, NY: The Graduate School Press, Syracuse University.

Sullivan, T. M. (1995). Creating and sustaining learning communities. In C. Dudgeon, T. M. Sullivan, & G. K. Wolfson, (Eds.). *PHE scholars program essays: Creating and sustaining learning communities* (pp. 13–30). Fort Lauderdale, FL: Center for the Advancement of Education, Nova Southeastern University. (ED386118)

Suskie, L. (2004). *Assessing student learning.* Bolton, MA: Anker.

Swing, R. L. (2009, October). Institutional researchers as change agents. In C. Leimer (Ed.), *Imagining the future of institutional research: New directions for institutional research* (no. 143, pp. 5–16). San Francisco, CA: Jossey-Bass.

Taylor, K., Moore, W., MacGregor, J., & Lindblad, J. (2003). *Learning community research and assessment: What we know now.* Olympia, WA: Washington Center for Improving the Quality of Undergraduate Education, Evergreen State College.

Thomas, L., & Adsitt, N. Z. (2010). Mentoring and the gateway learning community. In T. Peckskamp & C. McLaughlin (Eds.), *Building community: Stories and strategies for future learning community faculty and professionals* (pp. 93–98). Syracuse, NY: The Graduate School Press, Syracuse University.

Tinto, V. (1995). Learning communities, collaborative learning, and the pedagogy of educational citizenship. *AAHE Bulletin, 47*(7), 11–13.

Tinto, V. (1998, January). *Learning communities and the reconstruction of remedial education in higher education.* Paper presented at the Conference on Replacing Remediation in Higher Education at Stanford University sponsored by the Ford Foundation and the United States Department of Education. Available at http://faculty.soe.syr.edu/vtinto/Files/Developmental%20Education%20Learning%20Communities.pdf

Tinto, V. (2000, March–April). What have we learned about the impact of learning communities on students? *Assessment Update, 12*(2), 1–2, 12.

Tinto, V. (2003). Learning better together: The impact of learning communities on student success. In *Promoting student success in college*. Higher Education Monograph Series (pp. 1–8). Syracuse, NY: Syracuse University. Retrieved from http://faculty.soe.syr.edu/vtinto/Files/Learning%20Better%20Together.pdf

Tomlinson, C. A., & Germundson, A. (2007). Teaching as jazz. *Educational Leadership, 64*(8), 27–31.

Treisman, P. U. (1992). Studying students studying calculus: A look at the lives of minority mathematics students in college. *College Math Journal, 23*(5), 362–373.

Tribbensee, N. E., & McDonald, S. J. (2007, August 6). FERPA and campus safety. *National Association of College and University Attorneys NACUA Notes, 5*(4). Retrieved from http://troy.troy.edu/save/FERPA.html

Tsai, I., Laffey, J. M., & Hanuscin, D. (2010). Effectiveness of an online community of practice for learning to teach elementary science. *Journal of Educational Computing Research, 43*(2), 225–258.

Tussman, J. (1997). *The beleaguered college: Essays on education reform*. Berkeley: CA: University of California, Institute of Governmental Studies Press.

Upcraft, M. L., & Schuh, J. H. (1996). *Assessment in student affairs: A guide for practitioners*. San Francisco, CA: Jossey-Bass.

US Department of Health and Human Services, Office for Human Research Protections. (n.d.). *IRB Guidebook, Part III.D*. Available at http://www.hhs.gov/ohrp/archive/irb/irb_guidebook.htm

van Merriënboer, J. G., & Paas, F. (2003). Powerful learning and the many faces of instructional design: Toward a framework for the design of powerful learning environments. In E. Corte, K. Littleton, S. Strauss, & R. Wegerif (Eds.), *Powerful learning environments: Unraveling basic components and dimensions* (pp. 3–20). Oxford, UK: Elsevier.

Vermunt, J. D., & Verloop, N. (1999). Congruence and friction between learning and teaching. *Learning and Instruction, 9*, 257–280.

Visher, M. G., Schneider, E., Wathington, H., & Collado, H. (with Cerna, O., Sansone, C., & Ware, M.). (2010). *Scaling up learning communities: The experiences of six community colleges*. New York, NY: National Center for Postsecondary Research, Teachers College, Columbia University.

Vogel v. Felice, 127 Cal. App. 4th 1006 (Cal. App. 6th Dist., Mar. 24, 2005).

Vygotsky, L. S. (1978). *The mind in society: The development of higher psychological processes*. Cambridge, MA: Harvard University Press.

Wahlstedt, A., Pekkola, S., & Niemelä, M. (2008). From e-learning space to e-learning place. *British Journal of Educational Technology, 39*(6), 1020–1030.

Wallace, B., & Adams, H. B. (1993). *TASC: Thinking actively in a social context*. Bicester, UK: A B Academic Publishers.

Walvoord, B. E. (2004). *Assessment clear and simple: A practical guide for institutions, departments, and general education*. San Francisco, CA: Jossey-Bass.

Watson-Derbingy, M. (2007). Attending to cultural differences. In B. L. Smith & L. B. Williams (Eds.), *Learning communities and student affairs: Partnering for powerful learning* (pp. 71–80). Olympia, WA: National Association of Student Personnel Administrators and the Washington Center for Improving the Quality of Undergraduate Education.

Wenger, E. (1998). *Communities of practice: Learning, meaning, and identity.* Cambridge, UK: Cambridge University Press.

Wenger, E., McDermott, C. R., & Snyder, W. C. (2002). *Cultivating communities of practice: A guide to managing.* Cambridge, MA: Harvard Business School Press.

Whalen, D., & Shelley, M. (2010). *One-year, two-year, three-year, and four-year university retention rates associated with first-year participation in a learning community at Iowa State University by first-time, full-time students, fall 1998 to fall 2008 cohorts.* Ames, IA: Iowa State University. Available at http://www.lc.iastate.edu/pdfs-docs/University%20Retention%20Rates_LC_2010.pdf

Wiggins, G., & McTighe, J. (2005). *Understanding by design* (2nd ed). Upper Saddle River, NJ: Pearson.

Williams, F. E. (1970). *Classroom ideas for encouraging thinking and feeling.* Buffalo, NY: DOK.

Wisniewski v. Bd. of Educ. Weedsport Central Sch. Dist., 494 F.3d 34 (2d Cir. 2007), cert. denied 128 S. Ct. 1741 (2008).

W.K. Kellogg Foundation. (1998). *W.K. Kellogg Foundation logic model development guide.* Retrieved from http://www.wkkf.org/knowledge-center/resources/2006/02/WK-Kellogg-Foundation-Logic-Model-Development-Guide.aspx

Wolfson, G. K. (1995). Creating and sustaining learning communities: The electronic learning community. In C. Dudgeon, T. M. Sullivan, & G. K. Wolfson, *PHE scholars program essays: Creating and sustaining learning communities.* Fort Lauderdale, FL: Center for the Advancement of Education, Nova Southeastern University. (ED386118)

Young, J. R. (2008, August 18). When professors create social networks for classes, some students see a "creepy treehouse" [Blog post]. *The Chronicle of Higher Education.* Retrieved from http://chronicle.com/blogs/wiredcampus/when-professors-create-social-networks-for-classes-some-students-see-a-creepy-treehouse/4176

Zhao, C., & Kuh, G. D. (2004). Adding value: Learning communities and student engagement. *Research in Higher Education, 45*(2), 115–138.

ABOUT THE AUTHORS

Dr. Oscar T. Lenning is a retired academic and Director of Lenning Consulting Services. After 15 years of research, writing, and consulting in project leadership positions at ACT and the National Center for Higher Education Management Systems, he served 20 years as Academic Vice President and Dean at Roberts Wesleyan College in upstate New York, Executive Vice President and Academic Dean at Waldorf College in Iowa, and Special Assistant to the President responsible for institution-wide strategic planning and assessment, overseeing incorporation of the latest technologies throughout campus, and cochairing the regional accreditation self-study at Bacone College in Oklahoma. He then devoted nine years to leading development of innovative new programs at three quite different collegiate institutions; serving as Director of Special Projects for the College of Education at Iowa State University, Director of Program Development and Assessment for Bridgepoint Education, and Director of the Center for Learning and Advising at Thiel College.

In addition, Lenning has consulted with several dozen collegiate institutions of all kinds, and is author of more than 130 professional publications that includes serving as author, coauthor, or editor of 29 published books and monographs. His chapter titled "Assessment and Evaluation" in the 1981 and 1989 editions of Delworth and Hanson's *Student Services: A Handbook for the Profession* became the standard for the student affairs profession in that area during the 1980s and much of the '90s.

Denise M. Hill, JD, MPA, is Assistant Professor at Des Moines University teaching health law and ethics. She is also an adjunct faculty member at Drake University Law School and an "of counsel" attorney at the Whitfield and Eddy law firm in Des Moines. She is active in promoting cross-curricular and institutional learning opportunities and founded the first MHA student chapter in the nation of the American Health Lawyers Association. A trained mediator and frequent public speaker, previously she practiced law at two large law firms, was Manager of Public & Regulatory Affairs for the Iowa Medical Society and served as a labor relations attorney for the Iowa Department of Personnel.

Dr. Kevin P. Saunders is Director of Institutional Research and Assessment at Drake University. Previously he served as the coordinator of continuous academic program improvement, chaired the learning communities assessment subcommittee, and taught research and evaluation courses at Iowa State University. He is a former resource faculty member for the Evergreen State College Learning Community Summer Institute and is a current Teagle Assessment Scholar.

Dr. Alisha Solan is a Communication Studies instructor at Grossmont College in the Grossmont-Cuyamaca Community College District and Miramar College in the San Diego Community College District. She also teaches at the University of San Diego. In the past Solan has taught at Austin Community College, the University of Texas at Austin, Texas A & M University, Southwestern University and St. Edward's University in Texas. In addition to a focus on learning, she is a communication expert with a PhD in Communication Studies from the University of Texas at Austin. Dr. Solan also freelances as an editor and dissertation coach.

Dr. Andria Stokes is the director of the Center for Transformational Learning and Assistant Professor of Education at Avila University in Kansas City, MO. Her specialty is cognitive education; her focus has been on inquiry and constructivist learning that involves facilitating deep understanding and conceptual thinking systems.

Throughout her career, Dr. Stokes has designed and implemented numerous student and professional learning communities in both K–12 and higher education. Her recent publications include "Moving Toward Cognitive Excellence," a cognitive development program; "Finding Out Real Knowledge," a high school literacy program; and an art curriculum for Kookiedoodle Crafts, located in Overland Park, Kansas. She has been a University of Kansas Cohort member on Creating Digital Portfolio Assessments for Students with Special Needs and is currently working on creation of the new educational technology design program for her university.